ICSEA 2025

The Twentieth International Conference on Software Engineering Advances

September 28th - October 2nd, 2025

Lisbon, Portugal

ICSEA 2025 Editors

Luigi Lavazza, Università dell'Insubria - Varese, Italy

Roy Oberhauser, Aalen University, Germany

Printed from e-media with permission by:

Curran Associates, Inc.
57 Morehouse Lane
Red Hook, NY 12571

Some format issues inherent in the e-media version may also appear in this print version.

Printed with permission by Curran Associates, Inc. (2025)

International Academy, Research, and Industry Association (IARIA)
412 Derby Way
Wilmington, DE 19810

Phone: (408) 893-6407
Fax: (408) 527-6351

petre@iaria.org

Additional copies of this publication are available from:

Curran Associates, Inc.
57 Morehouse Lane
Red Hook, NY 12571 USA
Phone: 845-758-0400
Fax: 845-758-2633
Email: curran@proceedings.com
Web: www.proceedings.com

Table of Contents

ICSEA 2025

Forward

The Twentieth International Conference on Software Engineering Advances (ICSEA 2025), held on September 28 – October 1, 2025 in Lisbon, Portugal, continued a series of events covering a broad spectrum of software-related topics.

The conference covered fundamentals on designing, implementing, testing, validating and maintaining various kinds of software. The tracks treated the topics from theory to practice, in terms of methodologies, design, implementation, testing, use cases, tools, and lessons learnt. The conference topics covered classical and advanced methodologies, open source, agile software, as well as software deployment and software economics and education.

The conference had the following tracks:

- Advances in fundamentals for software development
- Advanced mechanisms for software development
- Advanced design tools for developing software
- Software engineering for service computing (SOA and Cloud)
- Advanced facilities for accessing software
- Software performance
- Software security, privacy, safeness
- Advances in software testing
- Specialized software advanced applications
- Web Accessibility
- Open source software
- Agile and Lean approaches in software engineering
- Software deployment and maintenance
- Software engineering techniques, metrics, and formalisms
- Software economics, adoption, and education
- Business technology
- Improving productivity in research on software engineering
- Trends and achievements

Similar to the previous edition, this event continued to be very competitive in its selection process and very well perceived by the international software engineering community. As such, it is attracting excellent contributions and active participation from all over the world. We were very pleased to receive a large amount of top quality contributions.

We take here the opportunity to warmly thank all the members of the ICSEA 2025 technical program committee as well as the numerous reviewers. The creation of such a broad and high quality conference program would not have been possible without their involvement. We also kindly thank all the authors that dedicated much of their time and efforts to contribute to the ICSEA 2025. We truly believe that thanks to all these efforts, the final conference program consists of top quality contributions.

This event could also not have been a reality without the support of many individuals, organizations and sponsors. We also gratefully thank the members of the ICSEA 2025 organizing committee for their help in handling the logistics and for their work that is making this professional meeting a success.

We hope the ICSEA 2025 was a successful international forum for the exchange of ideas and results between academia and industry and to promote further progress in software engineering research. We also hope that Lisbon provided a pleasant environment during the conference and everyone saved some time for exploring this beautiful city

ICSEA 2025 Steering Committee

Herwig Manaert, University of Antwerp, Belgium
Radek Koci, Brno University of Technology, Czech Republic
Sébastien Salva, University of Clermont Auvergne | LIMOS Laboratory | CNRS, France
José Carlos Metrôlho, Polytechnic Institute of Castelo Branco, Portugal
Luigi Lavazza, Università dell'Insubria – Varese, Italy
Hironori Washizaki, Waseda University / National Institute of Informatics / SYSTEM INFORMATION, Japan
Roy Oberhauser, Aalen University, Germany
Simona Vasilache, University of Tsukuba, Japan

ICSEA 2025 Publicity Chair

Lorena Parra Boronat, Universidad Politécnica de Madrid, Spain
Sandra Viciano Tudela, Universitat Politecnica de Valencia, Spain
Jose Miguel Jimenez, Universitat Politecnica de Valencia, Spain

ICSEA 2025

Committee

ICSEA 2025 Steering Committee

Herwig Manaert, University of Antwerp, Belgium
Radek Koci, Brno University of Technology, Czech Republic
Sébastien Salva, University of Clermont Auvergne | LIMOS Laboratory | CNRS, France
José Carlos Metrôlho, Polytechnic Institute of Castelo Branco, Portugal
Luigi Lavazza, Università dell'Insubria – Varese, Italy
Hironori Washizaki, Waseda University / National Institute of Informatics / SYSTEM INFORMATION, Japan
Roy Oberhauser, Aalen University, Germany
Simona Vasilache, University of Tsukuba, Japan

ICSEA 2025 Publicity Chair

Lorena Parra Boronat, Universidad Politécnica de Madrid, Spain
Sandra Viciano Tudela, Universitat Politecnica de Valencia, Spain
Jose Miguel Jimenez, Universitat Politecnica de Valencia, Spain

ICSEA 2025 Technical Program Committee

Tamer Abdou, Ryerson University, Canada
Morayo Adedjouma, CEA Saclay Nano-INNOV - Institut CARNOT CEA LIST, France
Abdullah Al-Alaj, Virginia Wesleyan University, USA
Ammar Kareem Obayes Alazzawi, Universiti Teknologi PETRONAS, Malaysia
Shabbab Algamdi, College of Computer Engineering and Sciences | Prince Sattam bin Abdulaziz University, Riyadh, Saudi Arabia
Washington H. C. Almeida, CESAR School, Brazil
Eman Abdullah AlOmar, Rochester Institute of Technology, USA
Sousuke Amasaki, Okayama Prefectural University, Japan
Talat Ambreen, International Islamic University, Islamabad, Pakistan
Amal Ahmed Anda, University of Ottawa, Canada
Daniel Andresen, Kansas State University, USA
Giusy Annunziata, University of Salerno, Italy
Jean-Paul Arcangeli, UPS - IRIT, France
Francesca Arcelli Fontana, University of Milano Bicocca, Italy
Oluwaseun Bamgboye, Edinburgh Napier University, Scotland
Jorge Barreiros, ISEC - Polytechnic of Coimbra / NOVA LINCS, Portugal
Leila Ben Ayed, National School of Computer Science | Lab. Hana, Tunisia
Marciele Bergier, Universidade do Minho | Research Center of the Justice and Governance, Portugal
Silvia Bonfanti, University of Bergamo, Italy
Mina Boström Nakicenovic, Paradox Interactive, Sweden

Khadija Bousselmi Arfaoui, University of Savoie Mont Blanc, France
José Carlos Bregieiro Ribeiro, Polytechnic Institute of Leiria, Portugal
Antonio Brogi, University of Pisa, Italy
Carlos Henrique Cabral Duarte, Brazilian Development Bank (BNDES), Brazil
Carlos A. Casanova Pietroboni, National Technological University - Concepción del Uruguay Regional Faculty (UTN-FRCU), Argentina
Olena Chebanyuk, National Aviation University, Ukraine
Fuxiang Chen, University of Leicester, UK
Hongmei Chi, Florida A&M University, USA
Dickson Chiu, The University of Hong Kong, Hong Kong
Rebeca Cortazar, University of Deusto, Spain
André Magno Costa de Araújo, Federal University of Alagoas, Brazil
Mónica Costa, Polytechnic Institute of Castelo Branco, Portugal
Yania Crespo, University of Valladolid, Spain
Luís Cruz, Delft University of Technology, Netherlands
Beata Czarnacka-Chrobot, Warsaw School of Economics, Poland
Hepeng Dai, Chinese Aeronautical Establishment, China
Giovanni Daián Róttoli, Universidad Tecnológica Nacional (UTN-FRCU), Argentina
Darren Dalcher, Lancaster University, UK
Andrea D'Ambrogio, University of Rome Tor Vergata, Italy
Patrizio Dazzi, University of Pisa, Italy
Guglielmo De Angelis, CNR - IASI, Italy
Thiago C. de Sousa, State University of Piauí, Brazil
Maria del Carmen de Castro Cabrera, Universidad de Cádiz, Spain
Kevin Delcourt, UPS - IRIT, France
Lin Deng, Towson University, USA
Anmol Deshpande, University of California at Irvine, USA
Fatma Dhaou, University of Tunis el Manar, Tunisia
Dario Di Dario, University of Salerno, Italy
Jaime Díaz, Universidad de La Frontera, *Chile*
Hyunsook Do, University of North Texas, USA
Dragos Laurentiu Dobrean, Babes-Bolyai University, Cluj Napoca, Romania
Diogo Domingues Regateiro, Instituto de Telecomunicações | Universidade de Aveiro, Portugal
Dimitris Dranidis, CITY College, University of York Europe Campus, Greece
Imke Helene Drave, RWTH Aachen University, Germany
Arpita Dutta, National University of Singapore, Singapore
Holger Eichelberger, University of Hildesheim | Software Systems Engineering, Germany
Ridha Ejbali, National Engineering School of Gabes (ENIS) / University of Gabes, Tunisia
Gledson Elias, Federal University of Paraíba (UFPB), Brazil
Fernando Escobar, University of Brasilia (UNB), Brazil
Mahdi Fahmideh, University of Southern Queensland (UniSQ), Australia
Kleinner Farias, University of Vale do Rio dos Sinos, Brazil
Thomas Fehlmann, Euro Project Office AG, Zurich, Switzerland
Alba Fernandez Izquierdo, Universidad Politécnica de Madrid, Spain
David Fernandez-Amoros, Universidad Nacional de Educación a Distancia (UNED), Spain
Estrela Ferreira Cruz, Instituto Politécnico de Viana do Castelo | ALGORIMTI research centre - Universidade do Minho, Portugal
Stefano Forti, University of Pisa, Italy

Jonas Fritzsch, University of Stuttgart | Institute of Software Engineering, Germany
Jicheng Fu, University of Central Oklahoma, USA
Stoyan Garbatov, OutSystems SA, Portugal
Jose Garcia-Alonso, University of Extremadura, Spain
Wided Ghardallou, ENISO, Tunisia / Hail University, KSA
Gwihwan Go, Tsinghua University, China
Elena Gómez-Martínez, Universidad Complutense de Madrid, Spain
Gregor Grambow, Aalen University, Germany
Chunhui Guo, California State University, Los Angeles, USA
Huong Ha, University of Newcastle, Singapore
Shahliza Abd Halim, UniversityTeknologi Malaysia, Malaysia
Atsuo Hazeyama, Tokyo Gakugei University, Japan
Hussein Hazimeh, Lebanese University, Lebanon
Qiang He, Swinburne University of Technology, Australia
Yifeng He, University of California, Davis, USA
Jairo Hernán Aponte, Universidad Nacional de Colombia, Columbia
Bogumiła Hnatkowska, Wrocław University of Science and Technology, Poland
Syeda Sumbul Hossain, Samsung Electronics, Bangladesh
Shintaro Hosoai, Institute of Technologists, Japan
Jie Hu, Arizona State University, USA
Fuqun Huang, Western Washington University, USA
LiGuo Huang, Southern Methodist University, USA
Rui Humberto Pereira, ISCAP/IPP, Portugal
Waqar Hussain, CSIRO - Data61, Australia
Gustavo Illescas, Universidad Nacional del Centro-Tandil-Bs.As., Argentina
Irum Inayat, National University of Computer and Emerging Sciences, Islamabad, Pakistan
Florije Ismaili, South East European University, Republic of Macedonia
Angshuman Jana, IIIT Guwahati, India
Marko Jäntti, University of Eastern Finland, Finland
Judit Jász, University of Szeged, Hungary
Laid Kahloul, Biskra University, Algeria
Hermann Kaindl, Vienna University of Technology, Austria
Yasushi Kambayashi, Sanyo-Onoda City University, Japan
Ahmed Kamel, Concordia College, Moorhead, USA
Chia Hung Kao, National Taitung University, Taiwan
Dimitris Karagiannis, University of Vienna, Austria
Dimitra Karatza, iov42, UK
Vikrant Kaulgud, Accenture, India
Siffat Ullah Khan, University of Malakand, Pakistan
Radek Koci, Brno University of Technology, Czech Republic
Christian Kop, University of Klagenfurt, Austria
Blagovesta Kostova, EPFL, Switzerland
Akrivi Krouska, University of Piraeus, Greece
Bolatzhan Kumalakov, Al-Farabi Kazakh National University, Kazakhstan
Tsutomu Kumazawa, Software Research Associates Inc., Japan
Rob Kusters, Open University, The Netherlands
Alla Lake, LInfo Systems, LLC - Greenbelt, USA
Stefano Lambiase, University of Salerno, Italy

Jannik Laval, University Lumière Lyon 2 | DISP lab EA4570, Bron, France
Luigi Lavazza, Università dell'Insubria - Varese, Italy
Maurizio Leotta, University of Genova, Italy
Abderrahmane Leshob, University of Quebec at Montreal (UQAM), Canada
Zheng Li, Queen's University Belfast, UK
Peng Liang, Wuhan University, China
Lan Lin, Ball State University, USA
Panos Linos, Butler University, USA
Alexandre Marcos Lins de Vasconcelos, Universidade Federal de Pernambuco, Recife, Brazil
Mingyi Liu, Harbin Institute of Technology, China
David H. Lorenz, Open University of Israel, Israel
Stephane Maag, Télécom SudParis, France
Silvana Togneri Mac Mahon, Dublin City University, Ireland
AKM Jahangir Majumder, University of South Carolina Upstate, USA
Frédéric Mallet, Université Cote d'Azur | Inria Sophia Antipolis Méditerranée, France
Herwig Mannaert, University of Antwerp, Belgium
Krikor Maroukian, Microsoft, Greece
Johnny Marques, Aeronautics Institute of Technology (ITA), Brazil
Célia Martinie, Université Paul Sabatier Toulouse III, France
Reshmi Maulik, Meghnad Saha Institute of Technology, India
Rohit Mehra, Accenture Labs, India
Kristof Meixner, Christian Doppler Lab CDL-SQI | Institute for Information Systems Engineering | Technische Universität Wien, Vienna, Austria
Vojtech Merunka, Czech University of Life Sciences in Prague / Czech Technical University in Prague, Czech Republic
José Carlos M. M. Metrolho, Polytechnic Institute of Castelo Branco, Portugal
Sanjay Misra, Covenant University, Nigeria
Mohammadsadegh Mohagheghi, Vali-e-Asr University of Rafsanjan, Iran
Atef Mohamed (Shalan), Georgia Southern University, USA
Miguel P. Monteiro, Universidade NOVA de Lisboa, Portugal
Fernando Moreira, Universidade Portucalense, Portugal
Óscar Mortágua Pereira, University of Aveiro, Portugal
Ines Mouakher, University of Tunis El Manar, Tunisia
Kmimech Mourad, Higher Institute for Computer Science and Mathematics of Monastir, Tunisia
Lucilene F. Mouzinho da Silva, Federal Institute of Maranhão, Brazil
Sana Ben Hamida Mrabet, Paris Nanterre University / LAMSADE - Paris Dauphine University, France
Kazi Muheymin-Us-Sakib, Institute of Information Technology (IIT) | University of Dhaka, Bangladesh
Marcellin Nkenlifack, University of Dschang, Cameroon
Thomas Nolte, Mälardalen University, Sweden
Alex Norta, Tallinn University, Estonia / Dymaxion Oy, Finland / University of Pretoria, South Africa
Marc Novakouski, Carnegie Mellon Software Engineering Institute, USA
Roy Oberhauser, Aalen University, Germany
Shinpei Ogata, Shinshu University, Japan
Flavio Oquendo, IRISA (UMR CNRS) - University of South Brittany, France
Smruti Padhy, Texas Advanced Computing Center (TACC) | University of Texas at Austin, USA
Marcos Palacios, University of Oviedo, Spain
Beatriz Perez Valle, Universidad de La Rioja, Spain
Quentin Perez, IMT Mines Alès, France

Michalis Pingos, Cyprus University of Technology, Cyprus
Monica Pinto, University of Málaga, Spain
Aneta Poniszewska-Maranda, Institute of Information Technology | Lodz University of Technology, Poland
Pasqualina Potena, RISE Research Institutes of Sweden AB, Sweden
Evgeny Pyshkin, University of Aizu, Japan
Claudia Raibulet, University of Milano-Bicocca, Italy
Raman Ramsin, Sharif University of Technology, Iran
Gilberto Recupito, University of Salerno, Italy
Stephan Reiff-Marganiec, University of Derby, UK
Fernando Reinaldo Ribeiro, Polytechnic Institute of Castelo Branco, Portugal
Catarina I. Reis, ciTechCare - Center for Innovative Care and Health Technology | Polytechnic of Leiria, Portugal
Wolfgang Reisig, Humboldt University, Berlin, Germany
Jose Ignacio Requeno Jarabo, Universidad Complutense de Madrid, Spain
Michele Risi, University of Salerno, Italy
Simona Mirela Riurean, University of Petrosani, Romania
Nelson Rocha, University of Aveiro, Portugal
José Raúl Romero, Universidad de Córdoba, Spain
António Miguel Rosado da Cruz, Polytechnic Institute of Viana do Castelo, Portugal
Adrian Rutle, Western Norway University of Applied Sciences, Norway
Ines Bayoudh Saadi, ENSIT - Tunis University, Tunisia
Gunter Saake, Otto von Guericke University of Magdeburg, Germany
Mohamed Aymen Saied, Laval University, Canada
Khayyam Salehi, Shahrekord University, Iran
Bilal Abu Salih, The University of Jordan, Jordan
Sébastien Salva, University of Clermont Auvergne | LIMOS Laboratory | CNRS, France
Hiroyuki Sato, University of Tokyo, Japan
Wieland Schwinger, Johannes Kepler University Linz (JKU) | Inst. f. Telekooperation (TK), Austria
Hans-Werner Sehring, Nordakademie, Germany
Vesna Šešum-Čavić, TU Wien, Austria
Mahaboob Subhani Shaik, Veristat, USA
Mohammad Shameem, IRCISS Research Center | King Fahad University of Petroleum and Minerals, Saudi Arabia
István Siket, University of Szeged, Hungary
Karolj Skala, Hungarian Academy of Sciences, Hungary / Ruđer Bošković Institute Zagreb, Croatia
Juan Jesús Soria Quijaite, Universidad Peruana Unión, Lima, Peru
Nissrine Souissi, MINES-RABAT School (ENSMR), Morocco
Maria Spichkova, RMIT University, Australia
Alin Stefanescu, University of Bucharest, Romania
Sidra Sultana, National University of Sciences and Technology, Pakistan
Yingcheng Sun, Columbia University in New York City, USA
Mahan Tafreshipour, University of California, Irvine USA
Abhishek Tiwari, University of Southern Denmark, Odense, Denmark
Jose Manuel Torres, Universidade Fernando Pessoa, Porto, Portugal
Christos Troussas, University of West Attica, Greece
Mariusz Trzaska, Polish-Japanese Academy of Information Technology, Poland
Masateru Tsunoda, Kindai University, Japan

Tugkan Tuglular, Izmir Institute of Technology, Turkey
Simona Vasilache, University of Tsukuba, Japan
Sylvain Vauttier, LGI2P - Ecole des Mines d'Alès, France
Rohith Yanambaka Venkata, Nokia Bell Labs, USA
Colin Venters, University of Huddersfield, UK
Laszlo Vidacs, Hungarian Academy of Sciences / University of Szeged, Hungary
Hironori Washizaki, Waseda University / National Institute of Informatics / SYSTEM INFORMATION, Japan
Bingyang Wei, Texas Christian University, USA
Mohamed Wiem Mkaouer, Rochester Institute of Technology, USA
Dietmar Winkler, Institute for Information Systems Engineering | TU Wien, Austria
Krzysztof Wnuk, Blekinge Institute of Technology, Sweden
Shuohan Wu (Tom), Hong Kong Polytechnic University, Hong Kong
Heitor Augustus Xavier Costa, Federal University of Lavras, Brazil
Kunpeng Xu, Université de Sherbrooke, Canada
Simon Xu, Algoma University, Canada
Rihito Yaegashi, Kagawa University, Japan
Guowei Yang, The University of Queensland, Australia
Yilong Yang, Beihang University, China
Haibo Yu, Kyushu Sangyo University, Japan
Zifan Yu, Arizona State University, USA
Mário Zenha-Rela, University of Coimbra, Portugal
Yutong Zhao, University of Central Missouri, USA
Xin Zhou, Nanjing University, China
Qiang Zhu, University of Michigan - Dearborn, USA
Martin Zinner, Technische Universität Dresden, Germany
Kamil Żyła, Lublin University of Technology, Poland

Copyright Information

How Digital Experiments Support Sustainability in a Forest Machine Operator Company: A Case Study

Marko Jäntti, Jarmo Koponen
School of Computing
University of Eastern Finland
P.O.B. 1627, Kuopio, Finland
Email: {marko.jantti, jarmo.koponen}@uef.fi

Markus Aho
Funlus Oy
Sepontie 15, 73300 Nilsiä, Finland
Email: markus.aho@funlus.fi

Markus Aho
UEF Business School
University of Eastern Finland
Yliopistokatu 2, Joensuu, Finland
Email: markus.aho@uef.fi

***Abstract*—Increasing number of organizations are adopting Green Information and Communication Technology (Green ICT) practices for their service operations. There are two main types of Green ICT in the organizational context. First, Green for ICT where ICT aims at reducing its own footprint and second, Green by ICT aiming at offering digital tools that reduce the environmental footprint of all business activities in the organization. In this paper, we present two digital experiments where green by ICT solutions for a forest machine operator company were engineered by software development practices. In this study, we aim to answer the research problem: How digital experiments support sustainability in a forest machine operator company? This embedded case study is based on two consecutive digital experiments conducted in Finland with a large scale forest machine operator company. The first digital experiment focused on tank level monitoring and the second experiment on mass monitoring. Our results highlight the challenges in receiving sustainability data from subcontractors and IT providers. Additionally, IoT-enabled monitoring services can eliminate traveling to remote storage areas and thus may reduce CO2 footprint remarkably.**

***Keywords*—Green ICT; software system; Internet of Things;**

I. Introduction

An increasing number of organizations are adopting green computing practices to transition their operations toward greater environmental sustainability. Green computing includes actions such as decreasing energy consumption, recycling e-waste and environmental friendly usage of devices [1]. A recent study [2] conducted in Finland showed that companies' awareness and understanding of green ICT varies a lot. According to Raja, green computing refers to sustainable, environment-friendly computing [3]. Chaudhari and Kothoke [4] have identified challenges in green ICT including inadequate ICT-based informed decision-making, low ICT and the least Green ICT awareness, lack of matured inter/multi-disciplinary software tools and issues related to availability and reliability of data. Cater-Steel and Tan [5] have established green IT service management (ITSM) framework that contains four pillars: Green procurement, consolidation of IT resources, power management of IT equipment, decommissioning of unused/obsolete equipment.

Widdicks et al. [6] report that ICT can enable reductions in global emissions in other sectors but there are continuous uncertainties regarding ICT's carbon impacts. The study of Dubey and Hefley [7] proposes green extensions to IT Infrastructure Library (ITIL). In supplier management, service vendors can be evaluated by using various green metrics. For example, when an organization decides to purchase datacenter services, one can use metrics, such as datacenter power usage effectiveness (PUE) and data center infrastructure efficiency (DCIE). Singh et al. [8] present a green and sustainable software model that can be used in green ICT practices. Cloud computing plays an important role in green computing by enabling more efficient and sustainable use of computing resources [9]. Cloud computing utilizes virtualization techniques that allow cloud providers run multiple virtual machines on a single physical server. Additionally, cloud computing enables on-demand usage of computing resources where resources are allocated only when needed. One of the key challenges in green ICT from IT company's perspective is that IT customers do not want to pay extra for greener services. Often, companies have to make trade-offs between costs and gains when they make decisions on implementing green and sustainable information systems [10]. If companies could assess and report their positive environmental contributions, it would provide more accurate knowledge and support for green initiatives [11]. The Internet of Things (IoT) represents a rapidly evolving network of interconnected devices that communicate and exchange data, offering huge transformation potential across various business domains. An IoT-based system consists of multiple configuration items, such as sensors, IoT devices, applications, cloud services, data networks and gateway devices. According to the definition by Dorsemaine et al. [12], IoT is "a group of infrastructures interconnecting connected objects and allowing their management, data mining and the access to the data they generate". Hatzivasilis et al. [13] discuss how IoT technology can be used for circular econonomy purposes, such as to administrate the lifecycle of the deployed electronic equipment and manage related supply chains. IoT provides significant improvement opportunities from green by ICT perspective. Tran et al. [14] have used IoT to collect vibration signals on engines of ships. Additionally, Gantert et al. [15] collect and use sounds produced by machine components to improve corrective maintenance of machinery.

Concerning the research gap, although IoT technologies have been widely used in several domains, existing research has not dealt with how forest machine operator companies are using IoT to increase automation and productivity. The novelty of our research lies in demonstrating how we applied IoT in our digital transformation experiments within a new business context—monitoring forestry assets as well as showing how these experiments supported the sustainability goals of the case organization.

The remainder of the paper is organized as follows: In Section 2, research methodology of the study is presented. In Section 3, case study results are provided. Section 4 is the analysis and finally, the conclusions are given in Section 5.

II. Research Problem & Methodology

This exploratory case study aimed at answering the following research problem: How digital experiments support sustainability in a forest machine operator company? The case study can be defined as "an empirical inquiry that investigates a contemporary phenomenon within its real-life context" [16]. Our research problem was divided into following three research questions:

- How sustainable and green practices are addressed by the forest machine operator's staff during digital experiments?
- How are the sustainability concepts visible in the service operation of the forest machine operator?
- What type of challenges are related to sustainability & green ICT from the perspective of a forest machine operator?

Regarding the case selection, the case organization was selected from the pool of industry partners and the university has collaborated several years with the case organization in EU funded projects. Additionally, the case organization participated in the green ICT research project carried out by the university. Thus, the project enabled an easy access to the case organization. While this case study was exploratory in nature and our first attempt to study green ICT, we used high level research questions focusing on green practices, visibility of sustainability concepts and challenges to answer our research problem.

A. Case Organization

Motoajo is one of the leading forest machine providers in Finland. The company is as a family-owned business with around 80 employees. The company operates almost 60 forest machines in North Karelia. Motoajo has a long expertise in the management and maintenance of forestry machinery, Motoajo provides professional services that enhance the efficiency and sustainability of forest operations. The services provided by Motoajo include harvesting, wood transportation, heavy machinery maintenance and repair; and excavator services, such as soil tilling. The company takes environmental responsibility into account, supports the circular economy, and has an up-to-date carbon footprint calculator. Motoajo is committed to providing logging services sustainably and profitably while respecting the environment and laws.

Motoajo was selected as a case organization because the Digital Innovation Hub network DIH World had announced the call for digital experiments and smart forestry was one the topics of that call. Together with Motoajo, our DIH applied funding for the tank level monitoring experiment The 2nd experiment focused on monitoring the mass of forestry assets (how many litres/kg of liquid remain in the container) by using industrial scale and IoT technologies. .

B. Data Collection Methods

Data for this study were collected from multiple data sources and multiple researchers between August 2021 - May 2025 by the university research team. Data was collected from two digital experiments related to applying IoT technologies. According to Eisenhardt [17] triangulation and usage of multiple data collection methods provides stronger substantiation of constructs and hypotheses. The following data sources, recommended by Yin [16] were used:

- Documentation: The sustainability report of the case organization, Tekelek tank level sensor product sheet, safety instruction documents, PCE RS 2000 specifications document
- Archival records: the public website of the case organization, a job onboarding questionnaire designed for case organizations employees, DEFRA GHG conversions factors spreadsheet used in calculating emissions for traveling between remote storage areas, online forms for truck drivers and forest machine operators
- Interviews/discussions: Green ICT group interview in May 2025 with CEO, foreman and quality manager; project discussions during work meetings with foreman of Motoajo, and interview with CEO related to digital transformation, online meetings with AWS consultants
- Participative observation: Digital experiment work meetings in target organization's facilities, multiple visits to the case organization, participative observations during visits in the organization's storage areas in Nurmes and Riistavesi, system testing workshop during the second experiment in the IT provider organization's facilities in Mikkeli
- Physical artifacts: videos that showcased how forestry liquids and forestry waste were stored and processed in the storage area: videos were shot while implementing a virtual job onboarding system; PCE RS 2000 industrial scale, various containers used for storing forestry liquids, such as marking dyes and diesel exhaust fluid; Tekelek tank level sensor
- Direct observations: Observations during physical visits to the case organization's main storage area and remote storage areas. A visit at the forest logging site during the winter.

III. Results

The research team including the first and second author and Motoajo received EU funding from DIH World project's Call for experiments. The funding enabled implementation of a digital experiment where the goal was to build a prototype for a solution that monitors and measures tank levels by using Internet of Things technologies. The experiment highlighed the following challenges in the forest service machine operator's operations. At that moment, Motoajo did not have accurate view on inventories of forestry liquids that forest machines consume. This resulted in situations that forest machine drivers may not get mandatory liquids. Frequent trips to remote storage areas were needed to check whether critical liquids consumed by forest machines are available. Additionally, better job introduction was needed for managing forestry liquids safely and according to green practices.

A. Green and digital forest service management experiment for tank level monitoring

Initial discussions on the experiment objectives addressed the need to monitor fuel containers in forest logging sites. We started studying external factors, such as legal, environmental and technical issues that affect fuel operations: "The process of transporting fuel to logging sites is tricky and might not be fully automated; typically a fuel truck driver needs to call anyway the forest machine driver to give location information." We observed that forest certificates prevent storing fuel containers in the forest in groundwater areas. Additionally, case organization's staff reported that forest machine settings and driving patterns affect the fuel consumption (also CO2 footprint of harvesting).

Due to complexity of fuel operations, we decided to focus on other business-critical liquids: Fungicide, marking colours and diesel exhaust fluid ADBlue. The case organization's representative stated: "We have many types of containers in several locations and dropping points: metal containers, plastic IBC containers". We also observed that the company had already invested in technology that helps collecting data on vehicles and analyzing factors that affect fuel costs: "Our vans have automatic driving logs where we can see where vehicles are and where they are moving. Additionally, we can observe driving behaviour and patterns."

Forest machine operations require various types of liquids (fuel, marking dyes, diesel exhaust fluid) and availability of those liquids is critical to Motoajo's harvesting business. Containers of liquids are stored in main storage area of Nurmes, Finland and remote storage areas. We observed that consumption of liquids is monitored manually and this activity requires frequent travelling to remote storage areas: "One employee spends at least one working day per month due to driving to remote storage areas and checking the availability of liquids and items".

In the specification phase, we asked user requirements for the monitoring system. The case organization's CEO addressed especially the usability requirements "The system should be very easy to use; even in a situation when a truck driver or a forest machine driver comes to the remote storage area during the winter gloves in his hand and when there is no daylight". Additionally, the CEO commented that it should be easy to interpret results provided by the monitoring solution "The mobile app could show the level of liquids with traffic light colour codes; additionally how much liquid a specific driver took from the container".

The research team made a visit to one of the remote storage areas during the winter and played the role of a truck driver. While the CEO had commented on data needs "If possible, a delivery truck driver should use the app to provide information about the refilling", we observed that there was a QR code attached to a container and opening the QR c led to an online form that was designed for both capturing data on refilling events and retrieving events. We opened the form during our field visit and observed that there was room for improvement

Fig. 1. TILHI application for tank level monitoring

in the usability of the form. We interpreted that in order to increase usability, it might be better to separate these forms from each other. This could be one root cause for missing data on liquid refills and retrievals.

Technical specifications for the IoT system were outlined based on the user stories. The key objectives of technical specification stage was to define the hardware and software requirements for the TILHI IoT system, including sensor calibration, dashboard interfaces, and data handling. The project team consumed a lot of time for selecting a right sensor for monitoring liquid levels. Meetings and discussions were organized with various sensor service providers and IoT platform providers. The sensor that was finally selected was Tekelek LoraWAN-enabled ultrasonic sensor. This sensor module had been used in many sensor projects in Finland and it was also available in the LoraWAN network provider's (Digita) sensor catalogue.

The core development of the IoT system took place over several months, culminating in the review of the completed development in February 2022. This phase covered both the mobile application and the web interface. Figure 1 shows the user interface of the tank level monitoring system TILHI that was implemented in the experiment. The key objective of this stage was to build the IoT system, including features such as sensor calibration, container management, and liquid tracking. We experienced minor challenges both in ordering the sensors and installing the sensors to the container.

The deployment of the system was performed February-April 2022. Deployment activities occurred after successful testing of the system. The deployment phase aimed at ensuring that the IoT system was integrated into the forestry operational processes, with all essential components functioning as expected. Our key objective was to roll out the tank level monitoring system to end users in forestry operations. In the end of the experiment, we found out that data submission frequency of sensor modules is every six hours, not hourly as we expected. We asked the reason in a telephone discussion with the service provider "Frequency on sending IoT data affects the sensor module battery duration." We also delivered this information to the case organization's representative that considered the data submission frequency adequate but not optimal. The IoT experiment ended with a Continual Improvement meeting with

Fig. 2. The context of the weight monitoring system for forestry liquids

a discussion on what went well and what could have been improved. The experiment was considered successful despite the slow start and many changes in monitoring target.

B. *Smart mass monitoring experiment*

At the end of the first experiment, the case organization provided idea for a new experiment. The main goal of the new experiment was to place an industrial-level 'scale' under a standardized IBC tank to allow for real-time mass measurement of the liquid content of the tank (see Fig. 2). Another use case was to measure the truck pallet containing hydraulic oil canisters. Initially, we selected the public LoRaWAN network for data transmission, however, this was changed later to the private LoraWAN because we wanted to minimize the number of third party services, such as public LoraWAN network provider.

The experiment started with studying which components were needed for the system. The main hardware components (industrial scale PCE RS 2000 [18] and Enless Wireless Signal Transmitter) were identified and selected by measurement technology unit located in Kajaani, Finland Hardware components were purchased and calibrated. After this, the research team initiated discussions with the cloud service provider. The public sector Amazon Web Services representative and cloud consultants helped the research team to identify which cloud services were needed to implement the system. The IoT reference architecture by AWS provided a good basis for discussions.

The next step in the experiment was to find an ICT company that could implement the system in AWS cloud. The first author of this paper participated in Solver X reverse pitching event and from the event we received eight potential IoT providers that were interested in implementing the system. We performed a public bidding process and selected the provider based on price and quality of implementation. The hardware components were transported from one city to another to the selected IT provider with a light commercial vehicle that could accommodate the industrial scale (1200 x 1200 x 100 mm; 85 kg). After few months, the research team had a small system testing workshop in October 11, 2023 (see Fig. 4) with the IT provider where the hardware (the scale and the signal transmitter) and software components (AWS cloud services) were tested together.

Fig. 3. A system testing workshop in IT provider's facilities

In May 14th 2025, the research team had a field visit to the case organization including discussions on green ICT and the monitoring target of the mass monitoring experiment. We asked whether they pay attention to sustainable choices while procuring IT equipment and they answered: "We purchase equipment to our own needs, not based on green ICT. If the system results in positive environmental impact, it is fine".

The case organization reported that they measure carbon footprint of their operations automatically from invoices by using an add-on ICT module installed in accounting software. The main challenges related to green approach seemed to be related to changing requirements: "The requirements in forest standards and legislation keep on changing. It will be increasingly challenging to get employees or forest machine drivers. Who has courage to start harvesting while there are so many requirements that you have to know?". The interviewees of the case organization commented that large customers are already asking information on sustainability and perhaps they should also start requiring information from their sub-contractors: "If our customers require sustainability information from us, we should have similar rights to request this information from our subcontractors."

During the visit we had an opportunity to see the storage facilities and observed that the mass monitoring target was an IBC container with metal frames and wooden truck pallet under the container (see Fig. 4). Discussion with the case organization's representatives showed that they would like to receive an alert when there is approximately 20 percent of liquid remaining in the container (200 litres). The case organization's representatives asked whether the system can be used also for other types of containers.

Additionally, the CEO stated that transporting the water causes CO2 emissions for them: "If we could transport only the chemical instead of water, this would definitely decrease CO2 emissions." It is mandatory for forest machine operators to take preventive actions for forest diseases, for example,

Fig. 4. Observing the monitoring target during the field visit to the case organization's facilities in Nurmes, Finland

chemical control is carried out with a strong urea solution and biological control with a solution of gray mold fungus: " Regarding monitoring operations, some customers have started to request information such as what is our portion on using gray mold fungus and urea solution."

If the remote monitoring service would be used in all remote storage areas of the case organization, carbon footprint of traveling could be reduced approx. 192 kg (2,66155 x 72 l = 191,63 kg CO2) based on driven kilometres (692 km) between several remote storage areas with a light commercial vehicle MB Sprinter, traditional diesel as fuel, calculated according to UK emission conversion factors [19]. This would be a significant saving. Additionally, the remote monitoring could save more than one working day per month .

IV. Analysis

Next, analysis of case study results reflecting the four research questions are presented. The source of evidence has been marked by the following abbreviations: IN= Interviews, AR= Archival Records, DI= Discussions, DO= Documentation, PO= Partic. observation, DOB= Direct observation, PA= Physical artefacts. Table 1 shows our findings from two experiments related to the first research question: How sustainable and green practices are addressed by the forest machine operator's staff? Our results showed that sustainability talks were closely related to the forestry operations, such as recycling, reusing the oil canisters and grease tubes. The company addressed that decision making on ICT purchases focuses on how well the system or the device supports their business objectives rather than how environmental friendly the system or the device is.

Table 2 shows our analysis on how sustainability concepts are visible in the organization based on the data from two experiments. Based on the interview with the CEO and foreman, we observed during the Experiment 2 that environmental concerns of the case organizations customers and knowledge requirements for forest machine drivers had increased since the Experiment 1. Sustainability issues were evolved remarkably after the first experiment: The company had introduced carbon footprint calculation and published a company-wide sustainability report. They had clear plans to start auditing their subcontractors and providers to receive sustainability data. They commented that some of their customers had also started to request sustainability data from them. Environmental issues were somehow visible in the company's marketing and communication during the first experiment but during the second experiment we observed that company was spreading the sustainability message more actively both inside the company and externally covering all the stakeholders of the organization.

TABLE I. Analysis related to RQ1: How sustainability concepts are addressed?

Finding	Source
Automatic driving diaries show the location driving behavior	IN, DI
The entire staff and subcontractors have been trained in responsible for sustainable operations and risk management.	IN, DO
We are committed to providing timber harvesting services sustainably and profitably, respecting the environment and adhering to laws.	IN, DO
We support the circular economy and recycle the most important waste generated in our ops, such as oils, metals, batteries, and tires	IN
When there is sufficient amount of liquids in containers, no extra trips are needed due to empty containers.	IN
Personnel is our most important resource, so employee well-being and safety are of utmost importance to us.	DO
We purchase equipment to our own needs, not based on green ICT. It is fine if the system results in positive environmental impact	IN
There are marked areas for forestry waste in the storage.	PA, IN

TABLE II. Analysis related to RQ2: Visibility of sustainability concepts in the organization

Finding	Source
The company has a quality and environmental management handbook	DOC, IN
Forest Act, the Nature Conservation Act, PEFC, and ISO standards used in harvesting	IN
The company invests in projects that optimize resource consumption	PO, IN
The entire staff and subcontractors have been trained in responsible operations and risk mgmt.	IN, DO
Sustainability is very visible in the company's values and marketing, such as 'Nature is our friend'	PO, AR
The company has a sustainability report on their website	AR
The company calculates carbon footprint for operations	IN
Sustainability and environmental friendly way of operating is communicated to new employees starting from job onboarding	AR, IN

Table 3 shows the analysis regarding the third research question: What type of challenges are related to sustainability and green ICT? We identified both Green ICT challenges that software or system engineers should pay attention to in the future. First, receiving data from subcontractors and IT providers is a precondition for succesful carbon footprint calculation. The organization calculates at the moment carbon footprint based on invoices from their financial management system. However, in order to calculate the CO2 emissions of the whole value chain or digital-enabled services where several forestry actors, platform providers and system providers participate in, reliable emission data is needed.

Second, more complicated the system structure, more difficult it will be to calculate the CO2 footprint. In the first experiment, we would need to calculate energy consumption of an AWS-backed mobile app, a third party IoT data ingestion platform, IoT sensor modules and receive data on system usage hours. Calculating the CO2 of the second experiment might be simpler because it uses only AWS cloud, AWS hosted Grafana and the industrial scale with a signal transmitter. Additionally, interviewees reported challenges in managing the knowhow

TABLE III. ANALYSIS RELATED TO RQ3: CHALLENGES IN SUSTAINABLE AND GREEN PRACTICES

Finding	Source
IT providers are not able to provide data on their CO2 emissions	PO
Cloud platforms provide CO2 reporting but allocating emissions for a specific customer or a service may cause challenges	PO
Frequent IoT data submission affects the battery of IoT sensor	PO, DO
The requirements in forest standards and legislation keep on changing	IN
It is difficult to recruit forest machine drivers because of ever increasing knowledge requirements	IN
Transporting the water causes unnecessary CO2 emissions	IN

because forest machine drivers must know forest machine settings, forest standards, requirements set by customers etc.

V. Conclusion

This study aimed at answering the research problem: How digital experiments support sustainability in a forest machine operator company? There were three research questions in the study. Regarding the first research question, we observed that sustainability &green practices were addressed by the forest machine operator's staff in terms of respecting the environment, promoting circular economy, such as recycling forestry assets and emphasizing safety and wellbeing of employees. While purchasing services, systems and devices, the company values their suitability to business over green IT causes.

Concerning the second research question, we found various ways how sustainability and green concepts were visible in the case organization and its service operations, such as improvement projects that advance digitalization and sustainability, the sustainability report and the environmental handbook and the carbon footprint calculator. The third research question highlighted the challenges, such as lack of emission data from IT providers, challenges in measuring carbon footprint of xomplicated systems, and increasing knowledge requirements for forest machine drivers.

There are certain limitations related to this case study. First, the second experiment is still in the work-in-progress status waiting for that software components, such as AWS cloud resources and Grafana dashboard are configured properly. Second, the results of the study might be difficult to generalize to other forest machine operator companies because the size of the company matters. Companies that operate only few machines do not need expensive monitoring mechanisms and they do not have so many remote storage areas. Third, data was collected during only two digital experiments from one organization. The results of this study may be used by software & system engineers to identify how digital transformation projects and experiments can contribute to sustainability thinking as well as how IoT-based systems can be designed, deployed and introduced to cater corporate sustainability objectives. Further research on this topic could focus on studying Green for ICT aspects of IoT-based monitoring services.

Acknowledgment

We would like to thank the case organization for valuable collaboration during the study. This paper is part of the results of the VICTIS - Green ICT from Eastern Finland UEF project co-funded by European Union (A91631, ELY Centre).

References

[1] V. Agarwal, K. Sharma, and A. K. Rajpoot, "A review: Evolution of technology towards green IT," in *Proceedings of the 2021 International Conference on Computing, Communication, and Intelligent Systems (ICCCIS)*, 2021, pp. 940–946.

[2] L. Abdullai, L. Partanen, A. Sipilä, S. Oyedeji, M. S. Haque, and J. Porras, "Co-design framework for green ICT ecosystem: A tale from the finnish green ICT ecosystem," in *2023 International Conference on ICT for Sustainability (ICT4S)*, 2023, pp. 207–215.

[3] S. P. Raja, "Green computing: A future perspective and the operational analysis of a data center," *IEEE Transactions on Computational Social Systems*, vol. 9, no. 2, pp. 650–656, 2022.

[4] Y. Chaudhari and P. Kothoke, "Green ICT and sustainable manufacturing: Economy of saving and saving of environment,," in *Strategic Technologies of Complex Environmental Issues -A Sustainable Approach*.

[5] A. Cater-Steel and W.-G. Tan, "The role of IT service management in green IT," *Australasian Journal of Information Systems*, vol. 17, 01 2010.

[6] K. Widdicks, B. Knowles, A. Friday, and G. Blair, "ICT under constraint: Exposing tensions in collaboratively prioritising ICT innovation for climate targets," *ACM J. Responsib. Comput.*, vol. 1, no. 2, Jun. 2024.

[7] S. Dubey and W. Hefley, "Greening ITIL: Expanding the itil lifecycle for green IT," in *2011 Proceedings of PICMET '11: Technology Management in the Energy Smart World (PICMET)*, 2011, pp. 1–8.

[8] S. Singh, A. Tiwari, S. Rastogi, and V. Sharma, "Green and sustainable software model for IT enterprises," in *2021 5th International Conference on Electronics, Communication and Aerospace Technology (ICECA)*, 2021, pp. 1157–1161.

[9] C. Sailesh, V. S. Praneeth, S. S. Koushik, V. G. N. Sai, N. Vurukonda, and V. K. Burugari, "A review on adoption of green cloud computing," in *2023 7th International Conference on Computing Methodologies and Communication (ICCMC)*, 2023, pp. 1–6.

[10] K. S. Savita, P. D. D. Dominic, and T. Ramayah, "The adoption of green information technologies and systems as a driver within green scm," in *2014 International Conference on Computer and Information Sciences (ICCOINS)*, 2014, pp. 1–6.

[11] V. Coroamă, P. Bergmark, M. Höjer, and J. Malmodin, "A methodology for assessing the environmental effects induced by ICT services: Part i: Single services," in *Proceedings of the 7th International Conference on ICT for Sustainability*, ser. ICT4S2020. New York, NY, USA: Association for Computing Machinery, 2020, p. 36–45.

[12] B. Dorsemaine, J.-P. Gaulier, J.-P. Wary, N. Kheir, and P. Urien, "Internet of things: A definition & taxonomy," 09 2015.

[13] G. Hatzivasilis, N. Christodoulakis, C. Tzagkarakis, S. Ioannidis, G. Demetriou, K. Fysarakis, and M. Panayiotou, "The CE-IoT framework for green ICT organizations: The interplay of CE-IoT as an enabler for green innovation and e-waste management in ICT," in *2019 15th International Conference on Distributed Computing in Sensor Systems (DCOSS)*, 2019, pp. 436–442.

[14] H.-L. Tran, D. Nguyen, Q.-H. D. Ba, and V.-N. Pham, "An implementation of IoT system for collecting vibration signals of ships engines to support engine failures detection," in *2024 Tenth International Conference on Communications and Electronics (ICCE)*, 2024, pp. 475–480.

[15] L. Gantert, M. Sammarco, M. Detyniecki, and M. Campista, "A supervised approach for corrective maintenance using spectral features from industrial sounds," in *2021 IEEE 7th World Forum on Internet of Things (WF-IoT)*, 2021, pp. 723–728.

[16] R. Yin, *Case Study Research: Design and Methods, Fourth edition*. Beverly Hills, CA: Sage Publishing, 2009.

[17] K. Eisenhardt, "Building theories from case study research," *Academy of Management Review*, vol. 14, pp. 532–550, 1989.

[18] PCE Instruments, "Platform scale pce-rs 2000," Online specification: https://www.pce-instruments.com/, 2025.

[19] Department for Energy Security and Net Zero, "UK government GHG conversion factors for company reporting," Conversion factors Excel Sheet, 2024.

Data-Driven Insights for Software Development Process Improvement: A Defect Analysis

Melike Takıl
The Scientific and Technological Research Council of Türkiye (TÜBİTAK) Informatics and Information Security Advanced Technologies Research Center (BİLGEM)
Ankara, Türkiye
email: melike.takil@tubitak.gov.tr

Zeliha Dindaş
The Scientific and Technological Research Council of Türkiye (TÜBİTAK) Informatics and Information Security Advanced Technologies Research Center (BİLGEM)
Ankara, Türkiye
email: zeliha.dindas@tubitak.gov.tr

Abstract— **This paper presents an analysis of defects found in a software project at a Capability Maturity Model Integration (CMMI) Level 5 public institution, required to manage and improve their processes using statistical and other quantitative techniques, develops software for other public organizations. A dataset of software defects collected via a task and issue management platform was analyzed, focusing on defect severity, defect type, detected activity and affected components. Defects were classified and a root cause analysis was conducted to identify defect-prone areas and underlying causes. The motivation of this work is providing a practical perspective on how public-sector software teams operating under governmental regulatory constraints can use defect data to fix defects and to support long-term process improvement and quality assurance. The results of this research are intended to contribute future projects of the organization and provide referenceable value to other governmental software units aiming to enhance their defect management capabilities.**

Keywords— software defect analysis; software quality; root cause analysis

I. INTRODUCTION

In software engineering, the identification, classification, and analysis of defects play a key role in providing product quality and maintaining process efficiency. Defects which are broadly defined as flaws, errors, or bugs in software have direct consequences on system reliability, maintainability and user satisfaction. Their early detection and resolution are crucial for reducing rework and cost while preserving the credibility of organizations, particularly in high-stakes public sectors. Defect analysis is an important component of software improvement process. It enables organizations to trace the origins of defects, understand the conditions under which they arise, and implement preventive measures to reduce their recurrence. Many studies have shown that systematic defect tracking and root cause analysis contribute significantly to achieving higher maturity in software processes, as seen in models such as the CMMI. Organizations at higher maturity levels (such as Level 5) are expected to leverage quantitative defect data for continuous process optimization and predictive quality management.

While defect analysis is a well-established practice in the private sector, its application within public-sector software development presents unique challenges and opportunities. Public institutions are often subject to greater regulatory oversight, extended stakeholder ecosystems, and longer procurement cycles. These factors underscore the importance of software quality and magnify the implications of defects. Moreover, since public-sector software is frequently reused, integrated, or interfaced with systems from other agencies, the downstream effects of unresolved or recurring defects can be profound.

The remainder of this paper is structured as follows. In Section 2, a review of the relevant literature and related works is presented in order to contextualize the study. In Section 3, the methodology is described, including the motivation for the study, its scope, the dataset and variables used, and the expected outcomes. In Section 4, the data is analyzed from multiple perspectives to uncover significant patterns and insights. Finally, in Section 5, the main conclusions are drawn and potential directions for future work are outlined.

II. RELATED WORK

Defect tracking is a critical component to a successful software quality effort. In fact, Robert Grady of Hewlett-Packard stated in 1996 that "software defect data is the most important available management information source for software process improvement decisions," and that "ignoring defect data can lead to serious consequences for an organization's business" [1]. Defect and problem metrics are among the few direct and quantifiable indicators of software process and product quality. Although customer perceptions of software quality may vary, the frequency of defects is widely recognized as being inversely proportional to quality. Such measurements provide objective insights into reliability, correctness, efficiency, and usability of the software system [2]. Preventing defects early in the software development lifecycle is more effective and less costly than detecting them later. Key defect prevention strategies—such as formal methods, process improvements (e.g., CMMI), training, and automation—play a crucial role in enhancing software quality. This proactive approach complements the focus on post-deployment defect analysis by underscoring the importance of early quality assurance practices [3]. Defect Causal Analysis (DCA) is a structured approach used to identify systematic errors that repeatedly cause software defects and failures. This technique aims not only to prevent similar defects in the future but also to enable their earlier detection through root cause analysis [4]. A common method within DCA is the use of defect classification data—such as Pareto charts—to identify the most frequent defect types, which often point to underlying process weaknesses [5]. Once these patterns are recognized, organizations can implement targeted process improvements to reduce recurrence of similar issues [6]. The present study follows a similar rationale by examining defect distributions and contributing factors to support software process improvement.

The outputs produced by a process can be characterized by some quality attributes, the values of which generally show some variation. The causes of variation can be classified as natural causes (also called common causes) or assignable causes (also called special causes). Natural causes are those that are inherent in the process and that are present all the time. Assignable causes are those that occur sometimes and that can be prevented. A process is said to be under statistical control if all the variation in the attributes is caused by natural causes [7][8]. Therefore, Statistical Process Control (SPC) control limits were used to detect defects throughout the software development process. Usage of control charts can lead to reduction in the control limits causing process improvements. It has been observed that rigorous monitoring of control charts plotted for process parameters like defect density and taking timely corrective and preventive actions would lead to process improvements [9].

III. METHODOLOGY

This section outlines the methodological approach adopted to investigate defect trends and root causes within a public sector software project. It describes the rationale behind the study, the scope and structure of the dataset, the selected variables, and the expected outcomes, all of which contribute to a systematic and data-driven defect analysis process.

A. *Rationale and Scope*

This study was carried out in response to a noticeable increase in software defects detected in the production environment of a public sector software project. Given the potential impact of such defects in public services, it became essential to investigate the nature, distribution, and timing of these issues. The primary objective was to identify critical defect patterns, root causes, and components most affected.

Software quality metrics are periodically monitored using dashboards visualized through a Business Intelligence (BI) tools. When defect counts began to increase, a more detailed investigation was required to identify trends, seasonal patterns, and component-level defect concentrations. Moreover, since data interpretation and context play a crucial role in defect analysis, the project's technical lead and project manager were actively involved in scoping the dataset. Their input ensured the inclusion of relevant variables and the exclusion of irrelevant entries, thereby improving the accuracy and relevance of the analysis. It is emphasized that the reactive aspect of defect management by analyzing already reported and resolved issues, aiming to support transition toward proactive quality assurance in future phases. It aligns with the principles of Total Quality Management (TQM) and CMMI, focusing on continuous improvement, data-driven decision-making, and stakeholder engagement [10].

B. *Dataset and Variables*

The dataset used in this study was obtained from a task and issue management platform employed by the institution to coordinate and oversee software development activities. This platform is deeply integrated into the organization's software lifecycle and serves as a central hub for managing project workflows, including backlog planning, sprint execution, issue tracking and quality assurance processes.

Acting as the authoritative repository for work-related records, the platform enables the systematic logging, categorization, assignment, and resolution of software issues. It facilitates end-to-end traceability by capturing detailed metadata for each issue, including attributes such as issue type, impacted components, severity, detected activity, sprint association, assignee and current status. Additionally, the system records all updates, comments, workflow transitions, and timestamps, allowing for detailed temporal analysis and retrospective evaluations. The tool is actively used by cross-functional teams comprising developers, testers, analysts, project managers, and technical leads. It supports both agile and hybrid project methodologies through features such as sprint boards, user story hierarchies, version tagging, and customizable workflows. This makes it possible to track the lifecycle of a defect from discovery through resolution with a high degree of transparency and consistency.

For the purposes of this analysis, the scope of the issues was narrowed to defects. The selection criteria included:

- Only resolved and closed issues were considered, to ensure that the analysis reflects confirmed defects rather than pending or misclassified reports.
- Only defects reported in production environments were included, as these are considered more critical due to their direct impact on end users and operational services. Issues identified in test environments were excluded, since their occurrence is expected and does not necessarily indicate process deficiencies.
- The analysis covers the period from January 2024 to April 2025, selected in collaboration with project's technical lead to focus on periods when defect trends increased.

A total of 147 defect issues met the inclusion criteria. Rather than including the entire dataset, we present a representative snapshot of the dataset and its fields in Table 1.

To ensure the relevance and reliability of the dataset, a preliminary validation process was conducted with the project's technical lead and project manager. This included reviewing ambiguous entries, verifying proper classification of defect types and deciding on the most appropriate variables. During pre-processing, a limited number of missing values were addressed by directly consulting project team, whose validated input was used to complete the dataset.

TABLE I DATASET SNAPSHOT FOR FIELDS

Field	Value
Issue Key	143
Issue Type	Defect
Sprint Period	01.04.24
Severity	Medium
Defect Type	Coding
Component/s	A
Detected Activity	System Monitoring
Resolution	Done
Status	Closed

The following key variables were extracted from the task and issue management platform and used in the analysis:

- Severity: This attribute indicates the relative criticality of the defect, typically ranked on a scale (e.g., minor, medium, major). It reflects the potential functional or user-facing impact of the issue.
- Detected Activity: This captures the specific development or operational phase in which the defect was discovered (e.g., Development, Integration Test, Code Review, System Monitoring). This variable supports root cause analysis by highlighting gaps in earlier detection efforts.
- Component(s): This denotes the subsystem(s) or modules affected by the defect. The platform allows for multiple components to be tagged per issue, enabling an analysis of module-level quality.
- Detected Sprint: This indicates the sprint during which the issue was logged. This supports time-based analysis, especially within agile projects where delivery and quality metrics are tracked in sprint cycles.
- Defect Type: This refers to the technical nature of the defect (e.g., coding, architectural design, data, integration, User Interface (UI), performance). Accurate classification in this field is crucial for identifying systemic weaknesses in development or architectural design practices.

Each of these structured variables was used to segment the dataset and support both descriptive and diagnostic analysis. By leveraging standardized fields available within the task and issue management platform, the study ensured traceable, reproducible, and context-aware outcomes. Nevertheless, several data quality considerations were taken into account:

- Timeliness and accuracy of data entry: As the platform relies on manual inputs from team members, discrepancies in timing or completeness of entries may affect the accuracy of the dataset.
- Subjectivity in classification: The interpretation of what constitutes a "defect" versus another issue type may vary across individuals or teams, potentially introducing inconsistency.
- Dataset size: Although the 147 production defects analyzed provide sufficient detail for meaningful pattern recognition, the moderate size limits the statistical generalizability of the results. Software engineering experiments often have small sample sizes [11]. One way to manage this challenge is through improving the dataset itself, as it has been noted that "the improvement of data sets through enhanced data collection, pre-processing and quality assessment should lead to more reliable prediction models, thus improving the practice of software engineering" [12].

Despite these limitations, the active use of a task and issue management platform significantly enhances the reliability and depth of the analysis. Its integration into daily workflows ensures that the defect data reflects the operational reality of software development in a complex institutional environment.

C. *Expexted Outcomes*

Identifying the conditions under which defects most frequently arise, determining whether specific modules or time periods exhibit elevated defect counts, and tracing the root causes behind these occurrences form the basis of this study. By leveraging this knowledge, the institution can reduce defect density—an outcome strongly correlated with maintainability and user satisfaction [13]. Improvements in defect management ultimately lead to shorter release cycles, lower maintenance costs, and enhanced end-user trust.

IV. ANALYSIS

This section presents a structured analysis of production defect data by leveraging variables extracted from the task and issue management platform. The aim is to identify defect trends, classify defect types, assess component-level impact, and examine detection patterns to support actionable quality improvement and data-driven decision-making.

A. *Monthly Defect Counts*

Several analyses were performed by using the available fields within the task and issue management platform. Monthly total defect counts and especially major defect counts were visualized in Figures 1a and 1b to monitor trends over time. It was observed that defect counts increased notably in certain months, prompting further statistical investigation.

To determine whether these increases were statistically significant or merely due to natural variation, an Upper Control Limit (UCL) was defined using the formula mean + standard deviation (1σ).

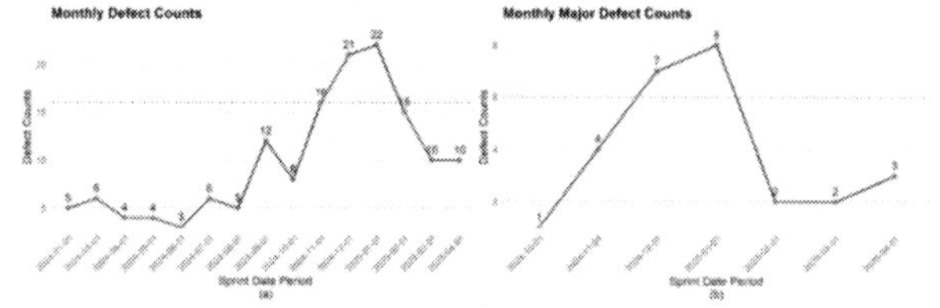

Figure 1. Monthly defect counts

This method provides a practical upper limit to identify months in which the defect count significantly exceeds the expected range, assuming a roughly normal distribution of the data. The rationale behind selecting the mean ± 1σ approach lies in its sensitivity to moderate but potentially meaningful anomalies. While traditional Shewhart control charts commonly employ mean ± 3σ, which encompasses 99.7% of all observations, such a strict threshold is more suitable for large datasets with high process stability, where false alarms must be minimized. A mean ± 2σ limit, capturing 95% of observations, offers a compromise but may still exclude relevant fluctuations in smaller or less stable datasets. In contrast, a mean ± 1σ threshold includes approximately 68% of data points under the normality assumption. This makes it particularly useful in exploratory analyses or early warning systems, where the primary aim is to flag unusual patterns for further review [14].

Using this method, the months of December 2024 and January 2025 were identified as exceeding the control limits, suggesting the presence of statistically unusual behavior. As a result, the possibility of seasonal effects influencing defect occurrences was explored. However, feedback obtained from the project team lead indicated that no seasonality was present. The variation was attributed to potential data entry adjustments or changes in reporting behavior. It was concluded that the increase in defects during these months likely stemmed from reporting-related factors rather than genuine increases in software issues. Then, it was agreed that team members should be provided with training or guidance on accurate and consistent data entry practices. Alternatively, the implementation of a control mechanism for validating input quality was proposed, aiming to improve the reliability of defect-related analytics in future reporting periods.

B. Defect Counts by Defect Type

Defects were categorized into standard types such as coding, functionality, architectural design, data, UI, performance, integration and system-related issues.

According to the Pareto analysis shown in Figure 2a Coding defects dominated the dataset (77%), suggesting significant opportunities for improvement in development practices, code reviews and developer training. Functional, architectural design and data-related defects followed, indicating lesser but still notable concerns. Understanding the origin of major defects is essential for effectively issue prioritization, establishing risk management practices and enabling teams to focus on areas with the greatest potential impact on system reliability and user satisfaction. As shown in Figure 2b, the majority of major defects are Coding defects. This can be taken into account when planning actions.

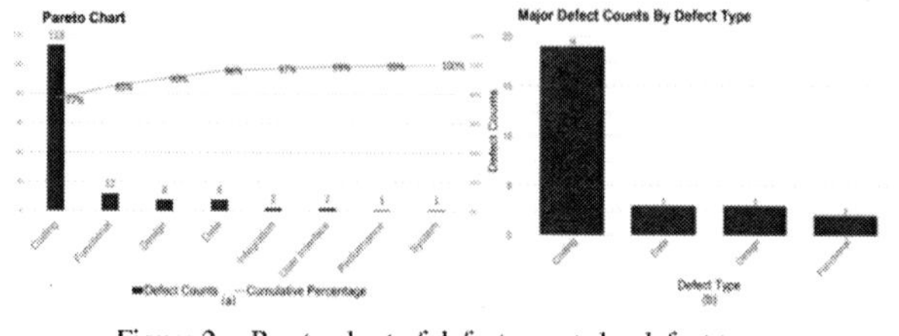

Figure 2. Pareto chart of defect counts by defect type

C. Defect Counts by Component

A defect issue can affect multiple components simultaneously. As teams conduct a defect analysis to understand root causes, it becomes increasingly important to identify which specific components are associated with higher defect frequencies. This level of granularity enables teams to detect recurring patterns, assess component-level stability and prioritize quality improvement efforts where they are most needed.

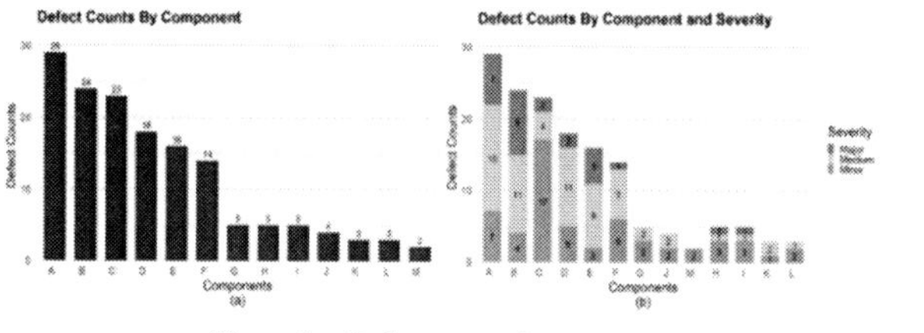

Figure 3. Defect counts by components

As illustrated in Figure 3a, a bar chart visualization was used to present the distribution of defects across different software components. The chart shows that three components exhibit a notably high concentration of defects compared to the others. Defect counts by severity level for each component displays in Figure 3b Identifying such major defect-prone components is critical, as it allows development teams to prioritize their efforts and conduct focused root cause analyses in the most problematic areas of the system. In the chart, although Component E exhibits a lower total number of defects compared to the others, it has a relatively high proportion of major defects. This aspect should be considered during task prioritization. Conversely, while Component C has a higher overall number of defects, the vast majority are classified as minor. Therefore, targeted interventions in this component may lead to a substantial reduction in the total defect count.

D. Defect Counts by Detected Activity

The activity during which a defect is detected serves as a critical indicator for understanding the effectiveness of quality assurance practices throughout the software development lifecycle. Conducting such analyses is essential for identifying defect patterns at a technical level and understanding in which activities defects are most frequently identified enables the implementation of targeted improvements and preventive measures.

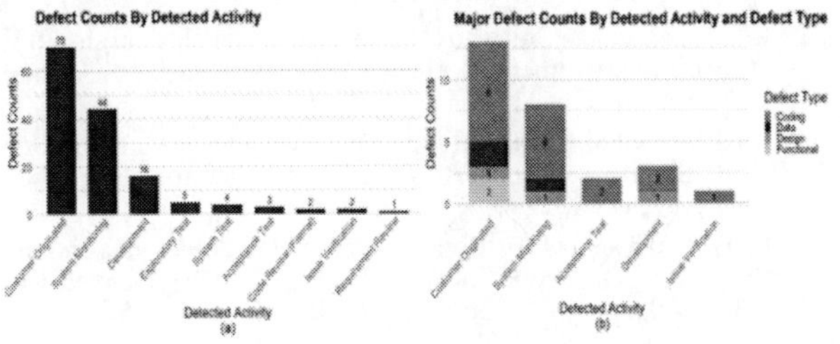

Figure 4. Defect counts by detected activity and defect types

To the Figure 4a, the analysis of defect detection activities revealed that the majority of defects were found after deployment, rather than during early development or testing stages. Specifically, the "Customer Originated" category accounted for the highest number of defects (70 cases), indicating that many issues were discovered directly by end users or stakeholders during actual system usage. The second most frequent detected activity was "System Monitoring"(44 cases), reflecting the role of automated monitoring tools in identifying runtime anomalies and system-level issues. While this demonstrates that monitoring mechanisms are effectively capturing failures in the production environment, it also reinforces the need for earlier detection to reduce operational risk and customer impact.

Figure 4b presents the distribution of major defects categorized by detected activity and defect type. As illustrated, Coding defects represent the predominant defect type across all detected activities. This suggests that efforts aimed at minimizing coding-related defects could lead to a substantial reduction in the overall number of major defects. It may also mean that fewer of them will leak to the customer.

E. Analysis of Defect Issue Summarries

As illustrated in Figure 5, detailed analysis of the defect issue summaries revealed that the most frequently reported defect issues were related to NULL (NPE) handling (26 instances), followed by business rule violations (23), and query-related defects (20). Additionally, a notable number of issues stemmed from incorrect data insertion operations (16), functional logic defects (13), and update operation failures (11).

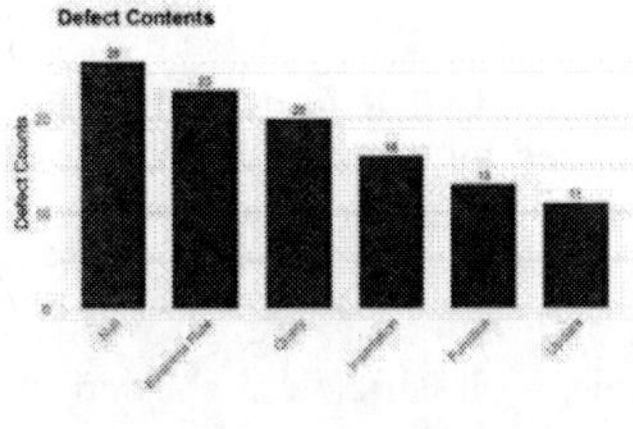

Figure 5. Defect issue summaries

This distribution indicates that a large proportion of the defects originate from NPEs, which typically occur when the code attempts to access or modify an object reference that has not been initialized. Previously, Figure 2 also highlighted that most defects were rooted in coding-related activities. The findings in this figure further corroborate that conclusion.

As for the null-related problems, static code analysis can detect some Null Pointer Exceptions (NPEs), particularly in cases where a method might return a null value, and the returned result is used directly—such as accessing a field or invoking a method—without checking for null. However, it cannot identify null values that originate from external sources such as databases or API inputs. In practice, many NPEs encountered during development tend to arise from such dynamic sources, which static analysis tools are generally unable to detect. Business rule violations rank as the second most common defect type after NPEs. Accordingly, allocating adequate resources and providing targeted training to address NPEs could significantly enhance code robustness. Furthermore, a detailed investigation into the origin of business rule violations specifically, whether they arise from customer miscommunication or analyst defects, would provide valuable insights to inform project decisions and process.

Ultimately, software defects are often the result of multiple, interrelated factors. Limited or superficial test coverage, insufficient domain knowledge, and time pressure can all contribute to quality issues. Late requirement changes and urgent requests disrupt planned workflows, reducing the time available for proper analysis and testing. Inadequate refactoring and poor adherence to clean code practices further degrade maintainability. Since many defects arise under complex conditions, identifying their root causes often requires detailed investigation.

V. CONCLUSION AND FUTURE WORK

In this study, a comprehensive defect analysis was conducted for a public institution engaged in software development for public organizations. Given the critical nature of software applications and their direct impact on end users, identifying and understanding defects was of high importance. Monthly analyses were performed both for total defects and major defects, using ±1 sigma control limits to identify significant increases. Defects were categorized by defect type, component, detected activity. A Pareto analysis revealed that the majority of issues stemmed from Coding defects. Components A and B were identified as the most defect-prone areas, both in terms of total and major defects.

When analyzed by detected activity, a significant portion of the defects, including major ones, originated from Customer Originated issues. The majority of these customer originated major defects were also related to coding. A deeper technical classification showed that most of the defects were associated with null-related problems, particularly Null Pointer Exceptions. Furthermore, a considerable number of defects resulted from misunderstandings of business rules, highlighting potential gaps in requirement analysis.

These findings highlight specific areas that require focused attention. The predominance of Customer Originated defects may indicate the need to intensify testing activities to identify issues prior to deployment. The high frequency of Coding defects related to null value handling suggests the necessity for targeted developer training and the establishment of best practices in coding standards. Additionally, relying solely on happy path testing is insufficient; comprehensive test coverage should include diverse input sets to ensure robustness against edge cases such as null values. The prevalence of business rule violations underscores the importance of conducting a thorough investigation into their root causes particularly to determine whether they stem from customer miscommunication or analyst errors. Such insights are expected to inform both project decisions and process improvements. The analysis presented here may serve as a foundation for future initiatives, such as increasing the involvement of analysts during early project phases.

While this study provides a detailed retrospective analysis of current defects, future efforts should shift towards predictive and preventive measures. To this end, a broader range of quality measures and metrics will be incorporated into the future work to demonstrate effectiveness and strengthen its scientific value. A potential direction for future research is the development of a predictive model capable of anticipating defect occurrences prior to deployment. Such a model would enable proactive mitigation strategies and contribute to enhanced overall software quality.

ACKNOWLEDGMENT

The authors thank TUBITAK BILGEM for supporting this work. Special thanks go to the project team for their valuable contributions throughout the research.

REFERENCES

[1] R. B. Grady, "Software failure analysis for high-return process improvement decisions," Hewlett-Packard Journal, vol. 47, no. 4, Aug. 1996.

[2] IEEE Standard for a Software Quality Metrics Methodology, IEEE Standard 1061-1990, Inst. Electr. Electron. Eng., New York, NY, USA, 1990.

[3] L. M. Laird and M. C. Brennan, "Software defect prevention," Proc. 14th Int. Symp. Softw. Rel. Eng. (ISSRE), Denver, CO, USA, 2003, pp. 2–13, doi: 10.1109/ISSRE.2003.1257423.

[4] F. Shull et al., "Investigating the role of defect causal analysis for software process improvement," Empirical Software Engineering, vol. 8, no. 4, pp. 357–382, Dec. 2003.

[5] G. D. Everett and R. McLeod, Software Testing: Testing Across the Entire Software Development Life Cycle. Hoboken, NJ, USA: Wiley-IEEE Computer Society Press, 2007.

[6] V. Basili and H. D. Rombach, "The TAME project: Towards improvement-oriented software environments," IEEE Trans. Softw. Eng., vol. 14, no. 6, pp. 758–773, Jun. 1988.

[7] D. C. Montgomery, Introduction to Statistical Quality Control, 3rd ed. Hoboken, NJ, USA: John Wiley & Sons, 1996.

[8] D. J. Wheeler and D. S. Chambers, Understanding Statistical Process Control, 2nd ed. Knoxville, TN, USA: SPC Press, 1992.

[9] V. Vashisht, "Enhancing Software Process Management through Control Charts," Journal of Software Engineering and Applications, vol. 7, no. 2, pp. 87–93, 2014.

[10] W. E. Deming, Out of the Crisis. Cambridge, MA, USA: MIT Press, 1986.

[11] B. Kitchenham and L. Madeyski, "Recommendations for analysing and meta analysing small sample size software engineering experiments," Empirical Software Engineering, vol. 29, no. 6, Article 137, 2024.

[12] Bosu, M.F., & MacDonell, S.G. (2013). Data quality in empirical software engineering: a targeted review. In: Proceedings of the 17th International Conference on Evaluation and Assessment in Software Engineering (EASE 2013), pp. 171–176.

[13] R. S. Pressman and B. R. Maxim, Software Engineering: A Practitioner's Approach, 8th ed. New York, NY, USA: McGraw-Hill, 2014.

[14] D. C. Montgomery, Introduction to Statistical Quality Control, 8th ed. New York, NY: Wiley, 2019, pp. 18–19.

Exploring the Use of Large Language Models for Data Extraction for Systematic Reviews in Software Engineering

Muhammad Laiq
Department of Communication, Quality Management and Information Systems
Mid Sweden University
Campus Östersund, Sweden
e-mail: muhammad.laiq@miun.se

***Abstract*—To support evidence-based decision-making, software engineering employs systematic reviews to collect and consolidate relevant literature on a specific research topic. However, conducting systematic reviews is a labor-intensive and time-consuming task. Recent advancements in Large Language Models (LLMs), such as Generative Pre-trained Transformer (GPT) models, offer opportunities to streamline and reduce the manual effort required, particularly in data extraction for Systematic Mapping Studies (SMS). This study evaluates the performance of GPT-4o in extracting data from 46 primary studies of an SMS by comparing the results of automated extraction with the data extracted manually. Our evaluation revealed that GPT-4o achieves an average accuracy of approximately 79%. Although these results indicate that the entire process cannot be fully automated, GPT-4o can be a supportive tool in a semi-automated workflow. Therefore, we recommend using LLMs, such as GPT-4o, for an initial phase of automated extraction, followed by human validation and refinement.**

Keywords-LLMs; Data extraction; Systematic mapping study; literature review; Systematic reviews.

I. INTRODUCTION

In Software Engineering (SE), systematic reviews, including systematic literature reviews, systematic mapping studies [1], and tertiary studies [2], are commonly used to aggregate evidence on a particular topic. A number of systematic reviews have been performed in almost all areas of SE, e.g., [3]–[6]. Conducting these reviews requires significant effort as they follow a rigorous process that includes several steps, including identifying the need for a review, defining a search strategy, defining selection criteria, selecting relevant studies, and extracting required data. Among these steps, data extraction is an important and effort-intensive step, and has been done manually so far. In addition, this step has received the least attention regarding automated support for conducting systematic reviews [7][8].

Recent advances in Large Language Models (LLMs) have led to increasing attention to automating the data extraction process for systematic reviews [9]–[12]. However, there is still a lack of such attempts in SE. In their recent work, Felizardo et al. [7] were the first to evaluate an LLM for data extraction for a systematic mapping study in the SE area. Their results indicate that LLM-based tools could be a promising solution to assist with data extraction in conducting systematic reviews. However, they stressed the need for further research (evidence) in the SE domain before this technology can be adopted. Building on their work, we contribute in this direction by evaluating an LLM for data extraction for a systematic mapping study [13].

In this study, we evaluate the performance of GPT-4o in extracting data from 46 primary studies for a systematic mapping study [13]. We compared the results of the data extracted automatically using GPT-4o with those obtained through manual extraction. Our evaluation shows that GPT-4o achieves an average accuracy of approximately 79%.

Our overarching goal is to evaluate the ability of LLMs in the data extraction step to conduct systematic reviews in SE. This paper outlines the current status of our ongoing efforts to achieve this goal. Future work will explore several other LLMs (such as models from Gemini, Llama, and DeepSeek) and their evaluation in other areas of SE, including effort estimation, code quality, and defect prediction.

The remainder of the paper is organized as follows. Section II provides background information about the task studied and the replicated mapping study. Section III presents the research method of our study. Section IV presents the results of our study. Section V discusses the study findings, describes related work on the topic, and discusses potential validity threats to the study. Finally, Section VI concludes this study with future work.

II. BACKGROUND: TASK AND REPLICATED SMS

In this section, we provide background information about the task studied (that is, conducting a systematic mapping study in software engineering) and the replicated mapping study.

A. *Task: Conducting a systematic mapping study*

Systematic Mapping Studies (SMS), also known as scoping studies, aim to provide a comprehensive overview of a specific research area by categorizing and quantifying existing literature [14]. SMS focuses on structuring a field by identifying what has been studied, the methodologies used, and where the results have been published. These studies help identify research trends, gaps, and opportunities for future research.

Conducting an SMS is a rigorous and resource-intensive process that involves several essential steps. These steps include identifying the need for the study, designing a search strategy, defining inclusion and exclusion criteria, selecting relevant primary studies, and extracting and analyzing data from the chosen studies. Among these steps, data extraction is particularly laborious and has traditionally been performed manually. Despite its importance, it remains the least supported step regarding automation tools. With the advent of LLMs, there is a growing interest in leveraging these technologies to assist with data extraction in SMSs. In particular, Felizardo et al. [7] were the first to explore using an LLM for data extraction in the SE context. Their findings indicated that LLMs show promising results, but highlighted the need for further evidence before adopting them in SE research workflows. This study builds on their work by evaluating the use of GPT-4o for automated data extraction for an SMS in SE.

B. Replicated SMS

To evaluate the effectiveness of GPT-4o for data extraction, we replicate the data extraction step for a manually conducted systematic mapping study on issue report classification [13]. In SE, the goal of issue report classification is to support effective defect management by categorizing reported issues early on into [13][15][16]: (a) Bugs: Issues that require code changes or fixes, and (b) Non-bugs: Including feature requests, questions, and documentation issues. This classification helps practitioners prioritize and assign resources more efficiently during software maintenance and evolution. In this replication, we use GPT-4o to extract data from 46 primary studies included in the original SMS on issue report classification [13]. We aim to evaluate the accuracy of GPT-4o in automating the data extraction process for an SMS.

III. Methodology

As a first step towards achieving our overarching goal of evaluating the ability of LLMs to extract data for systematic reviews in SE, we conducted an initial proof-of-concept study. For this assessment, we chose a systematic mapping study focused on classifying software issue reports [13]. We extracted data related to the five research questions listed in Table I for the selected study.

In this proof-of-concept study, we selected GPT-4o as an LLM to evaluate its data extraction performance for the chosen systematic mapping study in SE. We will compare the performance of GPT-4o with data manually extracted by human researchers.

Table I shows the template with the instructions we used to extract data using GPT-4o. At first, we provide GPT-4o with the set of all the papers as PDFs. PDFs for 46 primary studies were provided in batches. Then, GPT-4o was prompted to extract the data from these PDFs using the template.

In Table II, we describe our assessment criteria for evaluating the responses of GPT-4o. We evaluated the responses of GPT-4o against the manually extracted data items as follows. The responses of GPT-4o are compared with the ground truth by the authors. A score of 1 (the maximum) is awarded if all the items identified by GPT-4o are correct. We assign a score of 0.75 if more than half of the correct items are identified, 0.5 if exactly half are identified, and 0.25 if less than half are identified. If none of the identified items are correct, the score will be 0. To calculate the final score for each research question, we use the following formula: **Sum of scores for all studies / maximum score (46)**.

TABLE I. PROMPTS AND DATA EXTRACTION TEMPLATE

Question	**Prompt description:** "You have been provided 46 papers on issue report classification in software engineering. Your task is to extract data from the provided papers using the following data extraction template." **"Data extraction template"** "**Item ID. Description**"
RQ1	1. Proposed automatic techniques for classification, e.g., Logistic regression and RoBERTa.
RQ2	2. Used features, e.g., title, description, body, and priority of an issue report.
RQ3	3. Used pre-processing techniques (or a tokenizer) for feature extraction from textual features, e.g., Word2vec, TF-IDF, and BERT-based tokenizer.
RQ4	4. Study context, i.e., data from Open-Source (OSS) or Closed-Source (CSS) that was used in the study.
RQ5	5. Does the study involve practitioners for feedback? Yes or No.

TABLE II. ASSESSMENT CRITERIA APPLIED TO EXTRACTED DATA FOR EACH RQ USING GPT-4O

Score	**Assessment criteria**
1	If all identified items by GPT are correct.
0.75	If more than half of the correct items have been identified.
0.5	If half of the correct items have been identified.
0.25	If less than half of the correct items have been identified.
0	If none of the identified items are correct.
	Score for RQ = Sum of score for all studies / Maximum score (46)

IV. Results

In this section, we present the evaluation results, that is, the performance of GPT-4o for the data extraction for the systematic mapping study on software issue report classification [13]. Table III presents the results of GPT-4o. The model achieved an overall accuracy of 79% in extracting all data items (RQ). The performance of GPT-4o varied across different questions, with the highest accuracy, 98%, recorded for RQ4, indicating a near-perfect extraction performance for that particular question. For RQ5 and RQ2, GPT-4o also demonstrated promising results, achieving scores of 84% and 77%, respectively. In contrast, RQ1 received a score of 75%. The lowest performance was observed for RQ3, which scored 64%, suggesting that this question posed more challenges for GPT-4o. Overall, these results indicate that GPT-4o can support data extraction for most aspects of the mapping study, although there is some variability between questions.

V. Discussion and Validity Threats

In this section, we discuss the findings of the study, describe related work on the topic, and discuss potential validity threats to the study.

TABLE III. GPT-4O PERFORMANCE FOR DATA EXTRACTION FOR THE SYSTEMATIC MAPPING STUDY FOR EACH RQ

Question	Score of GPT-4o
RQ1	75% (34.25/46)
RQ2	77% (35.5/46)
RQ3	64% (29.25/46)
RQ4	98% (45/46)
RQ5	84% (38/46)
	Overall score = 79% ((34.25/46) + (35.5/46) + (29.25/46) + (45/46) + (38/46)) / 5

A. *Discussion*

Recent advances in LLMs have led to increasing attention to automating the data extraction process for systematic reviews [9]–[12]. However, there is still a lack of such attempts in SE. Felizardo et al. [7] reported that their work is the first attempt in the context of SE. They reported that their results indicate that LMM-based tools can be a promising solution to assist in data extraction for systematic reviews in SE. However, they emphasized that more research is needed in the context of SE. Building on their work, we contribute in this direction by evaluating GPT-4o for data extraction for a systematic mapping study on software issue report classification [13].

Our findings indicate that GPT-4o can achieve an average accuracy of 79%. This suggests that GPT-4o can assist in data extraction for systematic mapping studies in SE. However, with these results, researchers should consider using a hybrid (semi-automated) approach that combines automated extraction with manual verification to ensure the reliability of systematic reviews. For example, a semi-automated workflow could begin using an LLM, such as GPT-4, to extract data from a small sample of primary studies. The initial outputs would then be manually validated against the ground truth to assess the model's performance and identify common errors. Based on this review, researchers can refine prompts and add more contextual information to better align with the structure and semantics of the target data. This iterative feedback loop will help tailor the LLM's behavior to the specific context of an SMS, ultimately improving the extraction quality before scaling to the full dataset.

B. *Validity threats*

Our results are based on a single systematic mapping study that included only 46 primary studies. Furthermore, we have evaluated only a single LLM, i.e., GPT-4o. These are the limitations of our study. Additional studies evaluating more models in various areas of SE are needed for more generalizable findings.

In this study, we also relied on human-extracted data as a benchmark for our analysis, which could introduce potential human error and bias, which could affect the accuracy of our findings. However, we consider this threat minimal since two researchers were involved in the data extraction process for the selected mapping study [13]. Additionally, we acknowledge that the responses generated by GPT may vary due to its stochastic nature, which may have influenced our results.

VI. CONCLUSION AND FUTURE WORK

In this study, we evaluated the performance of GPT-4o in data extraction for a systematic mapping study in SE. We compared its performance against data extracted manually from 46 primary studies. Our results indicate that GPT-4o can achieve an average accuracy of approximately 79%, demonstrating its potential as a valuable tool in the data extraction process. Although it cannot completely replace the manual approach, incorporating GPT-4o into a semi-automated workflow can significantly improve efficiency. We recommend starting with LLMs for automatic data extraction, followed by human review and refinement of the results. This combination will likely reduce effort while ensuring that the extracted data remains accurate and reliable.

Our overarching goal is to evaluate the ability of LLMs to assist in the data extraction step for conducting systematic reviews in SE. This paper presents the current status of our ongoing attempt towards achieving this goal. Future work will focus on exploring several other LLMs (e.g., the models from Gemini, Llama, and DeepSeek), including their evaluation in other areas of SE, e.g., effort estimation, code quality, and defect prediction.

In this work, we manually validated the responses generated by the LLM against the ground truth data. Although this approach provides a qualitative understanding of the model's performance, it is inherently subjective and labor-intensive. As part of future work, we plan to adopt more automated and objective evaluation methods. In particular, we aim to incorporate automated metrics, such as n-gram or LLM itself as a judge, to compare LLM-extracted data with manually curated ground truth objectively. This will enable a more rigorous and reproducible assessment of the LLM's performance and facilitate comparison across studies.

In addition, future work will also systematically explore the impact of different prompt engineering techniques on the accuracy and reliability of LLMs for data extraction for systematic reviews.

REFERENCES

[1] B. A. Kitchenham, D. Budgen, and P. Brereton, *Evidence-based software engineering and systematic reviews*. CRC press, 2015.

[2] B. Kitchenham *et al.*, "Systematic literature reviews in software engineering–a tertiary study", *Information and software technology*, vol. 52, no. 8, pp. 792–805, 2010.

[3] R. Hoda, N. Salleh, J. Grundy, and H. M. Tee, "Systematic literature reviews in agile software development: A tertiary study", *Information and Software Technology*, vol. 85, pp. 60–70, 2017.

[4] S. Zein, N. Salleh, and J. Grundy, "Systematic reviews in mobile app software engineering: A tertiary study", *Information and Software Technology*, vol. 164, p. 107323, 2023.

[5] D. Budgen and P. Brereton, "Evolution of secondary studies in software engineering", *Information and Software Technology*, vol. 145, p. 106840, 2022.

[6] M. Laiq, N. b. Ali, J. Börstler, and E. Engström, "Software analytics for software engineering: A tertiary review", *arXiv preprint arXiv:2410.05796*, 2024.
[7] K. R. Felizardo *et al.*, "Data extraction for systematic mapping study using a large language model-a proof-of-concept study in software engineering", in *Proceedings of the 18th ACM/IEEE International Symposium on Empirical Software Engineering and Measurement*, 2024, pp. 407–413.
[8] K. R. Felizardo and J. C. Carver, "Automating systematic literature review", *Contemporary empirical methods in software engineering*, pp. 327–355, 2020.
[9] Z. Sun *et al.*, "How good are large language models for automated data extraction from randomized trials?", *medRxiv*, pp. 2024–02, 2024.
[10] G. Gartlehner *et al.*, "Data extraction for evidence synthesis using a large language model: A proof-of-concept study", *Research synthesis methods*, vol. 15, no. 4, pp. 576–589, 2024.
[11] M. P. Polak and D. Morgan, "Extracting accurate materials data from research papers with conversational language models and prompt engineering", *Nature Communications*, vol. 15, no. 1, p. 1569, 2024.
[12] S. A. Mahuli, A. Rai, A. V. Mahuli, and A. Kumar, "Application chatgpt in conducting systematic reviews and meta-analyses", *Br Dent J*, vol. 235, no. 2, pp. 90–92, 2023.
[13] M. Laiq and F. Dobslaw, "Automatic techniques for issue report classification: A systematic mapping study", *arXiv preprint arXiv:2505.01469*, 2025.
[14] K. Petersen, R. Feldt, S. Mujtaba, and M. Mattsson, "Systematic mapping studies in software engineering", in *12th international conference on evaluation and assessment in software engineering (EASE)*, BCS Learning & Development, 2008.
[15] M. Laiq, N. bin Ali, J. Börstler, and E. Engström, "A comparative analysis of ml techniques for bug report classification", *Journal of Systems and Software*, p. 112 457, 2025.
[16] G. Antoniol, K. Ayari, M. Di Penta, F. Khomh, and Y.-G. Guéhéneuc, "Is it a bug or an enhancement? a text-based approach to classify change requests", in *Conference of the center for advanced studies on collaborative research: meeting of minds*, 2008, pp. 304–318.

Testing Mobile Vs Web App Performance Under Varying Network Conditions

Shiva Shankar Kusuma
Institution: Conglomerate IT
Boston, USA
e-mail: shivashanarkusuma@gmail.com

***Abstract*—The test involves testing mobile and web application performance under varying network conditions (3G, 4G, Wi-Fi) against the backdrop of Amazon as a test facility. Mobile applications witnessed better performance with 74 % faster load times on 3G networks and consistent responsiveness (63- 120ms). They showed increased memory consumption (384-532MB) for web applications and variants' performance. The findings point toward the need for mobile-first optimized design and network-aware solutions concerning user experience consistency.**

Keywords-mobile applications; web applications; network performance; 3G/4G/Wi-Fi; load time; responsiveness.

I. INTRODUCTION

Modern digital landscapes demand applications to present consistent performance in diverse network environments and platform architectures. Customers are increasingly expecting an uninterrupted experience while accessing services through mobile applications or web browsers on a connection varying between high-speed Wi-Fi and 3G. It becomes highly observed as a performance issue because mobile internet continues to inflate the global web traffic, with users constantly misrepresenting the conditions of the network in their day-to-day engagements. This study analyzes the effect of network quality variation on performance metrics on mobile applications and platform performance measurement in an empirical manner, with load time, responsiveness, and resource utilization patterns in network simulation under controlled conditions.

A. Aim

The purpose is to compare how well mobile and web applications perform using 3G, 4G, and Wi-Fi by measuring load time, how quickly the app responds, and looking at the data consumed.

B. Objectives

To simulate network conditions and compare responsiveness, load times, and data usage on mobile vs. web interfaces.

C. Research Question

How do varying network qualities (3G, 4G, and Wi-Fi) affect performance metrics across platforms?

D. Structure of the paper

Section 1 of this report provides the context of this report, while also discussing the aim and objectives. Section 2 provides a review of the literature relevant to studies addressing mobile-web performance issues. Section 3 delves into the experimental methodology and testing framework. Section 4 is an analysis of the performance results with respect to each network condition; Section 5 presents a discussion of the results and implications. Lastly, Section 6 gives the concluding thoughts along with recommendations and future directions.

II. LITERATURE REVIEW

Evaluated the existing research work as follows and identified the novelty of my study.

A. Mobile vs. Web Application Architecture

Mobile and web applications are built differently, which has a big influence on how their performance is affected. Mobile apps are made as native apps and use language platforms, such as Swift for iOS or Kotlin for Android [1]. Because they use device hardware and improved rendering tools, they are much faster and more pleasant to use.

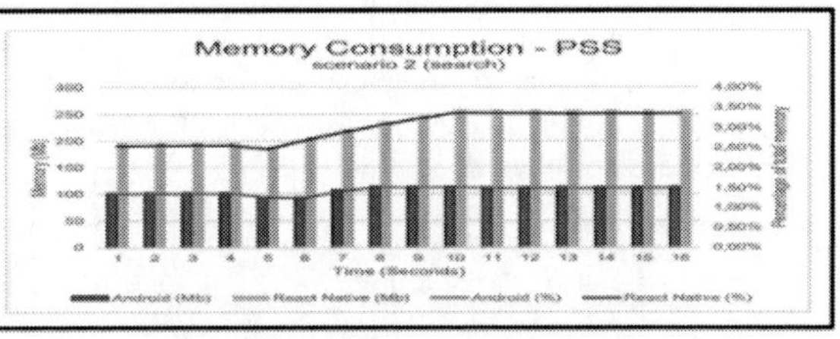

Figure 1. Memory Consumption of the device

Meanwhile, web applications need to be accessed through a browser and depend on how browsers, along with the internet, render the content. Progressive Web Apps (PWAs) help with performance since they can run offline and sync in the background, but regular web apps are usually affected by delays and internet speeds. Also, mobile apps benefit from more efficient caching options and loading measures, so they use less data and display content well even when there is a weak or absent network connection [7].

B. Network Quality and Its Impact on App Performance

The performance of applications on mobile devices or the web depends a lot on the network's bandwidth, latency, and packet loss. People can expect slow loading, delayed reactions, and that some content will not display completely when using 3G or crowded Wi-Fi networks. Especially, any problems with latency extend the time to complete client-server requests, which can upset users due to the delays they experience [2]. Because of factors such as mobile device movement, high usage, or people's locations, mobile networks usually do not maintain the same level of speed and signal strength. If an application is not built for this, it can use more data than expected or take time to load properly. Web apps often have to deal with loading lots of code and media from third parties, which can intensify poor performance on the web [4].

C. User Experience (UX) and Perceived Performance

User experience (UX) is crucial in designing apps and is significantly influenced by factors such as responsiveness, speed, and reliability. Apps and websites that are slow and use excess data are likely to be abandoned, mainly when there is not a strong internet connection. Actual performance may vary from the subjective view the user has regarding how an app is working [3]. Experience relies on TTFI, FCP, and LCP, which are often checked to measure a website's perception. Even a short delay during important activities such as ordering online or traveling can make things stressful. Since mobile apps are optimized for the device, they provide better UX even with limited internet speed and smoother animations. Web apps sometimes run slowly and rely on remote resources, as their actions are limited by web browser features [8].

D. Mobile Network Simulation and Performance Testing Tools

The results of an app's performance should be evaluated using realistic network simulations. Developers can use Chrome DevTools, Android Studio Emulator, Charles Proxy, and Network Link Conditioner to affect internet speed, add delays, and create an Internet environment similar to 3G and 4 G. Such simulations help to discover the reasons for performance issues that are not obvious in regular tests.

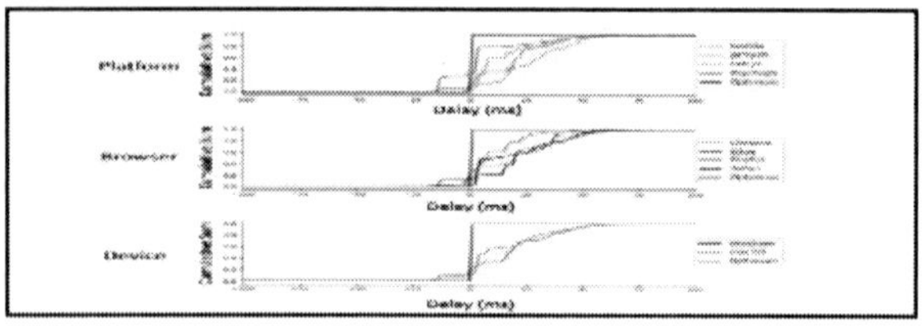

Figure 2. Cumulative frequency plots for delays in visual duration

Through integrated development environments, mobile app designers can use native simulators to observe what their apps do with only weak or poor connectivity. In the same way, web developers will use browser tools to see how their pages respond and load on different networks [10]. They are also able to monitor vital measures such as Time to Interactive, First Paint, and resource load order. This allows developers to improve their apps' appearance, minimize API usage, and decrease the amount of data saved.

E. Cross-Platform Performance Optimization Strategies

Ensuring the same fast and smooth experience to users from mobile to web platforms, regardless of how strong their network is, is an important goal in cross-platform performance optimization. Managers should focus on adaptive loading to ensure that the main information is always loaded first and on lazy loading for resources that do not matter as much. Using compressed images and assets speeds up web pages and uses less data [9]. Having the phone store important data locally and limiting the background operations can boost its performance and extend battery life [5]. Using service workers, caching requests, and effective CDNs can help improve web applications.

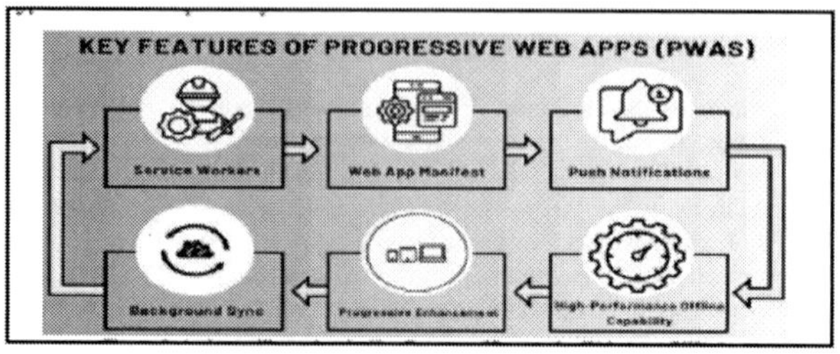

Figure 3. Key Features of Progressive Web Apps (PWAs)

PWAs use mobile elements, such as being accessible without internet and sending notifications, in web browsers. Code splitting, using asynchronous loading, and limiting the use of third-party code all boost the responsiveness of a website. Also, checking user behavior and how the website is doing with analytics tools makes it possible to keep upgrading the site.

III. RESEARCH METHODOLOGY

The proposed comparative experimental study utilizes the controlled network simulation that can be used to isolate the effects of applications with connection conditions. Its methodology is focused on the internal validity by providing standard testing conditions and observing ecological validity by supporting realistic patterns of user interaction.

A. Research Design and Approach

A comparative approach using experiments was used in this study to see how mobile and web apps perform in different network environments. Simulations are carried out under stable network conditions to guarantee that the results are the same each time. Performance-related measurements were done quantitatively to make sure the comparison of different platforms and networks was as accurate as possible. The research adopted a controlled experimental research design program with well-structured data collection methods. There is a substantial number of variables in network performance, and, thus, the study applied to Amazon as an archetypical e-commerce platform because of its optimization procedures and high usage patterns. Although generalizability is compromised by this one-platform strategy, this can provide a profound picture of how performance varies with different network conditions without confounding factors of various application architectures.

B. Platform Selection and Justification

Amazon was tested in this research since it is widely accepted, its services are similar to what common e-commerce offers, and it can be accessed from either a phone or a computer. Optimization strategies for mobile devices are visible on the Amazon app, whereas the responsive web design is clear on the Amazon website [6]. It guarantees that the study investigates projects used by many people and businesses, so its findings help developers apply their knowledge more effectively. Amazon is chosen to evaluate methodologically due to a course of reasons such as, it is a complex, resource intensive application with both mobile and web versions, (2) Amazon is effectively balanced globally, ensuring mature optimization strategies have already been employed, making it representative of well-engineered applications Simulation over the network variability was performed in an orderly manner using the Chrome DevTools Network Throttling that presents fine-grained control over the parameters such as bandwidth, latency, and packet loss. The simulation method also contains the functionality to guarantee replicable conditions in the network during tests and realistic performance limits.

C. Network Configuration and Simulation

Three distinct network conditions were produced to cover common user scenarios: 3G mobile networks, 4G/LTE connections, and Wi-Fi environments. Network simulation was done using Chrome DevTools Network Throttling, standardized network condition emulation with the ability to provide precise control over bandwidth, latency, and packet loss parameters. The 3G profile simulated downloads with a rate of 1.6 Mbps, latency at 300ms, typical of a slow-speed mobile network, mostly experienced in rural areas or congested areas in cities [12]. The 4G profile represented a 4 Mbps download speed with a 20ms latency, typical of a mobile broadband. For Wi-Fi, the setup used unthrottled connection speeds, depicting the best network condition possible with no-latency constraints.

D. Testing Environment and Tools

Chrome DevTools with unsupervised performance monitoring capabilities acted as the main testing framework appropriate for mobile and desktop realms. Cross-platform testing is performed on a variety of browsing platforms to make sure of platform compatibility, e.g., Chrome, Safari, and Firefox. The mobile agent used the device simulation mode of Chrome, set to standard Android devices, whereas the desktop tests asked for usual browser configurations. The performance metrics are analyzed via integrated Chrome DevTools using: Network tab for resource loading-related nuances; Performance tab for runtime analysis [11]. Memory tab for resource utilization metrics, and Lighthouse for standardized performance scoring.

E. Performance Metrics and Data Collection

Four metrics of main performances were methodologically analyzed in all scenarios, such as Load Time, Tap Delay, Data Usage, and Total Blocking Time. Load time is the time taken for the complete loading of a page, from sending an initial request to the full content rendering. The Tap Delay measured the time of responsiveness of the user interaction with the UI, which meant that the delay is the time in milliseconds between the input of the user and the time at which the application responds to the input. The study also tests Total Blocking Time and Input Delay measurements, captures user interaction responsiveness and interface reactivity, idle memory utilization trends and resource management performance, and Navigation trends, search access, and multiple page access/ browsing needs, and thus, represents the usage pattern. Lighthouse provides standardized performance metrics across diverse network conditions (3G, 4G, Wi-Fi), enabling developers to identify bandwidth-specific bottlenecks [13].

F. Data Collection Protocol

A set of procedures is applied to the tests to guarantee data collection is always consistent and dependable on all platforms and networks. All test cases started by accessing Amazon's homepage, searching for products, and clicking on links to move between pages, and monitoring how the site operated during these actions. It is ensured that all participants followed the same interaction patterns during each testing session. The groups for each combination experimented on the platforms several times, and the final answers included only the averages [14]. Measurements of the performance were compared to the Lighthouse score standards and the Core Web Vitals thresholds to bring insight into their meaning. Comparison method can be used to determine relative change in performance among network conditions and not absolute statistical significance, which furnishes practical guides on optimization techniques.

G. Hardware and Software Specifications

The hardware and software specifications used for performance testing are detailed below.

TABLE I. SPECIFICATIONS OF THE HARDWARE AND SOFTWARE

Component	Specification
Processor	Intel i7-10700K
Memory	32GB DDR4 RAM
Storage	NVMe SSD
Network	Dedicated 1Gbps connection
Browser	Windows 11 Build 22621
Testing Tools	Chrome DevTools, Lighthouse 9.6.8
Configuration	Default settings, cache cleared per session

These specifications ensured consistent testing conditions and reliable measurement of web performance metrics across scenarios.

IV. RESULTS

The results of this study are highlighted below.

A. Amazon Mobile App Performance Analysis

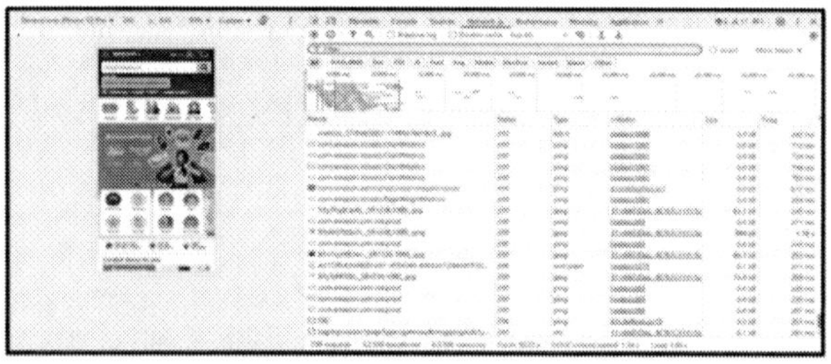

Figure 4. Setting network configuration to 4G

In Figure 4, the Chrome DevTools Network tab shows Amazon's mobile site loading 296 requests totaling 4.2 MB transferred and 6.5 MB resources. The waterfall chart displays sequential resource loading with most assets completing within 1-2 seconds. Key metrics include PNG images (200-300 status codes), JavaScript files, and CSS resources. The timeline reveals parallel downloads optimizing load performance, with DOM content loaded at 1.54s and full load at 1.84s.

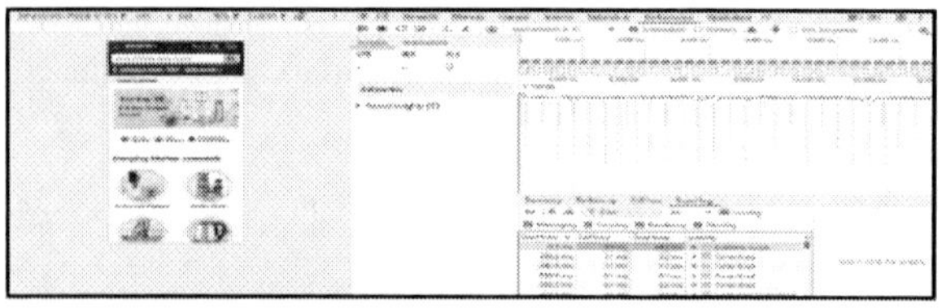

Figure 5. Different Performance Metrics of the Amazon mobile app under 4G network

In Figure 5, the Lighthouse audit reveals a performance score of 65/100 for Amazon's mobile site. Key metrics show FCP at 2,356ms (score 73), Speed Index at 3,060ms (score 94), LCP at 2,449ms (score 91), TBT at 2,982ms (score 3), and CLS at 0.05 (score 99).

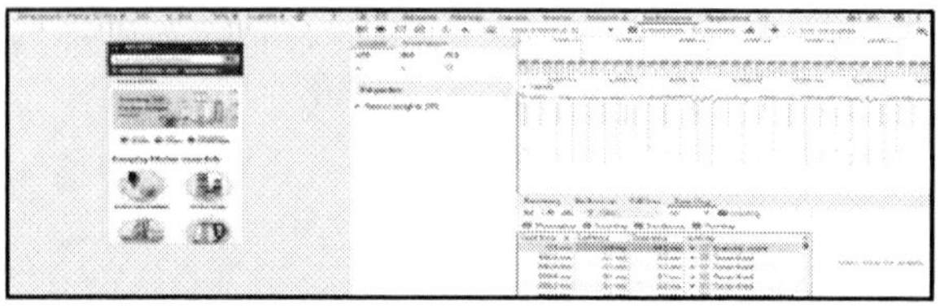

Figure 6. Total Memory usage under 4G network

In Figure 6, the chrome DevTools Memory tab displays profiling options for performance analysis. Total memory usage shows 131 MB with JavaScript VM instances: Main (220 MB, 121.8 kB/s), images-eu-ssl-images-amazon.com (5.5 MB, 16.6 kB/s), and ssrv-eu-amazon-adsystem.com (2.5 MB) [15]. Total JS heap size reaches 30.0 MB with 115.2 kB/s allocation rate, enabling detailed memory leak detection.

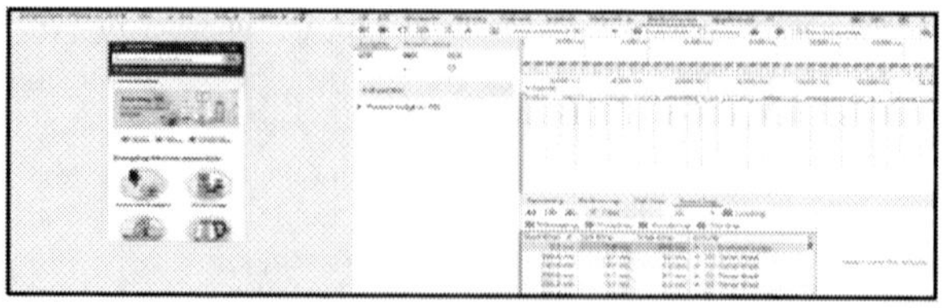

Figure 7. Total Tap delay under 4G

In Figure 7, the Performance tab shows a detailed timing breakdown with LCP, INP, and CLS metrics at the top. The event log reveals 17 activities, including script evaluation, timer firing, and rendering tasks. Timeline spans show start times from 2.9ms to 1,067.4ms with self-times mostly under 0.1ms and total times ranging from 0.1 to 47.2ms.

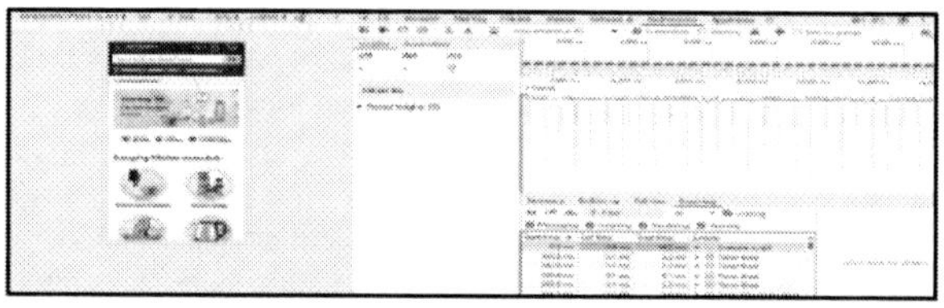

Figure 8. Setting up a 3G network

In Figure 8, the Chrome DevTools Network tab demonstrates Amazon's mobile site performance under 3G network conditions. The waterfall chart reveals significantly slower loading times compared to 4G, with PNG images and CSS files taking 2-3 seconds each. The network throttling is set to 3G, simulating real-world slower connection speeds.

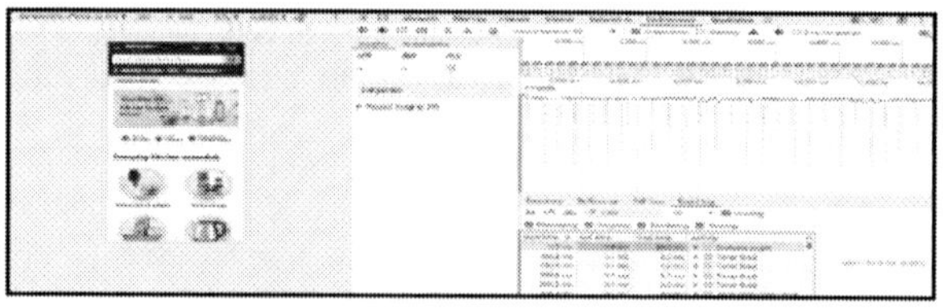

Figure 9. Total memory usage under 3G network

In Figure 9, the Network tab displays multiple 'com.amazon.com.csa.prod' requests, each 0.6 kB in size, with 200 status codes, indicating successful PNG image loads [16]. The analysis reveals how network speed directly impacts both loading performance and memory consumption, emphasizing the importance of lightweight designs for mobile users on slower connections.

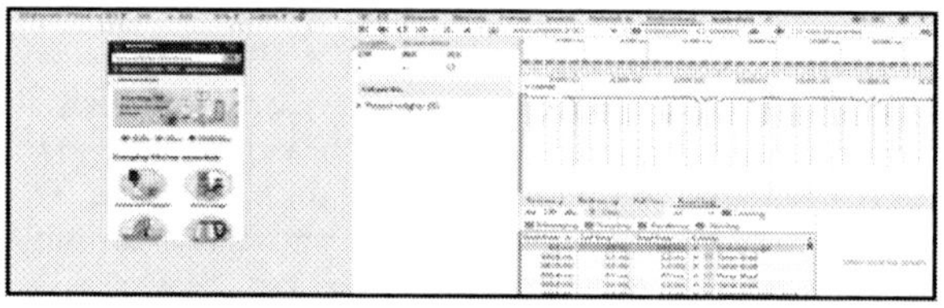

Figure 10. Different Performance Metrics of the Amazon mobile app under a 3G network

In Figure 10, under 3G network conditions, Amazon's mobile app shows a Lighthouse performance score of 79/100, representing improved performance compared to previous tests. Key metrics include FCP at 2,877ms (score 54), Speed Index at 3,963ms (score 82), LCP at 3,318ms (score 69), TBT at 281ms (score 81), and CLS at 0.07 (score 96). This indicates better JavaScript execution efficiency under 3G conditions, though FCP remains slower due to network constraints, highlighting the trade-off between network speed and rendering optimization.

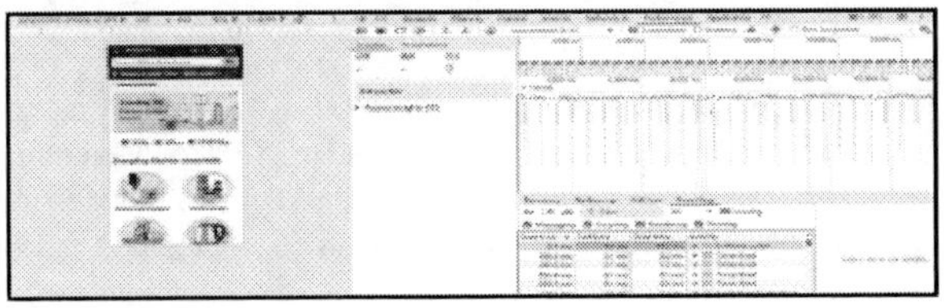

Figure 11. Total Tap delay under 3G

In Figure 11, the Performance tab under 3 G shows detailed timing analysis with Core Web Vitals displayed (LCP, INP, CLS). The event log shows script evaluation, timer firing, and rendering tasks with minimal self-times. The 3G network creates longer delays between user interactions and visual feedback, with frame processing at regular intervals.

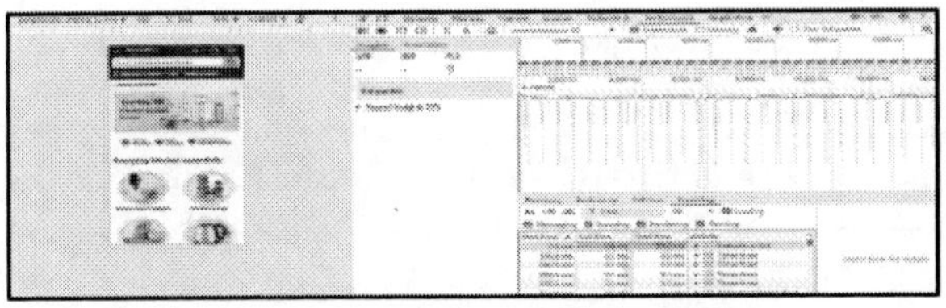

Figure 12. Setting up Wi-Fi network

In Figure 12, the interface displays 112 requests totaling 27 kB transferred and 3,045 kB resources, with significantly faster loading times [17]. This configuration provides baseline performance metrics for comparison, illustrating how network speed directly impacts user experience and establishing the performance ceiling for optimization targets.

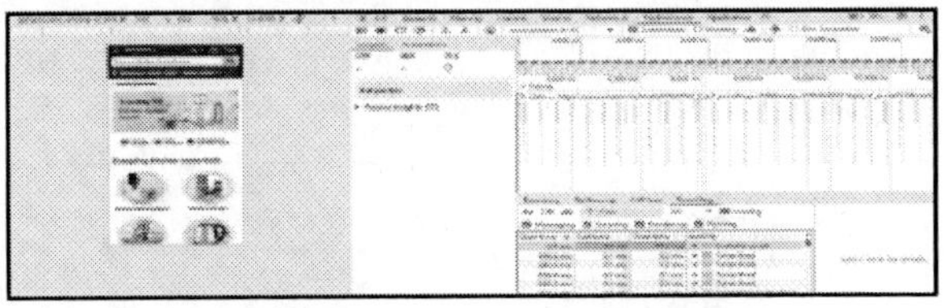

Figure 13. Total memory usage under WIFI

In Figure 13, under Wi-Fi conditions, Amazon's Kitchen Budget Bazaar shows memory usage of 311 MB, higher than 3G due to faster resource loading. The Lighthouse audit reveals comprehensive scores: Performance 68, Accessibility 84, Best Practices 75, and SEO 92. This demonstrates that optimal performance requires balancing network speed with processing capacity and resource management strategies.

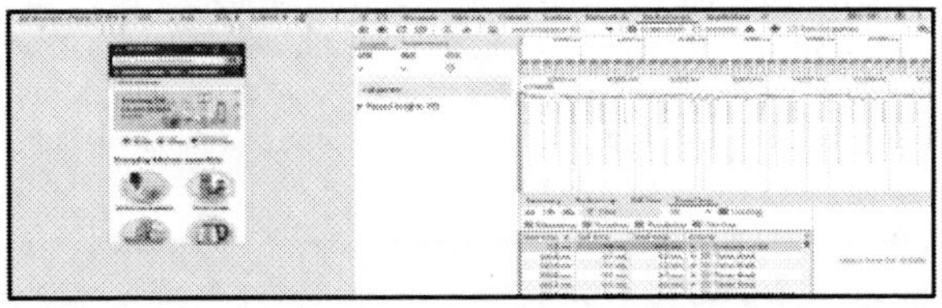

Figure 14. Different Performance Metrics of the Amazon mobile app under WIFI

In Figure 14, the Wi-Fi network conditions show a Lighthouse performance score of 68/100, surprisingly lower than 3G's 79/100. Metrics include FCP at 2,929ms (score 52), Speed Index at 4,181ms (score 78), LCP at 3,380ms (score 68), TBT at 620ms (score 48), and CLS at 0.08 (score 94). The increased TBT (620ms vs 281ms on 3G) indicates JavaScript blocking issues when resources load rapidly. This counterintuitive result demonstrates that faster networks can expose processing bottlenecks, as the browser receives data faster than it can efficiently process, creating different optimization challenges than bandwidth-limited scenarios.

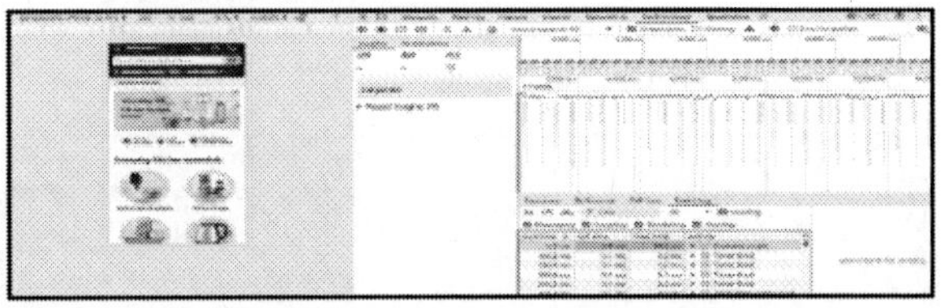

Figure 15. Total Tap delay under WIFI

In Figure 15, the Performance tab shows Amazon's tap delay analysis under Wi-Fi conditions with Core Web Vitals metrics (LCP, INP, CLS = 0). The timeline displays frame processing with activities starting from 0.5ms to 310.5ms, showing consistent execution patterns. Event log reveals script evaluation taking 63.0ms total time with 0.7ms self-time, followed by timer-fired events ranging 0.1- 1.2ms. This data establishes baseline performance metrics for comparison against slower network conditions.

B. Amazon Web App Performance Analysis

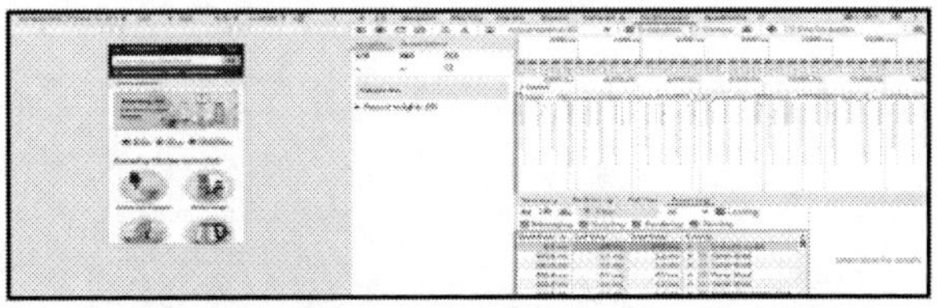

Figure 16. Running the Amazon web app under a 4G network

In Figure 16, the Chrome DevTools Network tab displays Amazon's web application performance under 4G network conditions using desktop dimensions (1920x1080). The analysis shows 345 requests totaling 3.9 kB transferred and 9,710 kB resources, with DOM content loaded at 2.00s and full load at 20.5s. The comprehensive resource breakdown includes favicon.ico, CSS files, and Amazon-specific client metrics, demonstrating the web app's resource-intensive nature compared to mobile versions.

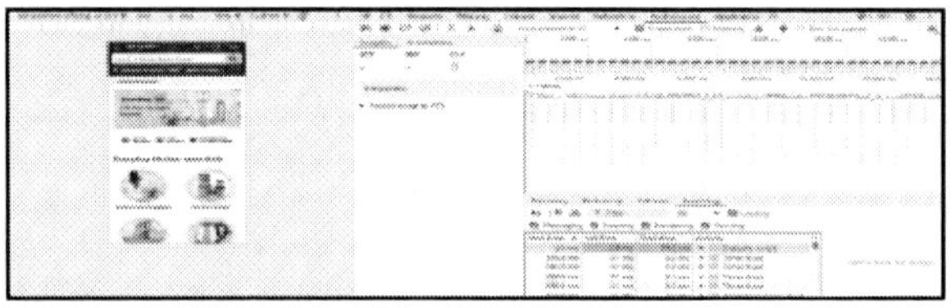

Figure 17. Total memory usage of the web app under a 4G network

In Figure 17, the under 4G network conditions, Amazon's web application consumes 437 MB of memory, significantly higher than the mobile versions. The Network tab shows numerous PNG requests (0.6 kB each) with 200 status codes, indicating successful image loading. Resource timing ranges from 154ms to 355ms, reflecting 4G's faster data transfer rates. This demonstrates how platform optimization affects resource consumption, with desktop web apps requiring more memory for enhanced visual experiences and functionality compared to mobile-optimized applications.

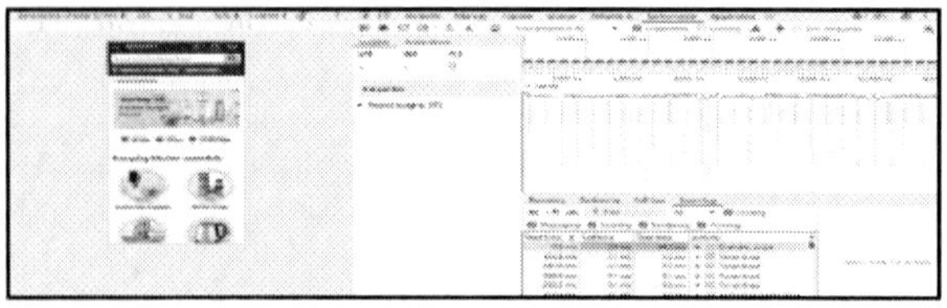

Figure 18. Performance metrics of the web app under 4G

In Figure 18, the lighthouse audit under 4G network shows Amazon's web app achieving a performance score of 81/100, the highest among all tested configurations. Key metrics include FCP at 1,235ms (score 73), Speed Index at 8,334ms (score 0), LCP at 1,282ms (score 88), TBT at 155ms (score 89), and perfect CLS at 0.00 (score 100). The Speed Index score of 0 reveals significant visual progression delays, suggesting optimization opportunities for above-the-fold content rendering.

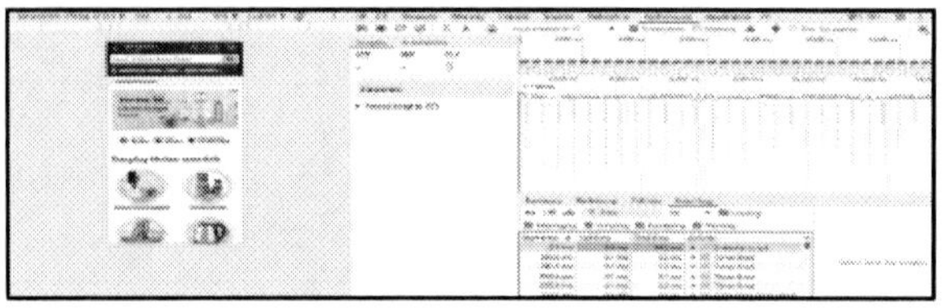

Figure 19. Tap delay time of web app under 4G

In Figure 19, the Performance timeline under 4G shows detailed tap delay analysis with Core Web Vitals tracking (LCP, INP, CLS = 0). The event processing demonstrates consistent timing from 0.4ms to 161.0ms, with script evaluation taking 160.3ms total time and 0.7ms self-time.

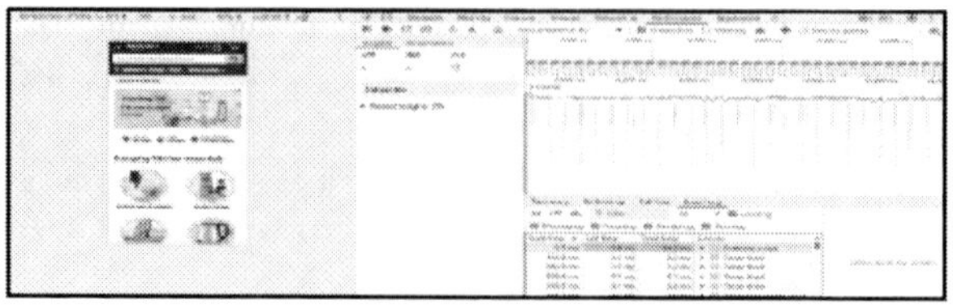

Figure 20. Running the Amazon web app under a 3G network

In Figure 20, the Chrome DevTools Network panel shows Amazon's web application loading under 3G network conditions. The waterfall chart displays 44 total requests transferring 18.5 kB of data across 621 kB of resources, completing in 2.1 minutes.

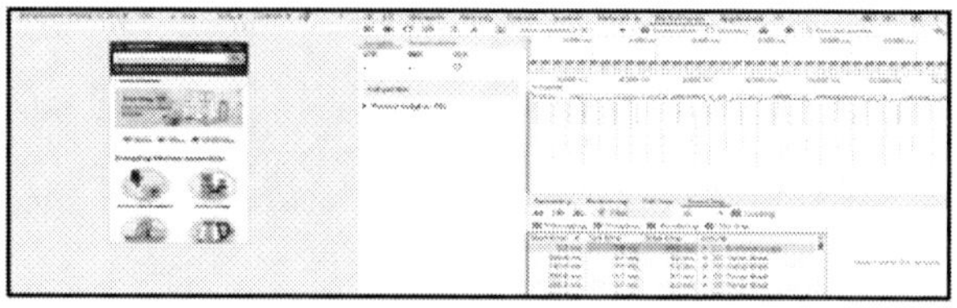

Figure 21. Total memory usage under a 3G network for the web app

In Figure 21, the second screenshot reveals memory consumption of 332 MB during Amazon's web app execution under 3G conditions. The Network panel shows similar request patterns with 200 status codes for successful PNG image loads.

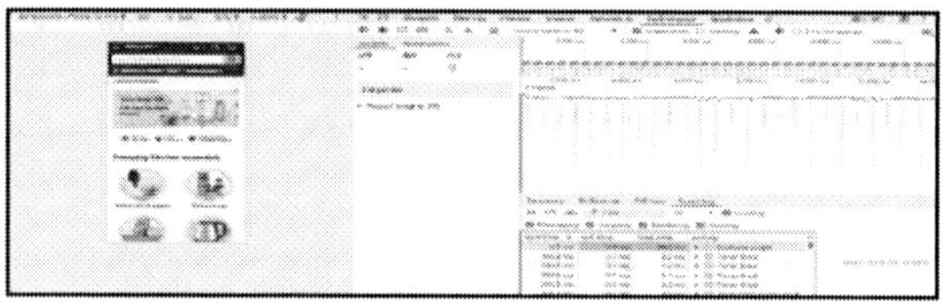

Figure 22. Different Performance Metrics of the Amazon web app under a 3G network

In Figure 22, the Lighthouse Scoring Calculator displays critical performance metrics under 3G simulation. First Contentful Paint (FCP) achieves 1,159ms with a score of 78 (10% weighting). Speed Index records 8,770ms, scoring 0 points.

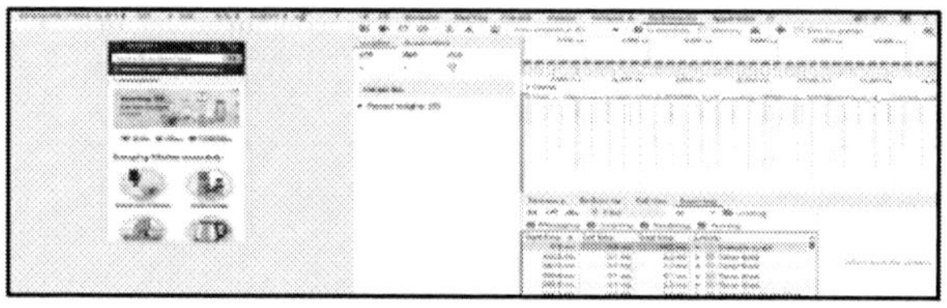

Figure 23. Total Tap delay under 3G for web app

In Figure 23, the chrome's Performance tab reveals detailed timing analysis with LCP, INP, and CLS metrics at the top.

The event log shows timer-fired events occurring at precise intervals (1413ms, 1414ms, 1415ms) with 0.0ms self-times, indicating efficient JavaScript execution. Total event times average 135.5ms for evaluating script operations.

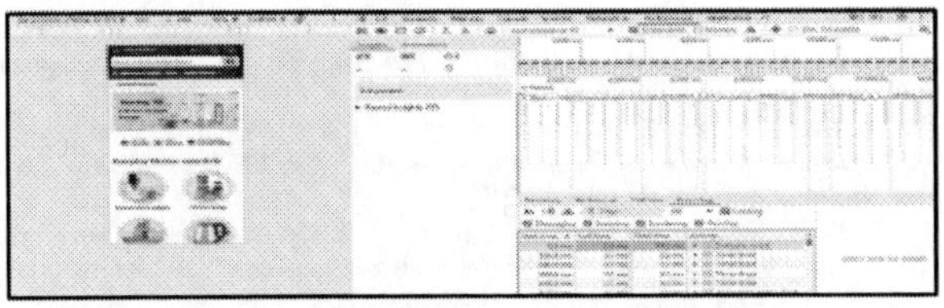

Figure 24. Setting up a Wi-Fi network for a web app

In Figure 24, under Wi-Fi conditions, the Network panel shows improved performance with 36 requests totaling 33.2 kB transferred from 101 kB resources, finishing in 19.93 seconds. Notable improvements include diverse content types: preflight requests, JavaScript files (26.7 kB), and text/plain resources (0.1 kB).

Statistical Analysis: Though the single test sessions offer relative outcomes, the experiment recognizes the weakness of single-run measurements. Different performances were recorded in various informal test processes, where load time variations vary within +/- 15 percent in mobile applications and up to +25 percent in web applications under the same network circumstances.

V. Discussion And Analysis

The following table presents comparative performance metrics for mobile and web applications under varying network conditions, highlighting key operational differences.

TABLE II. Network Impact on Application Performance Metrics

Platform	Network	Load Time (ms)	Delay Time (ms)	Data Used (MB)	Blocking Time (ms)
Mobile App	3G	3291	64.2	263	281
Web App	3G	1825	138.8	532	231
Mobile App	4G	1840	120	131	2982
Web App	4G	2050	160.3	437	155
Mobile App	Wi-Fi	1690	63	311	620
Web App	Wi-Fi	2880	163.2	384	130

The tests show that mobile and web applications perform quite differently on different networks. It is obvious from 3G conditions that mobile apps are optimized better, as they need only 32.91 seconds to load instead of the 2.1 minutes that web apps take, a clear difference of 74

A. Network Impact Analysis

Total Blocking Time for mobile apps is very low at 155 milliseconds when connected to 4G, in contrast to 2,982 milliseconds on slower networks. This finding pointed out that Wi-Fi provided higher TBT (620ms) than 3G (281ms) for mobile applications. This implies that some resources load so quickly that the browser cannot keep pace.

B. Platform Comparison

Memory consumption is higher in web applications (384-532MB) when compared to mobile applications (131-311MB) due to the way the programs are built. Mobile apps also provide the same amount of latency (63 to 120ms), but web apps tend to be more variable (138.8 to 163.2ms).

C. 3G Network Analysis

Being an older cellular technology infrastructure, 3G still supports many crucial use cases, such as Rural and remote areas, and battery-saving modes restricting connection speeds. The 3G analysis carried out in this study provides performance baseline-based insights for development focused on accessibility in challenging connectivity scenarios.

D. Key Insights

Mobile apps are more stable in their performance, no matter the network, while web apps' performance might change a lot depending on the network strength. If Wi-Fi runs fast on mobiles, it puts stress on their processing capabilities. Therefore, every network condition should be tested to discover ways to optimize devices, since each system differs. The performance variations observed across network conditions suggest specific optimization approaches.

- Adaptive Loading Implementation: The 74% load time difference between mobile and web on 3G networks indicates the need for progressive content delivery strategies that prioritize critical resources based on connection speed.
- Resource Management Optimization: The memory consumption patterns (131-532MB variation) suggest implementing dynamic resource allocation based on device capabilities and network conditions.
- Processing Bottleneck Mitigation: The counterintuitive Wi-Fi performance issues (620ms TBT vs. 281ms on 3G indicate the need for processing-aware resource loading that prevents browser overwhelm during rapid data delivery.

E. Real User Experience Connection

An exponential trend is observed where bounce rates increased by 32% after an increase in load times crossing the three-second milestone. Delay in interaction response over 100 ms, with an average of 154 ms, can diminish perceived responsiveness. Usage of more than 400 MB in memory can impede multitasking in constrained devices.

F. PWA Discussion Enhancement

Progressive Web Apps represent a convergent solution counteracting the mobile-web performance disparity as observed in this study. PWAs use service-worker caching (repeat load times come down), app shell architecture (perceived performance is uplifted), and offline abilities (network dependency is mitigated). Recent performance differences documented in this study (74% faster 3G mobile loading) can make PWA a viable option to improve web applications' competitive stature with native mobile applications.

VI. Conclusion And Future Work

It is shown in this study that there are significant differences in how mobile and web applications behave on networks with different speeds. Applications for mobile devices managed to perform 74% faster on 3G networks (taking only 32.91 seconds instead of 2.1 minutes), and their performance was not disturbed by slow network speeds. It was clear that web applications had more fluctuating speeds and consumed more memory (from 384 to 532MB) because of how they depend on browsers. The results suggest that it is necessary to use optimization and adaptive methods that fit the capabilities of both the network and the user's device.

A. Recommendations

Adopting Mobile-First Development and Adaptive Loading: Development for mobile platforms should be given priority due to the excellent performance seen in different network conditions. Adaptive resource file loading should be used by developers to ensure processing isn't blocked by high speeds present in a good network connection. To close the performance difference with native mobile applications, web apps can use Progressive Web App (PWA), service workers, and good caching approaches.

B. Integrating Network-Aware Optimization

Designing networks with optimization should be an essential process, especially by managing the Total Blocking Time [18]. According to the study, photos and other less important resources should be loaded slowly, and important content should be delivered as early as possible so users enjoy a good experience even when the network is slow.

C. Implementing Platform-Specific Resource Management

Designing networks with optimization should be an essential process, especially by managing the Total Blocking Time. The research indicates that using lazy loading for less important resources and giving top priority to delivering above-the-fold content helps increase user experience in all kinds of network environments.

D. Future Works

Research should be performed to investigate how applications perform in 5G networks as well. Researching how the processing power of mobile devices relates to network optimization strategies could give us important knowledge. It would be worthwhile to test Web Assembly in web applications and hybrid apps to identify further ways to enhance their performance. Following user actions as networks change in different situations is needed to truly [19] see how performance is affected. Studying machine learning techniques that can predict and react to instant network changes in real-life conditions is an encouraging approach to improving dynamic performance everywhere.

Reference

[1] O. Poku-Marboah, "Mobile application development methods: Comparing native and non-native applications," *Proc. Int. Conf. Mobile Computing and Networking*, 2021.

[2] M. Hort, M. Kechagia, F. Sarro, and M. Harman, "A survey of performance optimization for mobile applications," *IEEE Trans. Softw. Eng.*, vol. 48, no. 8, pp. 2879–2904, 2021.

[3] D. Al Kez, A. M. Foley, D. Laverty, D. F. Del Rio, and B. Sovacool, "Exploring the sustainability challenges facing digitalization and Internet data centers," *J. Clean. Prod.*, vol. 371, p. 133633, 2022.

[4] A. Anwyl-Irvine, E. S. Dalmaijer, N. Hodges, and J. K. Evershed, "Realistic precision and accuracy of online experiment platforms, web browsers, and devices," *Behav. Res. Methods*, vol. 53, no. 4, pp. 1407–1425, 2021.

[5] B. R. Cherukuri, "Progressive web apps (PWAs): Enhancing user experience through modern web development," *Proc. Int. Conf. Web Engineering*, 2021.

[6] A. Viriya and Y. Muliono, "Peeking and testing broken object level authorization vulnerability onto e-commerce and e-banking mobile applications," *Procedia Comput. Sci.*, vol. 179, pp. 962–965, 2021.

[7] Y. Lai, N. Saab, and W. Admiraal, "University students' use of mobile technology in self-directed language learning: Using the integrative model of behavior prediction," *Comput. Educ.*, vol. 179, p. 104413, 2022.

[8] R. Dangi, P. Lalwani, G. Choudhary, I. You, and G. Pau, "Study and investigation on 5G technology: A systematic review," *Sensors*, vol. 22, no. 1, p. 26, 2021.

[9] C. Yan, A. B. Siddik, L. Yong, Q. Dong, G. W. Zheng, and M. N. Rahman, "A two-staged SEM-artificial neural network approach to analyze the impact of FinTech adoption on the sustainability performance of banking firms," *Systems*, vol. 10, no. 5, p. 148, 2022.

[10] C. Magazzino, D. Porrini, G. Fusco, and N. Schneider, "Investigating the link among ICT, electricity consumption, air pollution, and economic growth in EU countries," *Energy Sources B*, vol. 16, no. 11–12, pp. 976–998, 2021.

[11] J. Vepsäläinen, M. Hevery, and P. Vuorimaa, "Resumability—A new primitive for developing web applications," *IEEE Access*, vol. 12, pp. 9038–9046, 2024.

[12] D. Jhala, "A study on progressive web apps as a unifier for native apps and the web," *Int. J. Eng. Res. Technol.*, vol. 10, no. 5, pp. 2278–0181, 2021.

[13] S. Weerasinghe, A. Zaslavsky, S. W. Loke, A. Hassani, A. Medvedev, and A. Abken, "Adaptive context caching for IoT-based applications: A reinforcement learning approach," *Sensors*, vol. 23, no. 10, p. 4767, 2023.

[14] Y. Ma, T. Li, Y. Zhou, L. Yu, and D. Jin, "Mitigating energy consumption in heterogeneous mobile networks through data-driven optimization," *IEEE Trans. Netw. Serv. Manag.*, 2024.

[15] J. Silva, E. R. Marques, L. M. Lopes, and F. Silva, "Energy-aware adaptive offloading of soft real-time jobs in mobile edge clouds," *J. Cloud Comput.*, vol. 10, no. 1, p. 38, 2021.

[16] A. Li, "Progressive web apps: Factors for consideration in development," *Proc. Int. Conf. Software Engineering and Applications*, 2021.

[17] V. B. Ramu, "Performance testing and optimization strategies for mobile applications," *Int. J. Perform. Test. Optim.*, vol. 13, no. 2, pp. 1–6, 2023.

[18] C. Petalotis, L. Krumpak, M. S. Floroiu, L. F. Ahmad, S. Athreya, and I. Malavolta, "An empirical study on the performance and energy costs of ads and analytics in mobile web apps," *Inf. Softw. Technol.*, vol. 166, p. 107370, 2024.

[19] A. S. Shethiya, "Scalability and performance optimization in web application development," *Integr. J. Sci. Technol.*, vol. 2, no. 1, 2025.

Designing for Quality in IoT: A User-Inclusive Approach to Non-Functional Requirements

Lasse Harjumaa
Jukka Määttälä
Kokkola University Consortium Chydenius
University of Jyväskylä
Kokkola, Finland
e-mail: {lasse.m.harjumaa | jukka.t.a.maattala}@jyu.fi

***Abstract*—The complexity of Internet of Things (IoT) systems highlights the critical need to address Non-Functional Requirements (NFRs) early in the development lifecycle. NFRs are essential to ensuring quality, yet they are often overlooked in favor of achieving core functionality. This paper presents an approach to elicit NFRs in an IoT context, using a pilot implementation in a vocational education setting focused on the food industry. The pilot of our approach demonstrated the importance of addressing the NFRs separately from functional requirements, raising new insights among participants. Role identification of stakeholders, interview structure and preciseness of documentation needed clarification after the pilot. Feedback from participants showed that the process not only captured key quality attributes but also fostered deeper understanding among stakeholders.**

Keywords-requirements engineering; Internet of Things; IoT systems; quality.

I. INTRODUCTION

The rapid expansion of Internet of Things (IoT) technologies has underscored the critical importance of non-functional requirements (NFRs) in system design and implementation. Unlike functional requirements, which describe what a system should do, NFRs – such as scalability, reliability, security, interoperability, and maintainability – define how a system performs under various conditions. They determine the crucial quality characteristic of an IoT system. In the IoT contexts, where heterogeneous devices, real-time data, and resource constraints are prevalent, the identification and specification of NFRs are particularly complex and could be insufficiently addressed during early development phases, because most attention is often focused on getting the system operational in the first place. This oversight can lead to costly redesigns or system failures.

The IoT context introduces challenges associated with eliciting and specifying non-functional requirements. It examines the specific nature of such systems, and involvement of diverse stakeholders in the requirements gathering process. Understanding these challenges is essential for improving engineering practices and ensuring that IoT systems meet not only their intended functionalities but also quality expectations in real-world environments.

This paper reports our experiences in *IoT Learning Environment* project, which aims at increasing students' knowledge of IoT technologies and their application in different domains. We conducted our experiment in the vocational education department specializing in the food industry.

The food industry exemplifies an environment where monitoring dynamic conditions – such as temperature, air quality, hygiene, and equipment status – is critical. Many of these conditions are also subject to strict regulations, such as mandated temperature ranges for food preservation or time limits for cooling prepared food. IoT technologies enable continuous monitoring and visualization of operational conditions. By embedding sensors and connected devices within the learning environment, IoT systems can collect and transmit data that reflect real-time conditions, providing more immersive and data-driven educational experiences for students of the food industry, thus enhancing learners' understanding of quality and safety parameters related to their work.

We first created an approach to gather non-functional requirements through stakeholder interviews, based on experiences reported in literature. Once the process was defined, we conducted a pilot run in a real-world setting to evaluate its practicality and to obtain feedback for improving the process. Following the pilot, we organized a postmortem analysis involving key participants to reflect on outcomes, and to identify challenges and deviations from the intended process.

The remainder of this paper is organized as follows. Section 2 briefly summarizes research carried out in the area. Section 3 summarizes special characteristics of IoT systems that need to be addressed when gathering NFRs. Section 4 depicts our approach for gathering the NFRs in the IoT context. Section 5 summarizes the observations from a pilot run of the process. Section 6 concludes the paper.

II. RELATED WORK

The elicitation of non-functional requirements in the IoT context has not received much attention in research. Most of the studies concentrate on understanding functional requirements, and a typical method for gathering those is through user scenarios use cases. For functional requirements engineering, formal approaches have been introduced, such as the four-phased model-driven development methodology for IoT applications introduced by Sosa-Reyna et al. [1] and UML-based requirements and specification method called IotReq [2], but methods, tools and techniques for eliciting non-functional requirements for IoT systems are limited.

According to Gupta [3], non-functional requirements, such as performance, reliability, availability, scalability, maintainability, security and privacy, may have crucial impact on success of adopting the edge computing paradigm within the IoT systems. Paiva et al. [4] have recognized the lack of methods for evaluating NFRs in IoT context and the need for developing systematic approaches to target NFRs for IoT applications.

Mahalank et al. [5] propose a checklist and a template for documenting non-functional requirements for smart traffic management system. Brito et al. [6] describe a procedure for eliciting NFRs in the context of a smart city project providing electric bicycles to the academic community. Tabassum [7] suggests an approach extending use case models, soft goal models and behavioural models for addressing non-functional requirements, especially interoperability and context-awareness for IoT systems, in order to increase the adaptability.

IoT systems are often under pressure to achieve rapid time-to-market. Furthermore, they are commonly developed with agile methods, which utilize user stories for gathering requirements. User stories emphasize functionality, and quality attributes (NFRs) may be even ignored. Sachdeva and Chung [8] state that NFRs should be introduced early in the software lifecycle, including in projects involving cloud and IoT. They also emphasize the importance of quantifying the requirements and setting clear acceptance criteria for them.

Tools to automate requirements elicitation have also been presented. For example, Khurshid et al. [9] introduce a machine learning algorithm to extract the non-functional requirements from documentation, in order to reduce the possibility of missing NFRs during the requirements engineering phase, and to promote security and performance of healthcare systems utilizing IoT.

Security is the most frequently addressed quality characteristic of IoT applications. Alhirabi et al. [10] surveyed the empirical research on security and privacy requirements for IoT, and concluded that using human-centred design might help in integrating these capabilities into systems. They also identify several challenges related to privacy in IoT systems, including the lack of tools, methods and notations for modeling these quality attributes.

III. Non-functional requirements in IoT Context

Non-Functional requirements are the quality attributes that the system must conform to, often referred to as -ilities. They describe how the system should work and consist of qualities that can be observed at run time, such as usability or security, and qualities that are embodied in the system structure, such as testability, scalability or extensibility. Defining non-functional requirements in a measurable way is necessary to determine whether the development work has achieved its goals. [11]

IoT systems tend to be more complex than traditional software or embedded systems, since they consist of a variety of hardware and software components, services and communication solutions. There may be a vast number of combinations involving wireless and wired sensors, actuators, networks, and smart objects – each with varying levels of computing capability. Stakeholders from different groups may access the system in completely different ways, using varying devices and services, which can potentially cause conflicts in requirements specification [12].

IoT systems typically evolve or change during their life cycle, as more advanced technology becomes available and new features are requested by the users. Finally, certain constraints and external factors must be addressed—such as ensuring the privacy of users' personal data, dependencies on specific service providers, and the limitations of existing infrastructure. Figure 1 summarizes the special characteristics of IoT systems. In the figure, the main issues – change, complexity and constraints – are exemplified with a few characteristics that distinguish the development of IoT systems from that of traditional systems.

Figure 2 summarizes the quality attributes that address the challenges set by change, complexity and constraints. Of course, all aspects of quality need consideration, but attributes listed here can be straightforwardly derived from the characteristics of IoT systems. Evolving user needs require flexibility in interaction, and technology upgrades emphasize the need for scalability and maintainability. To improve system understandability, analyzability should be addressed. Integrations to external services require interoperability, and modularity makes the system architecture extendable and manageable. Performance efficiency, security and reliability help in dealing with technological and regulatory constraints.

IV. The NFR Gathering Process for IoT

Figure 3 depicts the process that we have used in our project to gather non-functional requirements. The first phase involves inviting stakeholders from different groups to an interview. The participants should be able to represent views of future users, maintainers and business owners. After the interview, the results are analysed and summarized by the development team. Interpretations and the summary report are validated in a workshop. If all stakeholders have common view of the requirements, they are documented and signed off.

A. *The Interview*

We created a set of interview questions to elicit non-functional requirements related to the quality attributes identified earlier: interaction capability, maintainability, scalability, analyzability, interoperability, modularity, performance efficiency, security and reliability. Since discussions with stakeholders in IoT projects often focus on the measurements and data, these NFRs often remain implicit unless explicitly addressed during requirements elicitation. We decided to use open-ended questions to encourage detailed responses. Questions were be designed to uncover constraints, expectations, and existing practices, enabling the development team to translate qualitative insights into measurable system attributes. We derived the questions from experiences and documentation

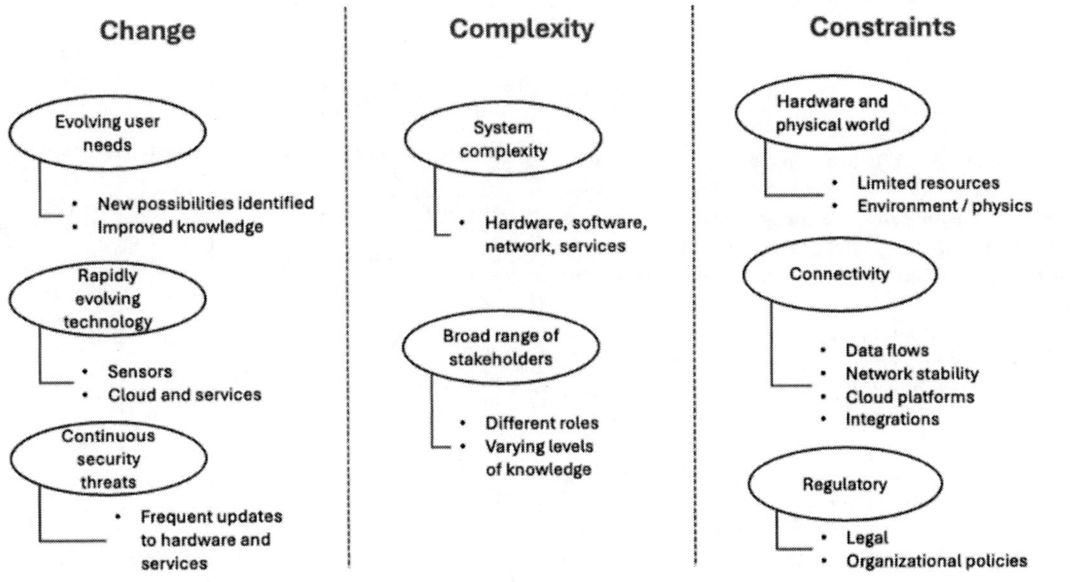

Figure 1. Characteristics of IoT Systems.

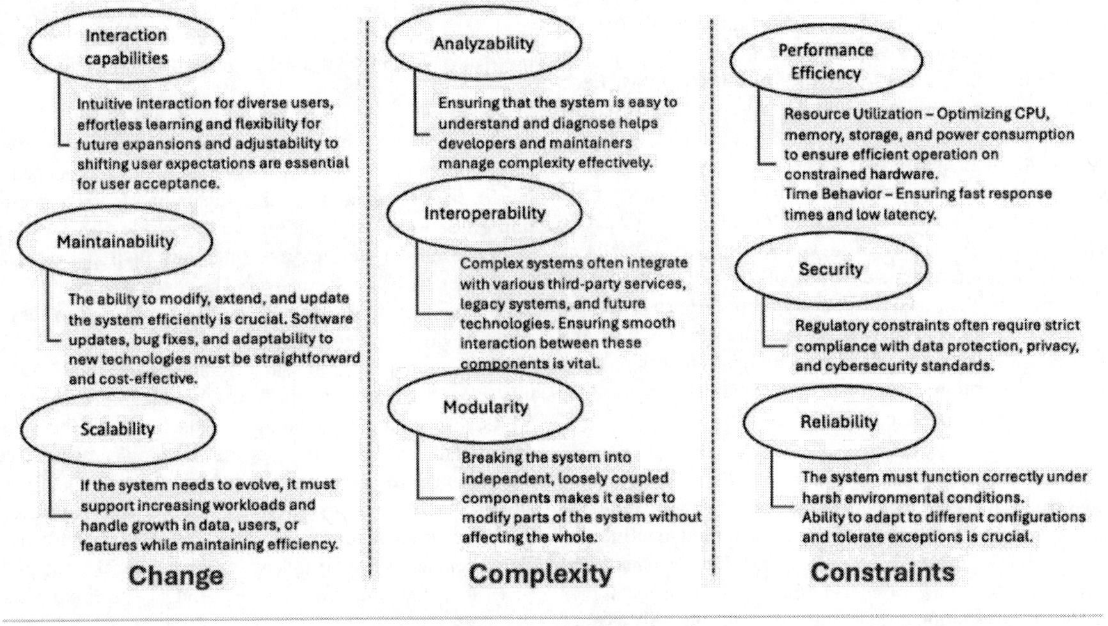

Figure 2. Quality attributes to address in IoT system design.

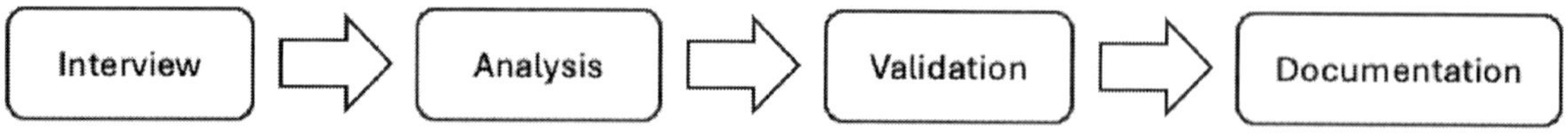

Figure 3. Process of Gathering Non-Functional Requirements.

from dozens of sensor network projects previously implemented in collaboration with the local industrial and educational partner organizations. We focused on operational goals, environmental constraints and stakeholder needs to ensure alignment with technical feasibility and real-world deployment challenges.

To assess interaction capability, questions focus on user interface expectations, system responsiveness, exceptional situations, and means to interact with the system. For maintainability, questions explore how frequently the system is updated and what documentation practices have to be followed. Interoperability questions focus on data exchange standards, third-party system integration, and API usage. Security is addressed by inquiring about necessary authentication mechanisms, data access, and compliance with regulatory standards. For analyzability, questions concern logging practices, monitoring tools, and diagnostic capabilities. Questions about modularity explore how the system is divided into components, the independence of modules, and the ease of updating subcomponents without breaking the whole. Performance efficiency questions address acceptable response times, resource usage under varying loads, and performance thresholds during operational peaks. Finally, reliability questions investigate error recovery mechanisms and system behavior under failure conditions.

A total of 58 questions were introduced in the first version of interview. Table 1 shows examples of the questions. Each question addresses certain aspects of IoT-specific challenges – Change, Complexity and Constraints – and related quality attributes: Maintainability (M), Scalability (S), Analyzability (A), Interoperability (I), Modularity (Mo), Performance Efficiency (PE), Security (Se), Reliability (R), Interaction Capability (IC). The questions were designed so that persons without deep knowledge on technical details of the system would be able to provide their insights. In addition to answering the questions, we wanted to encourage storytelling by the interviewees. Real-life examples, experiences and preferences provide important information about the concerns and expectations that different stakeholders have.

B. Analysis

Analyzing interview responses is a critical step in identifying themes and eliciting the most important qualities to guide the development of the system. Qualitative data gathered through interview often contains implicit insights into stakeholder expectations, concerns and priorities. To extract meaningful information, responses must be evaluated systematically. Answers given by interviewees should be coded and categorized according to the related quality attributes. This process can involve open coding, where recurring ideas are highlighted. The experience and technical expertise of the participants, together with contextual factors must be taken into account when making interpretations of the answers.

TABLE I. EXAMPLE QUESTIONS TARGETING SPECIFIC ASPECTS OF QUALITY.

Question	Change	Compl.	Constr.
Can you describe any challenges or frustrations you have previously experienced with IoT systems?	IC, M	A	PE, R
How many devices do you currently use, and how do you expect this number to grow?	S	I	PE
Should different user groups have access to different system modules?	S	Mo	Se
What existing systems should the IoT system integrate with?	S	I	-

The mapping of interview questions to specific quality targets helps distinguishing functional and non-functional requirements, as the users of the system tend to concentrate on system features in their storytelling. Performing analysis on the stakeholder needs and expectations early on the project helps to plan the development more effectively and reduces the risk of overlooked constraints and misunderstandings.

C. Validation

The purpose of the validation phase is to ensure that all stakeholders have common understanding of the needed qualities of the system, and that developers have correct interpretation of the users' expectations. In this phase, the development team presents a summary of interview findings, categorized by themes found in the answers. They can also bring out pain points, conflicting goals or insights and experiences they have from previous implementations.

The summary report should be concise and organized into clear thematic sections. Even though the focus is on NFRs, organizing the summary report around the system's operational features may improve stakeholder understanding. For instance, requirements related to latency or performance are closely tied to the user experience and interface, and could be grouped under headings that reflect those aspects. This thematic structuring can make technical content more accessible and relatable to non-technical stakeholders, while still preserving the integrity of the NFRs.

Stakeholders or participants confirm the accuracy of interpretations and if there are misunderstandings or misrepresentations, they are corrected. If project scope or resources are limited, prioritization may be necessary. Shared understanding ensures the next steps are grounded in actual user needs.

D. Documentation

The documentation and sign-off phase serves as the formal agreement between stakeholders and the development team. This phase ensures that all identified requirements are approved before design and implementation begin. By systematically documenting and approving non-functional requirements alongside functional ones, development team can better manage risks and ensure that the final system meets both operational goals and user expectations. However, explicit documentation of non-functional requirements may be difficult, as the user needs are often imprecise.

We used a simple template for documenting the NFRs, including the following items: Requirement ID, Requirement Type, Description, Priority, Acceptance Criteria, Dependencies, Assumptions, and Verification Method.

The sign-off process acts as a formal validation checkpoint, ensuring all stakeholders agree on the documented requirements. This alignment not only helps guide the development effort but also supports accountability and traceability throughout the project lifecycle.

V. Observations from the Pilot Run of the Process

The project in which the research is being carried out, aims at developing teaching and learning materials for vocational secondary education. As digitalization affects more and more people's daily lives, their working lives will also change. Various IoT solutions are already in use in many sectors and this development is expected to accelerate dramatically in the future. Understanding the potential of IoT is essential to remain competitive in the future labor market. Today, most students do not have sufficient experience in applying IoT solutions, and at the same time these technologies are increasingly taken advantage of in workplaces.

The project explores how IoT-enabled systems can support learning and visualization in food industry training environments. It focuses on the design and implementation of interactive tools that translate complex sensor data into intuitive visual formats. During the project, we will also examine how such systems can improve situational awareness, decision-making, and compliance with industry standards, ultimately contributing to a more skilled future workforce.

Learning environments in the food industry school participating in our project consist of two distinct areas: food production and bakery (confectionery) training environments. In food production, meat and other food products are prepared in various processing facilities where temperature fluctuations play a critical role during both the production and storage phases. In the bakery environment, temperature and other conditions are essential not only for successful baking, but also for ensuring that ingredients are stored under appropriate conditions.

In both learning environments, materials and ingredients are stored in freezers and cold storage units, with their temperatures monitored in real time using sensors. Real-time temperature monitoring of the production facilities is also essential. Threshold values have been defined for each environment, and alerts are triggered if these limits are exceeded, notifying the staff. Additionally, for legally mandated self-monitoring (HACCP), daily temperature values – most commonly the daily average – are recorded for reporting purposes. In the bakery room, flour dust is monitored, while in the food production area, spice dust is tracked using fine particle sensors to assess air quality.

Currently, the temperatures of various rooms and cooling units are monitored, as the cooling of finished products must be completed within four hours. In future, the goal is to enable real-time monitoring of the entire production process from the initial preparation phase through to the end of the cooling phase. This could even be extended to include tracking up to the end user.

During this project, we carried out a pilot round of our NFR gathering process. The participants' roles in the interview phase included a domain expert (teacher) and a project coordinator. The interviewer and interviewees were physically present in the same location, while the note-taker participated remotely. This setup allowed for direct interaction between the main participants while ensuring accurate documentation of the session. Participants' knowledge of IoT systems and general information technology was significantly higher than that of the system's future "basic users." Consequently, this interview alone does not allow for substantial conclusions regarding the influence of different roles on the formulation of questions. The expertise of the interviewees may have introduced a bias in responses, highlighting the need for further interviews with users possessing varying levels of technical proficiency. A more comprehensive analysis requires diverse perspectives to ensure balanced insights into desired system characteristics.

We found that having two interviewers made the process seamless, and will continue this practice, especially if some participants join remotely. At least one of the interviewers should be familiar with the subject or people in order to enhance engagement, while allowing the other interviewer to concentrate on documentation allows for a more structured and inclusive discussion.

It is advisable to allocate more than an hour for the interview to ensure all perspectives are covered. Beginning with informal conversation helps set the stage for discussion. Afterward, comments are transcribed. A summary report must be provided to the interviewees to ensure clarity and transparency in the process.

A postmortem held after an interview session serves as a structured review to assess the execution of the interview, identify strengths and weaknesses, and enhance future practices. This reflective discussion focused on clarifying how the interview was conducted and evaluating the quality of the questions. During the postmortem analysis, we refined the interview process to improve clarity and consistency.

If an individual can analyze an issue from multiple role

perspectives, it is essential to specify the perspective alongside their response. Clearly identifying the viewpoint prevents ambiguity and enhances the reliability of the findings. This practice alwo significantly eases the analysis phase of the process.

The interview questions were perceived by the participants as providing comprehensive coverage of the system. According to the interviewees, the structure and content of the interview allowed for a thorough exploration of key aspects, and relevant areas were adequately addressed. Moreover, the interview questions encouraged participants to consider new perspectives on issues that had not previously been examined. This reflective aspect of the interview highlighted its value not only as a data collection method but also as a tool for enhancing understanding and fostering critical insight among participants.

Before the interview, concerns arose regarding the large number of questions. However, all questions were addressed, albeit some more superficially than others. Based on feedback, the order of questions should be improved and grouped according to the respondents' roles and topics. Grouping the questions according to thematic areas will make the questionnaire more coherent and encourage more accurate responses from the interviewees.

During the documentation phase, we identified the need to more precisely define threshold values for alerts, normal operating ranges for various measurements, and constraints imposed by organizational policies or legislation. To address this, the documentation template was revised to explicitly incorporate these elements.

As a summary, after the first interview:

- Six questions were removed, as they were deemed to add little value compared to others.
- Another six questions specifically related to interfaces and maintenance were merged into two clearer ones.
- The wording of several questions was refined for clarity.
- Each question was reviewed to determine which respondent role would provide the most insightful answers.
- NFR template was refined to target aspects of threshold values and legislation issues more specifically.

VI. Conclusion and Future Work

IoT applications consist of different types of hardware and software components that are required to work together under varying and often demanding conditions. Future users of the system, or other stakeholders, on the other hand, may have very little knowledge on the implementation of the system. This complexity may lead to putting more emphasis on achieving the functionality at the expense of quality aspects.

Clearly, the process of eliciting NFRs in the IoT context requires greater focus. In our ongoing project, we have developed and experimented with a four-phase process to systematically gather NFRs, aiming to create more robust and adaptable IoT architectures. Our work extends prior research on NFRs by offering guidelines that address quality aspects particularly relevant in the IoT context, while also enhancing the involvement of future users in the requirements engineering phase of IoT systems.

Based on our initial experiences, we believe that IoT projects significantly benefit from a well-defined NFR gathering process, which acts as a vital bridge between stakeholder expectations and technical implementation – ensuring that essential non-functional aspects are thoroughly addressed throughout system design and development.

Acknowledgement

This work was supported by the Economic and Social Research Council through the Centre for Economic Development, Transport and the Environment of Central Finland [project number S30655] and the City of Kokkola.

References

[1] C. M. Sosa-Reyna, E. Tello-Leal, and D. Lara-Alabazares, "Methodology for the model-driven development of service oriented iot applications," *Journal of Systems Architecture*, vol. 90, pp. 15–22, 2018.

[2] G. Reggio, "A uml-based proposal for iot system requirements specification," in *Proceedings of the 10th International Workshop on Modelling in Software Engineering*, ser. MiSE '18, Gothenburg, Sweden: Association for Computing Machinery, 2018, pp. 9–16.

[3] S. Gupta, "Non-functional requirements elicitation for edge computing," *Internet of Things*, vol. 18, p. 100503, 2022.

[4] J. Paiva, R. Andrade, and R. M. Carvalho, "Evaluation of non-functional requirements for iot applications," in *Proceedings of the 23rd International Conference on Enterprise Information Systems.*, 2021, pp. 111–119.

[5] S. N. Mahalank, K. B. Malagund, and R. M. Banakar, "Non functional requirement analysis in iot based smart traffic management system," in *2016 International Conference on Computing Communication Control and automation (ICCUBEA)*, 2016, pp. 1–6.

[6] I. S. Brito, A. Moreira, and J. Araújo, "Handling nonfunctional requirements for smart cities.," in *CIbSE*, 2020, pp. 334–341.

[7] M. R. Tabassum, "Addressing non-functional requirements of adaptive iot systems: A model-driven approach," in *Proceedings of the 25th International Conference on Model Driven Engineering Languages and Systems: Companion Proceedings*, ser. MODELS '22, Montreal, Quebec, Canada: Association for Computing Machinery, 2022, pp. 195–200.

[8] V. Sachdeva and L. Chung, "Handling non-functional requirements for big data and iot projects in scrum," in *2017 7th International Conference on Cloud Computing, Data Science Engineering - Confluence*, 2017, pp. 216–221.

[9] I. Khurshid *et al.*, "Classification of non-functional requirements from iot oriented healthcare requirement document," *Frontiers in Public Health*, vol. Volume 10 - 2022, 2022.

[10] N. Alhirabi, O. Rana, and C. Perera, "Security and privacy requirements for the internet of things: A survey," *ACM Trans. Internet Things*, vol. 2, no. 1, pp. 1–37, Feb. 2021.

[11] K. Wiegers and J. Beatty, *Software Requirements*, 3rd. Redmond, WA: Microsoft Press, 2013.

[12] B. Costa, P. F. Pires, and F. C. Delicato, "Specifying functional requirements and qos parameters for iot systems," in *2017 IEEE 15th Intl Conf on Dependable, Autonomic and Secure Computing, 15th Intl Conf on Pervasive Intelligence and Computing, 3rd Intl Conf on Big Data Intelligence and Computing and Cyber Science and Technology Congress*, IEEE, 2017, pp. 407–414.

Performance Evaluation of Software Transactional Memory Implementations

Dániel Urbán
Bell Labs, Nokia, Network Systems and Security Research
Budapest, Hungary
email: daniel.urban@nokia-bell-labs.com

Péter Fazekas
Bell Labs, Nokia, Network Systems and Security Research
Budapest, Hungary
email: peter.fazekas@nokia-bell-labs.com

***Abstract*—Software Transactional Memory (STM) was introduced as a promising technology to handle memory conflicts in parallel computing. In this paper, a performance comparison of various STM engine implementations is presented. The well-known Lee's algorithm was used for benchmarking ten different Scala based STM API variants, and one written in Kotlin. Results compare how these implementations scale in terms of the number of processor cores available and how they perform in terms of running time, compared to each other and a single threaded baseline implementation.**

Keywords – Software Transactional Memory; parallel computing; concurrent programming; functional APIs; performance measurement.

I. Introduction

Parallel computing has a decades long history from emerging concepts to practical applications already in early mainframe systems. Nowadays, concurrent programming is applied in almost all domains from end user applications, enterprise software to exascale computing workloads.

Concurrent threads using shared resources (such as memory) have been identified early as a critical aspect. Straightforward solution is to prevent threads using the resource at the same time, therefore plethora of solutions and approaches have been designed and implemented in various architectures, such as using critical sections in the code, atomic operations, locks, semaphores, mutexes, etc.

Most aforementioned approaches are using some form of locking based solution (preventing threads to execute while some conditions apply), which brings well known shortcomings such as potential deadlocks, livelocks, convoying, priority inversion, starvation, etc.

To overcome these issues, several solutions were proposed and implemented, which are basically building on special representation of data or programming phenomena to avoid reading/writing shared information at the same time. The main directions are using lock-free or wait-free data structures, such as queues, ring buffers or stacks among others; or to basically prevent using shared context data and apply messaging among threads instead, such as actor model, or message passing channels. Furthermore, several approaches are targeting the complete avoidance of using shared mutable data, hence eliminating the root of the problem, such as data partitioning, thread-local storage or immutability in functional programming.

Transactional memory was introduced in the early 90's [1] to overcome shared memory challenges in concurrent programming. This approach is motivated by how transactions work in database systems. Basically, transactions are defined as serializable atomic instructions, that read and ultimately tentatively write shared memory spaces. Then, a *validate* operation is needed to ensure that there are no conflicts, that is, the memory content read for the computations and to be written as result is consistent. If validation is successful, the thread tries *committing* the changes. If the validation fails, the transaction aborts and retries. Commit is successful if no other transactions have modified the process's read set and no other transaction has read the write set, i.e., contention has not occurred since the last validation. When the commit is successful, the changes are made visible to other processes, otherwise the transaction *aborts* and tentative changes are reverted. This transactional model for memory operations was introduced as a low-level Application Programming Interface (API) in [2], so that the transactional memory is implemented in software (Software Transactional Memory, STM). Since then, numerous implementations have appeared, which provide these transactional functionalities over their APIs. These differ in various basic algorithms, data structures and optimizations provided; in Sections III and IV, we detail the ones relevant for our work.

The rest of this paper is organized as follows. Section II introduces the basic algorithm used for evaluating various STM implementations' performance and some related work. Section III summarizes various implementations evaluated with this work. Section IV addresses some important details of the implementations behind our analysis and the hardware and software environment used. Section V shows and analyses numerical results.

II. STM Performance Related Work

The main contribution of this paper is to provide a comparison on the performance of various STM implementations, focusing on the execution time of certain multi-threaded computation tasks.

To assess STM performance, one may select proper multi-threaded applications, for example, the authors of [3] list an excessive number of those. Their focus is on evaluating how the applications themselves behave with STM, in terms of size of read/write sets, transaction lengths statistics and depth of nested transactions, but the emphasis is not on comparing different STM engine implementations. Another suggestion is described in [4] as STMbench7, which is a synthetic benchmark defining a multitude of operations on a shared data structure.

However, we wanted to use a computing problem that has practical significance and enables a comparable

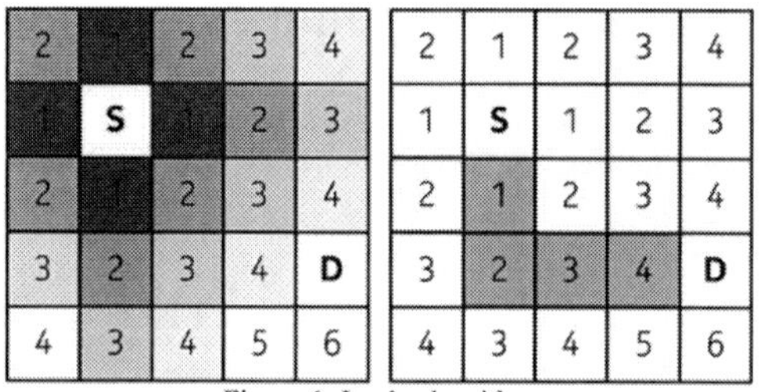
Figure 1. Lee's algorithm

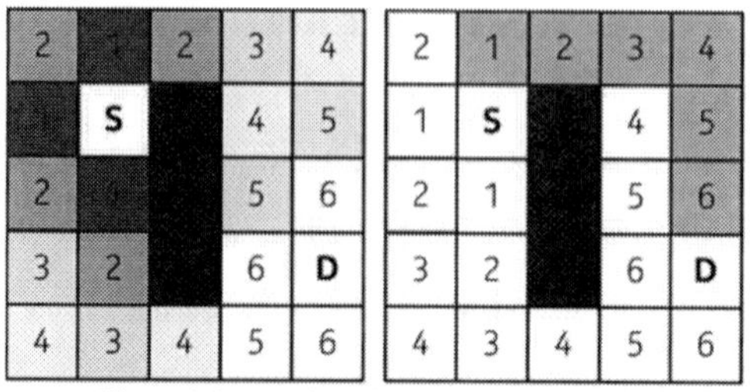
Figure 2. Lee's algorithm with occupied cells

benchmarking between various STM engine implementations; thus, the problem should be well parallelizable, the effect of concurrency should be significant, and the level of concurrency should be controllable via setting the inputs to the problem.

Therefore, as in [5]-[7], we selected the well-known circuit-board routing problem and used Lee's algorithm [8] to solve it. Circuit routing has practical significance when designing connections among electronic components on a surface, where crossing of connections (routes) is forbidden or has significant extra cost. In its simplest form, the surface is represented as a two-dimensional grid of square cells, representing potential insertion points of components and potential placeholders for connections.

Lee's algorithm has a number of source-destination pair cells (endpoints needing connections) as input. For a given source-destination pair, the algorithm starts with an expansion phase. This basically starts a "wave" from the source, searching all neighboring (along the edges of the square) cells and enumerating them with their distance from the source. This breadth-search continues from every neighboring cell to the neighbors of those (which are second neighbors to the source), until the search reaches the destination or the edge of the surface. In general, any cell might be occupied by an already existing route; these cells are not enumerated and not taken into account in the next phase of the algorithm.

The second phase is the backtracking, when from the destination to the source a list of cells is found, their enumeration should be in decreasing order. As there are multiple such routes, the particular implementation should rank those and select the optimal one. Typically, the shortest route, or the route with the least turns, or routes that are closer to blocked cells, etc. could be selected. This final phase of the algorithm is referred to as laying the route. As mentioned above, if a cell is already occupied by a route, it is not considered in the expansion phase, hence the backtracking will efficiently find routes avoiding occupied cells. Naturally, a laid route will occupy its cells for any later runs of the algorithm. Figure 1 shows a basic example of Lee's algorithm without occupied cell, the left Figure shows the expansion phase, while on the right the backtracking is represented with a laid route between source (S) and destination (D). Figure 2 visualizes the algorithm in the case where there are already occupied cells on the board (denoted by black).

As for parallel computing, it is apparent that this algorithm can be implemented in a way that multiple source-destination pairs are being calculated in parallel, using a shared data representing the grid of cells. It is easy to see how contention is occurring if a thread reserves a route in backtracking, while the other counts it in expansion. It is also evident that a grid with large number of cells but short routes (source-destination are close to each other) is well parallelizable with lower chance of contention, while in smaller grids with relatively long routes, contention will occur with higher probability.

As mentioned, [5] proposed Lee's algorithm as a benchmark for STM. The authors implemented the algorithm using Java and evaluated various optimizations in handling the transactions, assessing the number of routes the algorithms found. That work was expanded in [6], and evaluated STM performance in terms of abort ratio, wasted work and number of transactions in realistic large circuits. In [7], a Ruby based STM implementation was evaluated, in terms of finding the routes on modest difficulty grids.

III. IMPLEMENTATIONS

Due to the practical significance of STM, naturally there is rich support in various programming languages, in the forms of various libraries, or being implemented in the standard library. Without the need to be exhaustive, some examples are as follows. Haskell, as a purely functional language suitable for parallel programming, has native STM support through its standard library. Similarly, Clojure has this kind of built-in STM support. In C/C++, STM is not natively supported, but throughout the years several libraries were built, such as *stmmap*, or *cpp_stm_free*, etc., but none of the implementations were standardized yet. Similarly, Java offers several STM implementation libraries, examples are *JVSTM*, *Deuce* or *DSTM2*. Naturally, these extensions exist in all the other popular languages as well, such as in Ruby, Rust or Golang.

During our evaluations we focused on STM implementations in Scala and one written in Kotlin; in the following we briefly recap these. We selected Scala as our main focus, because of its popularity as a functional programming language supporting concurrent and parallel programming on the Java Virtual Machine (JVM). Scala offers a variety of STM APIs to test. We also looked at Kotlin, as a similar, but less functional programming language. Our goal was to compare both purely functional and imperative STM APIs.

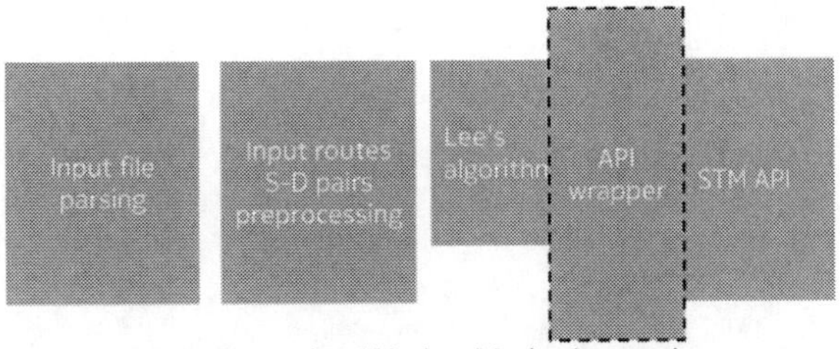

Figure 3. Functional blocks of the implementation

Cats STM [10] is a Scala library enabling composable in-memory transactions. It implements fine grained optimistic concurrency handling with no global locks; automatic retries and composing complex transactions out of elementary ones with its purely functional API. Cats STM supports using multiple runtimes. Also, Cats STM does not have a built-in transactional array, or similar type, so in the implementation we store grid matrices in array of transactional variables.

CHOAM's *Rxn* [11] is our own Scala based implementation. It does not use locks, instead it uses a lock-free multi-word compare-and-swap algorithm [17] to commit transactions. It has both a purely functional, and an imperative API; these use the same underlying engine, so we were able to compare their performance. *Rxn* is technically not a full-featured STM, but it is close enough: it does not have Haskell-style modular blocking (i.e., the *orElse* combinator), but that is not necessary for parallelizing Lee's algorithm. It has a built-in *Ref.Array* type (transactional array), which we use for the board matrices.

The next implementation we tested is based on Kyo [12], a library for algebraic effects in Scala. One of its built-in effects is STM. This STM implementation uses fine-grained locking and has a purely functional API. We run the transactions on Kyo's own runtime with its default configuration. For the board matrices we use an array of transactional variables (*Array[TRef[A]]*), because Kyo does not have a built-in transactional array type.

ScalaSTM is a lightweight STM implementation [13][14] inspired by the STM API in the Haskell standard library. It has a mostly imperative API and uses fine-grained locking. It also has a sophisticated contention manager for retrying conflicting transactions. We use ScalaSTM's built-in *TArray* (transactional array) for the board matrices.

ZSTM is an implementation in the ZIO concurrency framework [15]. It has a purely functional API, similar to the one in the Haskell standard library. We run the ZSTM transactions on their own *zio.Runtime* and we use ZSTM's *TArray* for the board matrices.

The Kotlin implementation we tested is within the Arrow concurrency framework [16]. The algorithm is written in Kotlin, with a thin Scala wrapper. The API of *arrow-fx-stm* is inspired by Haskell's STM package, but it is nevertheless mostly imperative. We run the STM transactions on the default coroutine dispatcher of Kotlin. We use *TArray* for the grid matrices.

During the evaluation of results in Section 0, we refer to two possible basic solutions for STM with regards to the implementations listed above, that is *opacity* and *early release*. *Opacity* [19] is a consistency property specifically for STM systems. The consistency of committed transactions is usually guaranteed by all STM systems (e.g., by performing a validation step during commit). However, an opaque STM also guarantees the consistency of all running transactions. That is, a transaction in an opaque STM is never able to observe an inconsistent view of memory. Conversely, a transaction in a non-opaque (i.e., transparent) STM might observe such an inconsistent view, and then later (e.g., when trying to commit) detect the inconsistency, roll back, and retry. Depending on the specific logic of a transaction, the lack of opacity could lead to observing violation of invariants, which in turn could lead to, e.g., out-of-bounds reads or infinite loops. On the other hand, if an STM guarantees opacity, it will typically need to roll back and retry transactions more often, which could lead to performance degradation.

The authors of [18] proposed early release as an optimization for STM transactions. This is a mechanism to remove items from the read set of a transaction, in effect releasing those memory locations earlier than the commit of the transaction (because the transaction does not need them anymore). On one hand, this has the potential to reduce the number of conflicts the transaction encounters, thus potentially increasing performance. On the other hand, the released memory locations will not be part of any later automatic validation (e.g., during commit), so early release must be used with care, to preserve the correctness of the transaction.

IV. IMPLEMENTATION ARCHITECTURE AND TEST ENVIRONMENT

To enable better understanding of the results, main design and implementation considerations are introduced in the following subsections.

A. Design and implementation

The bases of main building blocks of the software implemented to test performance of various STM implementations is shown in Figure 3. The first block is responsible for parsing the input file given to the algorithm; that contains the description of the board (grid) and the source-destination (S-D) pairs between which the routes are to be laid. Then there is an initial optimization, as for all the source-destination pairs a simple grid-distance is calculated, and S-D pairs are sorted in increasing order. For those pairs that have the same grid-distance, a pseudorandom shuffling is applied, to reduce the number of trivial conflicts (because S-D pairs with coordinates close to each other are often also specified close to each other in the input files). Lee's algorithm will be then executed on the S-D pairs in this order.

In this implementation, a small generalization of Lee's algorithm is introduced, compared to the basics shown in Section II. Namely, in this version, we still allow routes to cross in the grid. In terms of route laying on a circuit board, this mimics the case when there can be multiple layers. However, in this version of the algorithm we assign a cost to the routes. That is, we assign a unit cost to each cell allocated for a route and if another route crosses an already existing one,

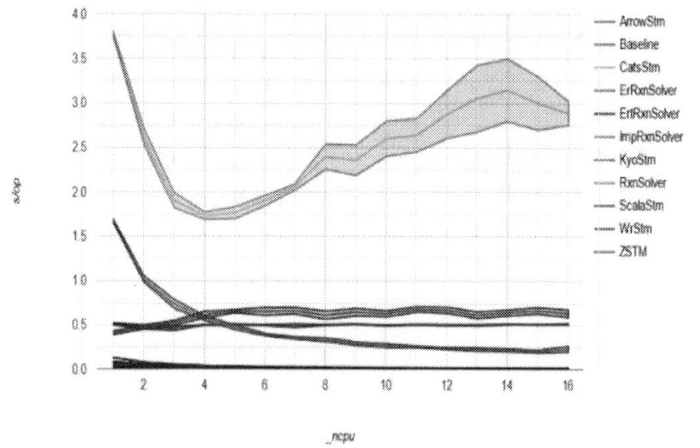

Figure 4. Completion time for simple input

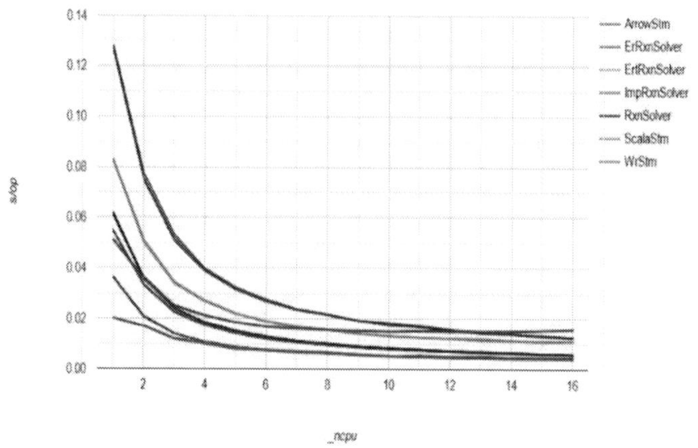

Figure 5. Completion time for simple input, zoomed

there is a double cost associated to that cell within this next route. Similarly, if a third route is to be laid using this same cell, that would again double this cell's cost (hence it would cost four units) and so on, each layer doubles the cost (exponentially rising cost). Finally, the algorithm selects the route with the lowest cost. Note that the original version of the algorithm that does not allow route crossing is a subset of this approach with allocating infinite cost to route crossing.

The parallelization is handled in the following manner: the S-D pairs are evaluated in parallel batches that have the size equivalent to available CPU threads. Whenever a thread finishes (a route for an S-D pair is laid), the next one from the ordered list starts. Note that the algorithm finishes when an S-D route is found; when the transaction should abort and restart for example due to validation error or commit error, that is handled by the STM engine itself.

In Figure 3 the functional blocks of the algorithm, the tested STM API (listed in Section II) and a block labelled as "API wrapper" are interwoven. This is because we have implemented the algorithm for each STM API in a way that the implementation natively uses the API and its data structures, therefore, the very implementation code is specific to the given API. For example, for a functional API a function itself can be passed, hence the STM engine itself can call "back" to the algorithm.

The API wrapper part in the Figure is specific to testing the ScalaSTM API. Namely, ScalaSTM was tested in an idiomatic way, using its default imperative API. However, as in general we would like to harness the strengths of functional programming, we have also implemented and tested a thin layer, that wraps the ScalaSTM API in a monadic (purely functional) API similar to that of Cats STM. This way we can also get some ideas about the overhead of a monadic ("programs as values") API in Scala. (We have considered creating a unified API for *all* the STM libraries, and implementing Lee's algorithm only *once*, using this API. However, as measurements on the wrapped ScalaSTM API showed significant performance degradation due to the wrapping, we have not done this.) We summarize all the variants we implemented, and the STM libraries we used in Table I.

CHOAM has both a purely functional and an imperative API; it also has various optimization options. To compare the performance effect of these variations, we have implemented four versions of Lee's algorithm with CHOAM:

- One using the default (purely functional and safe) API (*RxnSolver*).
- An optimized one, which uses "early release" [18] to make the transaction log smaller (*ErtRxnSolver*). This optimization would not be safe in arbitrary transactions, but as discussed in [5], it is safe for Lee's algorithm. This version also uses non-opaque (i.e., "transparent") reads [19], to further decrease the probability of conflicts.
- Another optimized version, which uses "tentative reads", as an alternative implementation of early release (*ErRxnSolver*).
- A version which (unlike the other three) uses the imperative API of CHOAM (*ImpRxnSolver*). It has no early release, or other extra optimization (thus, it can be seen as the direct imperative equivalent of *RxnSolver*).

We run the various implementations on asynchronous runtimes they are designed for. When they are not designed for a specific runtime, we run them on the thread-pool of Cats Effect. We configure these runtimes by turning off features which could have a negative performance impact.

The transactions in these implementations of Lee's routing algorithm are read heavy, but at the end they always write to some locations (to lay a route). This means that read-only transactions, and transactions which only access a very small number of memory locations are not measured.

We also have implemented a sequential (non-parallelized) version of the same algorithm, which serves as the *baseline* for comparison to the parallel ones. This sequential implementation is intentionally not very well optimized, because we wanted to compare it to similarly high-level and easy-to-use STMs.

All the implementations used for this benchmarking are available as open source [20].

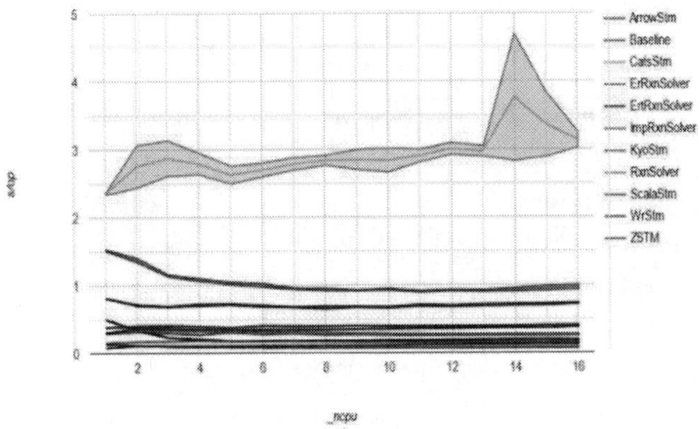

Figure 6. Moderate complexity input

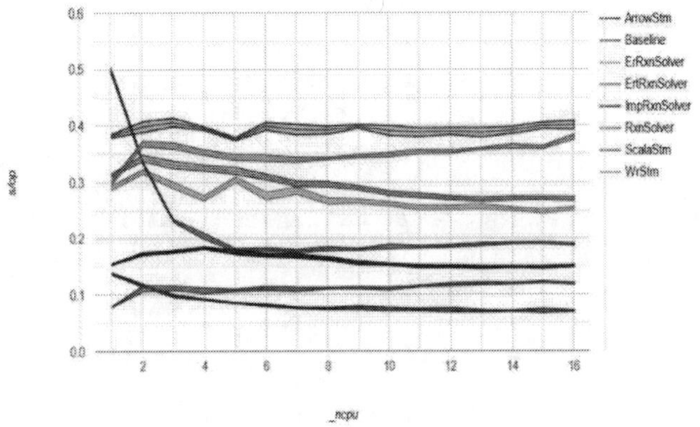

Figure 7. Moderate complexity input, zoomed

B. Experimental setup

We run the benchmarking software described above on the Java Virtual Machine (JVM). This is packaged into a Docker container, because we wanted the measurement software to be portable and easily automatable, and the measurement easily reproducible.

The server used has two Intel Xeon E5-2680 v3 processors running at 2.5 GHz, with 12 physical cores, that is 24 cores in total. During the measurements hyperthreading was disabled, therefore each thread is running on a physical core. Turbo boost was also disabled. During the measurements, one control parameter is the number of cores allocated to the JVM, and the software itself implements parallelization in a way that the number of available cores is queried from the JVM.

The server is equipped with 256 Gbytes of physical memory, but the JVM heap size was configured to be 16 Gbytes. All the implementation is based on Scala 3.7.0 and OpenJDK 21.0.7 (Corretto).

We used three inputs (circuit boards for laying routes) with different sizes in terms of the number of cells in the grid and number and length of routes to be laid, as will be discussed in the next section: a well parallelizable simple synthetic input, a modest one, and a complex one coming from real circuitry.

The algorithm for laying routes in the simple and moderate complexity boards was continuously run for 300 seconds for each input, and for each implementation, for a given number of available CPUs. Based on the completion times needed for solving an input (see next section), this results in several hundreds to several thousands of runs for each data point. For the complex input, due to its excessive complexity, 20 runs were performed for each data point.

We used the Java Microbenchmark Harness (JMH) [21] to perform the measurements, in its default time-based "average time" benchmark mode. In this mode JMH repeatedly calls a benchmark method until a timeout of 10 seconds is reached (JMH calls this 1 iteration). JMH performs the measurements in a forked JVM (i.e., it launches a separate process just for the measurement); we configured it to repeat this forking 6 times. We performed 5 warmup iterations and 5 measurement iterations (that is, 50+50 seconds total per fork); the measurement results of the warmup iterations are ignored, and the execution times of the benchmark method during the measurement iterations are averaged. (An exception to this is the last complex input, where we used the "single-shot" mode of JMH, resulting in the average of 20 benchmark method executions, as mentioned above.) The purpose of the warmup iterations is to avoid measuring in a "cold" JVM, i.e., in which the just-in-time compiler (JIT) did not yet optimize the running methods.

V. RESULTS AND EVALUATION

The charts in this Section show the results of our measurements. On the vertical axis, we show the completion time, i.e., the time required (in seconds) to solve one particular input board. The curves show the average time required to run on the input; the shaded area shows a 99.9% confidence interval (it is not visible on some of the curves). The horizontal axis shows the number of CPU cores available to the solvers. This way we can analyze the scalability of the various STM engines when used for parallelization.

Figures 4 and 5 show measurement results for a 200×200 circuit board with 90 routes (i.e., source-destination pairs), which is the simple input. The routes are all very short (10), the solutions are trivial (each is a straight line), and they never cross each other. (This board is a smaller version of the board called "simple" in [6].) Thus, solving this synthetic input is, in theory, perfectly parallelizable. While this is not a realistic circuit board, we use it to measure the ability of the various STM engines to exploit the potential parallelism (which is very high here). Figure 4 shows results for all the STM engines and variants we measured. The smaller results (i.e., results for the faster implementations) are not visible on that chart, so they are shown in Figure 5 (which is essentially the zoomed in version of the bottom of Figure 4).

In Figure 4, we can see that the slowest STM implementation on this particular input is Cats STM (labeled *CatsStm*). As we increase the number of cores, at first it scales well until around 4 cores; then performance starts to degrade. We suspect the reason for this is the behavior of the locks used under higher contention (Cats STM uses the built-in locks of Cats Effect, which use a single atomic reference). Even at the best point in the chart (at 4 cores), this engine is slower than the non-parallelized baseline implementation (*Baseline* in the chart). The reason for this is probably (at least in part) the high

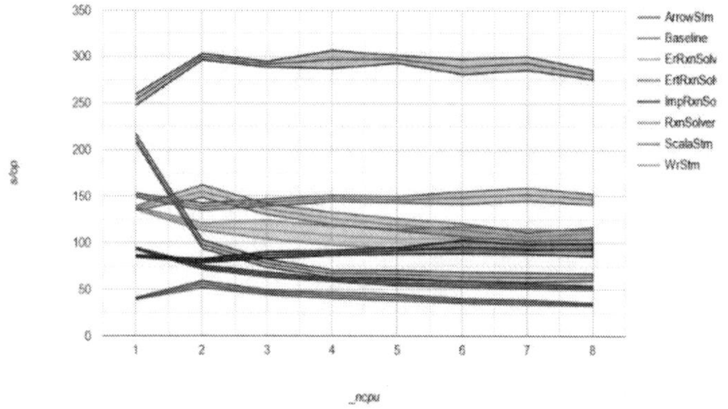

Figure 8. Completion time of complex realistic board

overhead of the immutable and purely functional data structures used by Cats STM.

In the same chart, we can see that the STM engine of Kyo (labeled *KyoStm*) seems to scale well with the number of processors, although there is less and less improvement the more cores are used (this is expected of any parallelization scheme that requires some coordination between cores). On the other hand, ZSTM seems unable to scale beyond 2 cores; we suspect the reason is that the locks it uses are blocking physical threads, and its runtime does not seem to start other threads, or compensate somehow for these threads that are not doing useful work.

On Figure 5 we can see the implementations which are able to solve this input much faster. All of them show a scaling curve similar to *KyoStm* (i.e., they scale well, but the improvements are smaller and smaller). If we compare the default ScalaSTM implementation (*ScalaStm*), and its variant wrapped in a purely functional API (*WrStm*), we can see that the purely functional API has a very significant overhead (around 2-3 times slower). We see similar, but smaller differences between the solvers using the functional and imperative APIs of CHOAM (*RxnSolver* and *ImpRxnSolver* respectively). The variants using the various forms of early release (*ErRxnSolver* and *ErtRxnSolver*) show little or no performance advantage over *RxnSolver*; this is expected, as early release is used to decrease the number of conflicting transactions, and due to the nature of the input, there are no (or very few) conflicting transactions here. (*ErtRxnSolver* is even slower here, due to the overhead associated with that particular implementation of early release.)

Figures 6 and 7 show results for another input with moderate complexity, a "small but realistic board" (*testBoard.txt* from [7]). This board is 75×75, and has 203 routes to solve, both short and long. This input has lots of potential conflicts, so we expect solving it to scale worse with the number of cores. (As before, some implementations are significantly faster than others, so Figure 7 shows the zoomed-in lower part of Figure 6.)

As expected, we see the implementations becoming only modestly faster as the number of cores increases, or not at all. An interesting exception to this is *ErtRxnSolver*, which seems to scale very well from 1 to 5 cores (and it is mostly flat after that). We suspect this is due to the relatively high overhead of

TABLE I. SUMMARY OF THE IMPLEMENTED VARIANTS

Name	STM library	API style
CatsStm	Cats STM	functional
RxnSolver	CHOAM	functional
ErRxnSolver		functional
ErtRxnSolver		functional
ImpRxnSolver		imperative
KyoStm	Kyo	functional
ScalaStm	ScalaSTM	imperative
WrStm		functional
ZSTM	ZIO	functional
ArrowStm	Arrow	imperative

implementing early release this way, which is then able to be overcome by more parallelism (allowed by using early release and non-opaque reads to decrease transaction conflicts).

As Figure 6 shows, the slowest implementation is Cats STM as previously. The fact that it is the slowest on both inputs suggests that it has very high single-threaded overhead (probably due to the immutable data structures used and the purely functional API).

The STM engine of Kyo shows some limited ability to scale, but despite this, it is slower than ZSTM, which (as before) does not scale well. This contrasts with the previously discussed results, where Kyo's superior scalability was able to overtake ZSTM at 4 cores.

Interestingly, none of these three implementations (*CatsStm*, *KyoStm*, *ZSTM*) is faster than the baseline non-parallelized implementation (on this input).

In Figure 7 we see the results of the faster implementations on the same input. All of them are faster than the *Baseline* (non-parallelized) version. The fact that they are faster even on a single core (i.e., no parallelism) is because we did not bother optimizing the baseline (we wanted to compare "conveniently coded", high level implementations). As mentioned before, all of them show no or limited scaling. Interestingly, *ScalaStm* (and its *purely* functional variant, *WrStm*) show only performance degradation with more cores (i.e., they are fastest with 1 core). This suggests that they are unable to exploit the very limited potential parallelism of this input.

RxnSolver and *ErRxnSolver* show modest scaling, (but still, they are slower than ScalaSTM). Of the two, *ErRxnSolver* is the faster: as expected, using early release helps to reduce transaction conflicts.

The fastest implementation (on this input) is *ArrowStm*, which scales reasonably well, and overtakes ScalaSTM at 3 cores.

Figure 8 shows our measurement results on a complex real circuit board of a memory module (board "mem" in [6]). This is a 600×600 board, with 3101 routes to solve. As this board is much bigger and more complicated than the previous two, solving it requires orders of magnitude more time (minutes instead of fractions of seconds as before). For this input, we do not show results for Cats STM, ZSTM or Kyo as they showed limited performance even for the moderately complex board.

As for the previous input, we see all the (faster) implementations improving on the *B*aseline (even at 1 core). ScalaSTM is the fastest here, showing an interesting curve: when running on multiple cores, it is first slower than on 1 core, but slowly getting faster, and overtaking its single-core performance at 6 cores. We suspect ScalaSTM has some optimizations specifically for single-threaded execution. (Its purely functional version, *WrStm* shows the same scaling behavior, but with a significant overhead due to the API wrapping). As before, *ArrowStm* performs well, and scales well, but in this case, cannot overtake ScalaSTM.

Comparing the various versions implemented with CHOAM, we see the unoptimized, purely functional variant (*RxnSolver*) being generally the slowest (and much slower than Scala STM). The variant *ErRxnSolver* (using early release) shows a significant improvement, which grows as the number of cores increases (this is expected, as the potential for conflicts is bigger with more cores, and early release reduces these conflicts). *ErtRxnSolver* (which uses both early release and non-opaque reads) starts slower (as before, due to the bookkeeping overhead of this particular implementation), but scales much better, overtaking all the other CHOAM variants, but it is still unable to overtake *ArrowStm*. Again, this scaling behavior is expected, like for testBoard.txt.

VI. Conclusions and Future Work

Considering all the measurement results detailed in the previous section, we make the following observations.

Comparing purely functional APIs with their imperative counterparts (i.e., *WrStm* with *ScalaStm*, and *RxnSolver* with *ImpRxnSolver*), we see overheads from around 30% to around 300% for the purely functional APIs. This is probably due to the purely functional APIs allocating an enormous amount of very small objects, which stresses the garbage collector of the JVM.

If we compare all the functional APIs with all the imperative ones, we see a similar trend: imperative ones tend to be faster (as expected). However, there is a significant difference in performance between the functional ones themselves, so there is clearly a way to decrease their overhead.

The Kotlin implementation (*ArrowStm*) performs consistently well and scales well. This is probably in part due to its imperative nature, but we suspect it might also have something to do with it being executed on the Kotlin coroutine scheduler. All the other implementations run on runtimes of Scala effect systems, which tend to schedule tasks differently from the coroutine scheduler. We leave examining the precise effect of the scheduler behavior on STM performance for future work.

On inputs where we expect transaction conflicts, using early release (and non-opaque reads) shows a clear performance advantage. This is expected, as these optimizations aim to decrease the number of conflicts, and they succeed at that goal.

Preliminary profiling shows that both Cats STM and ZSTM spend a considerable portion of their execution time maintaining the transaction log. This is not surprising, as the transactions we measured here are relatively big (i.e., their logs contain a lot of entries), especially for the last input (the memory module). Thus, optimizing their log data structures is a potential future performance improvement for these STM engines.

References

[1] M. Herlihy, J. E. B. Moss, "Transactional Memory: Architectural Support for Lock-Free Data Structures" ACM SIGARCH Computer Architecture News, Volume 21, Issue 2, 1993, pp. 289 - 300.

[2] M. Herlihy, V. Luchangco, M. Moir, and W. N. Scherer, "Software transactional memory for dynamic-sized data structures", PODC '03: Proceedings of the twenty-second annual symposium on Principles of distributed computing, 2003, pp. 92 – 101

[3] J. Chung et al., "The common case transactional behavior of multithreaded programs", Proceedings of the Twelfth International Symposium on High-Performance Computer Architecture, 2006, pp. 266–277

[4] R. Guerraoui, M. Kapalka, and J. Vitek, "STMBench7: a benchmark for software transactional memory", ACM SIGOPS Operating Systems Review, Volume 41, Issue 3, pp. 315 - 324

[5] I. Watson, C. Kirkham, and M. Lujan, "A Study of a Transactional Parallel Routing Algorithm," 16th International Conference on Parallel Architecture and Compilation Techniques (PACT 2007), Brasov, Romania, 2007, pp. 388-400

[6] M. Ansari et al., "Lee-TM: A Non-trivial Benchmark Suite for Transactional Memory". In: Bourgeois, A.G., Zheng, S.Q. (eds) Algorithms and Architectures for Parallel Processing. ICA3PP 2008. Lecture Notes in Computer Science, vol 5022.

[7] C. Seaton, "Context on STM in Ruby", online https://chrisseaton.com/truffleruby/ruby-stm/ accessed: 17/6/2025

[8] C. Y. Lee, "An Algorithm for Path Connections and Its Applications," in *IRE Transactions on Electronic Computers*, vol. EC-10, no. 3, pp. 346-365, Sept. 1961, doi: 10.1109/TEC.1961.5219222

[9] R. Guerraoui, M. Kapalka, and J. Vitek, "STMBench7: A benchmark for software transactional memory". EuroSys '07: Proceedings of the 2nd European Systems Conference, pp. 315–324. ACM Press, March 2007.

[10] T. W. Spence, Cats STM, online https://github.com/TimWSpence/cats-stm/, accessed: 18/6/2025

[11] D. Urban, CHOAM, online: https://github.com/durban/choam , accessed: 18/6/2025.

[12] Online: https://getkyo.io/ , accessed: 18/6/2025

[13] N. Bronson, Scala-STM, online: https://github.com/nbronson/ accessed: 18/6/2025.

[14] N. Bronson, H. Chafi, and K. Olukotun, "CCSTM: A Library-Based STM for Scala". Proceedings of the First Annual Scala Workshop. Lausanne, 2010

[15] Online: https://github.com/zio/zio/tree/series/2.x/core/shared/src/main/scala/zio/stm , accessed: 18/6/2025

[16] Online: https://arrow-kt.io/learn/coroutines/stm/ , accessed: 18/6/2025

[17] R. Guerraoui, A. Kogan, V. Marathe, and I. Zablotchi, "Efficient Multi-word Compare and Swap," in Proceedings of

the 34th International Symposium on Distributed Computing, Virtual Event, Oct. 2020.

[18] M. Herlihy, V. Luchangco, M. Moir, and I. William N. Scherer, "Software transactional memory for dynamic-sized data structures". In Proceedings of the twenty-second annual Symposium on Principles of Distributed Computing, pages 92–101, 2003.

[19] R. Guerraoui, M. Kapalka, "On the Correctness of Transactional Memory". In PPoPP '08: Proceedings of the 13th ACM SIGPLAN Symposium on Principles and Practice of Parallel Programming, pages 175–184, New York, NY, USA, 2008. ACM.

[20] D. Urban, stm-benchmark, online: https://github.com/nokia/stm-benchmark, accessed: 19/6/2025 Online: https://openjdk.org/projects/code-tools/jmh/ accessed: 19/6/2025

[21] Online: https://openjdk.org/projects/code-tools/jmh/ , accessed: 19/6/2025

Protocol-aware Cloud Gateway with Adaptive Rate Control

Ivana Kovacevic
Faculty of Technical Sciences
University of Novi Sad
Novi Sad, Serbia
email: kovacevic.ivana@uns.ac.rs

Vasilije Milic
Faculty of Technical Sciences
University of Novi Sad
Novi Sad, Serbia
email: milic.ra208.2019@uns.ac.rs

Isidora Knezevic
Faculty of Technical Sciences
University of Novi Sad
Novi Sad, Serbia
email: knezevic.ra47.2019@uns.ac.rs

Tamara Rankovic
Faculty of Technical Sciences
University of Novi Sad
Novi Sad, Serbia
email: tamara.rankovic@uns.ac.rs

Milos Simic
Faculty of Technical Sciences
University of Novi Sad
Novi Sad, Serbia
email: milos.simic@uns.ac.rs

***Abstract*— As cloud computing has emerged as the next-generation architecture for IT enterprises, it is challenging to envision a well-configured cloud environment that delivers services without adequate mechanisms for maintaining high availability, minimizing latency, and ensuring robustness. A notable feature of distributed cloud systems is their need to support a wide range of data formats and communication protocols. The pivotal role of communication protocols in facilitating seamless interactions among distributed components depends on their capability to perform real-time data and protocol conversion, ensuring interoperability without data loss while considering latency and reliability constraints. This paper proposes a prototype of open-source components designed to enhance distributed cloud infrastructure, including a protocol-aware gateway that performs configurable protocol transcoding. Additionally, the gateway component is connected to a rate-limiting service that ensures high availability and mitigates network congestion. These components are seamlessly integrable, preserving protocol features without performance trade-offs. Their effectiveness is demonstrated through integration into the open-source Constellations (C12S) platform, validating their flexibility and practical value in real-world cloud environments.**

Keywords-Gateway; Service discovery; Rate-limiting; Protocol transcoding; Distributed cloud.

I. INTRODUCTION

In the present era, cloud computing offers extensive computational capabilities and facilitates on-demand access to a shared pool of both hardware and software resources. It has been introduced as the next-generation architecture of IT enterprises and gives great capabilities that ensure improved productivity with minimal costs while offering a better level of scalability and flexibility in comparison to traditional IT systems [1]. High performance, high availability, and scalability present promising features guaranteed by the migration to cloud computing. To minimize complexity and ensure a stable environment conducive to future adaptations, both business and regular users choose to leverage the hardware or software resources offered by cloud providers, aiming to enhance cost-effectiveness and simplify maintenance.

It is not easy to envision a well-configured cloud environment delivering services without incorporating mechanisms for maintaining high availability, minimizing latency, and ensuring robustness. Moreover, addressing resource exhaustion and network congestion introduces a new set of rules that require careful consideration to ensure the overall health of cloud services and protect them from common misuse. To mitigate such risks, implementing a rate-limiting service serves as a viable solution, as a rate-limiting mechanism helps prevent resource exhaustion by temporarily blocking requests or placing them in sleep mode once a maximum limit has been reached. On the other hand, a distributed cloud aims to accommodate a wide range of data formats and protocols, facilitating seamless integration among applications. While existing cloud solutions are typically optimized for inter-service communication through RPC in a binary format, the same approach is not always suitable for external web clients. The Constellations platform is no exception. It follows the pattern of loosely coupled Dockerized micro-services, but it does not support out-of-the-box request handling beyond RPC, limiting straightforward interaction with external clients. For such scenarios, an integration of the component responsible for data and protocol conversion becomes crucial. Such a component ensures proper routing to the destination service without data loss, considering the overall network response time.

This paper centers on the design, implementation, and evaluation of two integrated, open-source, platform-independent components to maintain performance features crucial for a distributed cloud environment. Specifically, the goal is to ensure high availability and elasticity of communication between users and services, while protecting the system from excessive misuse. We propose a prototype gateway as the primary entry point to the system, which exposes Remote Procedure Calls (gRPC) as Hypertext Transfer Protocol (HTTP) endpoints by transcoding one protocol to another in a configurable manner. This service demonstrates that protocol awareness can be centralized at the entry point of a distributed cloud environment. It features dynamic client discovery and utilizes flexible configuration files for managing Application Programming Interfaces (APIs), eliminating the need to modify source code when a new service is discovered. Furthermore, the gateway is connected to a rate-limiting service to ensure availability and mitigate potential attacks. This service enforces limitations based on both system and user levels, leveraging priority queues and algorithms, such as token bucket, leaky bucket, and sliding window, to enforce fair rate control. To assess the proposed solution, both components are integrated with an open-source Constellations platform [2], which operates as a module within the distributed cloud infrastructure.

The paper is organized as follows: Section 2 presents the related work for this research on performance in distributed cloud, with a particular focus on gateways that ensure low latency and high availability. Section 3 provides an overview of rate-limiting algorithms, their advantages, and applications. In Section 4, the gateway is described. Section 5 explains the implementation of a protocol conversion service, a rate-limiting service, and their integration with the open-source platform for configuration dissemination in a distributed cloud. The usability, interoperability, and limitations of the proposed solution are discussed in Section 6. Finally, Section 7 presents the conclusion and future directions of the conducted research.

II. RELATED WORK

In their study, El Kafhali et al. [1] presented a thorough overview of cloud computing mechanisms, offering a systematic literature review specifically focused on cloud computing security issues and frameworks through a comprehensive survey. Their paper provided an overview of the fundamentals of cloud infrastructure, reflecting on the mechanisms to achieve scalability and availability, while considering proper defense against attacks. Latha et al. [3] conducted research that addresses challenges in distributed applications, focusing on client satisfaction, confidence, and preventing revenue losses by ensuring service availability. Their study developed an overload protection technique that relies on a URI configuration file, in conjunction with the Zuul gateway, which can filter requests before obtaining tokens. The token bucket rate-limiting algorithm is implemented to ensure traffic limitation while improving the reliability and availability of the cloud platform service. Despite integrating the gateway with rate-limiting to enhance availability, this research remains protocol-dependent and lacks protocol transcoding, which would enable flexibility and broaden its usage. Distributed cloud control approaches are also demonstrated in papers by Raghavan et al. [15] and in "Load balancing vs. distributed rate limiting: a unifying framework for cloud control" written by Stanojevic Rade et al. [16]. However, they do not describe a holistic approach with an integrated API gateway for monitoring and filtering requests that could also be protocol-agnostic.

Ranawaka et al. [14] emphasized the need to provide a scalable microservice architecture that offers highly available and fault-tolerant operations. They implemented Custos, which exposes services through a language-independent Application Programming Interface that encapsulates science gateway usage scenarios. This work primarily focuses on science-specific gateways in a research domain, tailored for computational experiments while hiding the complexities of accessing and using cyberinfrastructure. Although the necessity for such a solution is evident, the paper lacks an explanation on how to ensure scalability as the number of requests increases while protecting the platform from malicious Denial-of-Service (DoS) attacks.

III. RATE-LIMITING IN THE CLOUD ENVIRONMENT

To ensure service availability and achieve high scalability, cloud services must protect themselves against excessive usage, whether it is expected or not. Cloud services should be developed with rate limitations in mind to ensure the system operates properly and avoids cascading failure. For increasing throughput and decreasing end-to-end delay over large distribution systems, rate limiting on either the client or server side is critical [3]. Our approach in this research is to implement a prototype rate limiting at the OSI layer 7, to prevent resource exhaustion and maintain system resilience. We propose rate control at the entry point level, paired with the gateway. By integrating rate limiting within gateways, API usage can be centrally controlled across all deployed nodes, ensuring uniform policy enforcement and simplifying management.

Rate limiting helps prevent resource exhaustion by temporarily blocking requests or placing them in sleep mode once a maximum limit has been reached. After the sleep time, the request can be forwarded from the rate limiter to the handling server [4]. Rate limiting has found use in various cases, including improving overall system performance, protecting against brute force or Distributed Denial-of-Service (DDoS) attacks, preventing web scraping, and preventing resource starvation. Scalable rate limiting is achieved using various algorithmic approaches, including the leaky bucket algorithm, the token bucket algorithm, the fixed window, the sliding log, and the sliding window [3]. This paper focuses on the leaky bucket algorithm, the token bucket algorithm, and the sliding window, all of which are implemented within our rate-limiting service. The token bucket algorithm provides solutions for traffic shaping in packet-switched networks [5]. In this algorithm, when a new request arrives, the bucket grants one token to the requester, based on the availability [6]. If there are available tokens, the service accepts the request and removes one token from the bucket. If no tokens are available, the system rejects the request. This algorithm also requires a parameter for the refill rate, as it adds tokens to the bucket at a fixed rate defined by this parameter. It is a common choice in distributed systems, primarily due to its memory efficiency and ease of implementation.

The sliding window algorithm imposes limits within fixed time intervals, allowing for precise control over requests in smaller time windows. It admits a specified number of requests in a given timeframe L. As each request arrives, a request counter is incremented by one. This process continues as long as the request counter is less than a specified fixed number. At the end of a window interval, the request counter resets. Intervals are half open, i.e., [t, t+L) [7]. The leaky bucket is a counter that increases by one up to a maximum capacity C for each arrival and decreases continuously at a given drain rate D to as low as zero; an arrival is admitted if the counter is less than or equal to C- 1 (so that after the arrival it will be less than or equal to C) [7]. The leaky bucket algorithm is designed to provide clients with smooth and steady throughput by delaying requests rather than rejecting them outright. While this approach may increase latency due to its lack of drop behavior, it remains well-suited for use cases like background processing or metrics collection. That said, we also support two additional rate-limiting algorithms, giving clients the flexibility to choose the strategy that best fits their specific needs.

The proposed solution emphasizes implementing API rate-limiting as a centralized, independent component, which differs from traditional methods that integrate rate-limiting algorithms directly into individual services. By applying rate limiting on a system-wide basis, we gain finer control, allowing for multiple configurations for each request or service. Additionally, this approach can be developed and deployed separately, offering greater flexibility and ease of management. Having a single, global limit also avoids common problems related to communication and synchronization among multiple, distributed rate-limiting services [7].

IV. Transcoding HTTP to gRPC

While HTTP is a very popular choice due to its simplicity and stateless nature, some studies have shown that RPC outperforms HTTP in terms of response time and data volume [8], [9]. Moreover, 80% of the public APIs available follow most Representational State Transfer (REST) conventions, and developers are accustomed to that pattern, implying the need for gRPC APIs also to follow REST convention [10]. Additionally, having multiple cloud providers joined in a distributed cloud, cross-platform compatibility issues, and inconsistent call standards arise. Placing separate components as an API gateway alleviates these problems to some extent. To enhance user experience and minimize development costs, we propose a configurable rate-limiting gateway that is designed to fully comply with the REST while retaining the advantages of remote procedure calls. With this, existing REST endpoints can be efficiently transcoded to use the RPC protocol, guaranteeing no data loss. Remote procedure calls heavily rely on Protobuf, an open-source technique for serializing structured data [10]. Unlike JavaScript Object Notation (JSON), Protobuf is optimized and runs in binary format, which is why it is often the preferred choice. Additionally, Protobuf offers a mechanism to segregate context and data, allowing data to be transmitted repeatedly without duplicating context, such as field or property names, as often occurs in JSON or eXtensible Markup Language (XML). In practice, both gRPC APIs and HTTP/JSON APIs serve distinct purposes, and an ideal API platform should offer robust support for both types.

For protocol transcoding, the proposed gateway component leverages gRPC client reflection to dynamically discover methods, ensuring interoperability across services and reducing the need for manual adjustments. Given a hostname and port provided in the configuration scheme, the gateway attempts to establish a connection to the specific gRPC server and dynamically discover available services and methods without prior knowledge. Discovered services are later used in the process of protocol transcoding in order to forward data from the original HTTP request to the corresponding RPC service method. Moreover, by providing a transcoding feature, it is possible not only to determine what formats (i.e., which Protobuf messages) a server's method uses but also how to convert messages between a human-readable format, which is dominant in HTTP, and the binary wire format.

V. Implementation and the Use Case

Configurable, highly available cloud services, namely a gateway and rate-limiting service, are integrated within the configuration dissemination tool in the distributed cloud. This tool is part of the Constellations, an open-source, distributed cloud platform [2]. The main objective of the tool is to enable cloud-like services for users who would benefit from highly elastic deployments, while also taking latency and privacy requirements into account. To achieve so, the tool offers streamlined processes for infrastructure provisioning, application life cycle, and behavior management [10]. As the platform has multiple services distributed across the cloud that communicate using gRPC protocol, adding a rate-limiting gateway only increased its heterogenity and improved the response rate.

A. Gateway

The gateway solution offers a flexible approach for exposing gRPC calls as REST endpoints. Instead of burdening each service with boilerplate code to enable transcoding, this approach delegates the protocol conversion logic to a dedicated service acting as a proxy between the platform's end clients and the internal services. It uses the flexibility of the configuration file to avoid source code alterations that would otherwise be mandatory and are common in other prominent gateway implementations [12].

Within the configuration file, the highest level of API description is an API group, which encompasses versioned descriptions for the gRPC methods intended for exposure. These methods are grouped based on their purpose, allowing for the inclusion of gRPC methods from various services and applications. Bundling the APIs into API groups simplifies access to the methods needed for specific purposes, eliminating the need to search through an extensive list of APIs from each service to locate a particular method. A description of each gRPC method includes the REST route, HTTP method type (e.g., GET, POST), and the gRPC service that hosts it. The method's name serves as a key in a map during the dynamic generation of routes, and it must match the name in the source service. The configuration also includes the port of the gateway and the addresses of the gRPC services used. These addresses are kept internal to the gateway and are inaccessible from outside sources, meaning they cannot be directly reached via either gRPC or HTTP requests. The example of the configuration file is shown in Figure 1. The service registry, as a separate component within the gateway, allows services to register their endpoints, which are then stored in a configuration file. In the event of a failure, the gateway utilizes this configuration file to route

```
gateway:
  route: /apis
  port: 5555
services:
  Kuiper: kuiper:5000
  ExampleService: example:9001
  RateLimitService: rate_limiter_service:8080
groups:
  core:
    v1:
      CreateExample:
        method_route: /example-route
        type: POST
        service: ExampleService
      PutStandaloneConfig:
        method_route: /configs/standalone
        type: PUT
        service: Kuiper
```


Figure 1. Example of a YAML gateway configuration.

requests, eliminating the need to ping each service individually to collect routes.

Upon initializing the gateway, the configuration file is loaded, and for each gRPC service listed, a corresponding Client object is instantiated. Each client object includes an attribute called *DescriptorSource*, which is derived from the gRPC reflection mechanism and participates in obtaining a list of exposed gRPC methods from each client. However, this solution relies on gRPC services having reflection enabled, which allows clients to access detailed information about the Protobuf APIs they expose, including the specifications of each request and response, as well as their attributes. To invoke gRPC calls, this service depended on the Go library *grpcurl* [13]. This decision was beneficial because *grpcurl* efficiently converts HTTP data to gRPC data, simplifying the procedure. Moreover, *grpcurl* supports request headers during invocation, which was crucial for later authorization between services.

The process of HTTP route generation consists of several parts:

1. Generation of sub-routers for every group,
2. Sub-routing groups based on the version,
3. Assigning a path to each route based on the method name from the configuration file,
4. Creating a middleware that integrates a handler function and HTTP method type for each route.

The second step provides fine-grained configuration of routes, combining group and version, resulting in each method being mapped with its version and group, allowing for easier maintenance of clients in the future, based on the current API version. All of these parameters are required to create a complete path for each method. The full path is created in the third step, using the exact method name previously read from the configuration file. The final step is to prepare the router for gRPC method invocation. To achieve this, HTTP endpoints are wrapped into the middleware, which performs preprocessing and validation before the actual gRPC call. The transcoding process is validated against GET, POST, PUT and DELETE HTTP methods, with and without custom HTTP headers. To extract parameters from routes, the gateway uses regular expressions and then performs implicit type conversion. To prevent unauthorized access, the middleware includes a check for authorization tokens, verifying each request before directing it to the destination service. This process helps eliminate redundant calls to services with restricted access, enhancing security and improving response time. Once the gRPC method is invoked and completed successfully, the response is returned as a byte buffer. Additionally, the gRPC status codes are mapped to their corresponding HTTP response codes. This mapping is particularly helpful in case of errors, as it enables the provision of informative messages that explain why the error occurred.

B. Rate limiter

The rate-limiting service provides customizable rate-limiting mechanisms per request at both the application and system layers. Limitations are designed per client. In our scenario, clients refer to end users of the constellation platform. However, distinct rate limiters can be created based on the requirements of cloud services, irrespective of client types. Full support for managing rate limiters is also provided, enabling rate or type updates, safe deletion, and optional parameters. To support flexible request control, the prototype offers multiple rate-limiting algorithms that clients can choose from based on their specific needs. To apply safety measures against API overuse, we first define a rate-limiting strategy. Every rate limiter is assigned a unique ID in the format of user_id-method_id. For seamless integration, method_id corresponds to a method name retrieved from gRPC clients in the gateway. As this data is already extracted and prepared for routing to the desired service, no further querying or communication with other services is necessary. Given that this ID is treated as a regular expression, any notation is allowed, making it usable not only for gRPC methods but also for users or organizations that require limited access to resources. For instance, it is possible to configure access limitations for authenticated users and request origins, forbidding usage from multiple devices simultaneously. Apart from ID, the rate limiter is also described with TYPE, REQ_LIMIT, PRIORITY, PERIOD, and BURST. Attribute TYPE is directly related to supported rate-limiting algorithms, currently limited to

```
&pb.RateLimiter {
        id: "user1-PutStandaloneConfig",
        Name: "PutStandaloneConfig",
        UserName: "user1",
        Type: "tokenBucket",
        Priority: 1,
        ReqLimit: 1,
        Period: 60,
        Burst: 1,
        Idle: 2
    }
```

Figure 2. Code snippet demonstrating a rate limiter object

token bucket, leaky bucket, and sliding window. The total number of allowed requests within a specified period is determined by the combination of the attributes REQ_LIMIT and PERIOD. A period of time can be expressed in seconds. This additional parameter enables services to create rate limiters tailored to internal service metrics. These metrics might incorporate temporal factors, such as the number of served requests during specific periods of the day. Parameter BURST stands for the maximum number of concurrent requests that the API can handle, and it is used to regulate throttling in the token bucket algorithm. With larger bursts, the network may need to allocate more resources per connection [7].

The rate limiter also supports a priority queueing mechanism that can be utilized to favor users who are most frequently rejected due to system limitations. Priority can be handled at either the method or user level, where critical, time-sensitive methods have higher priority, while tracking or monitoring methods can be accessed with a delay. A lower PRIORITY value means a higher priority in the queue; thus, a value of 1 indicates the highest priority. If the userName is not provided, PRIORITY refers to the method. It is also possible to define an IDLE parameter for slow connections. This parameter and priority queueing are optional and can be deactivated based on system needs. The example of a rate limiter is shown in Figure 2. This rate limiter is set to allow only one request per minute, using the token bucket algorithm. It is defined for the user with the highest priority. Only one rate limiter can be active per client–request combination. This aligns with the notion of a fixed number of requests per user, as offered by cloud provider subscription plans. Any changes made to the rate limiter will override previous settings and reset the number of available tokens.

To minimize response time, a caching mechanism is implemented in the rate-limiting service. This mechanism stores the current state of the rate limiter in a cache memory for a specified period, reducing the number of calls to the database. The cache is updated each time a service modifies the rate limiter object. However, inconsistencies can arise due to network delays and concurrent updates, which may allow clients to exceed rate limits before the state is synchronized. Achieving strong state consistency can introduce significant overhead, resulting in longer processing times and reduced performance. To address this issue, we decided to integrate with Redis due to its ability to perform operations in memory, which reduces latency and makes it suitable for high-traffic environments where rate limits need frequent checking and updating.

C. Integration with the Constellations platform

As an evaluation, developed components are integrated with an open-source platform within a distributed cloud infrastructure to facilitate two-way protocol conversion and manage resource availability by enforcing rate control. To illustrate the flow of the transcoding process, Figure 3 depicts a scenario in which two clients send identical requests within a predefined timeframe. Requests are sent to the service responsible for configuration management within the Constellations platform. The service responsible for this feature is represented as a constellation service in a diagram. For example, in Figure 3, we demonstrate two calls to an endpoint that has a system rate limit of one request per minute. After receiving a request, the gateway uses *DescriptorSource* to determine the actual method name bound to the received HTTP request. Based on the configuration file, it maps parameters (if any) and

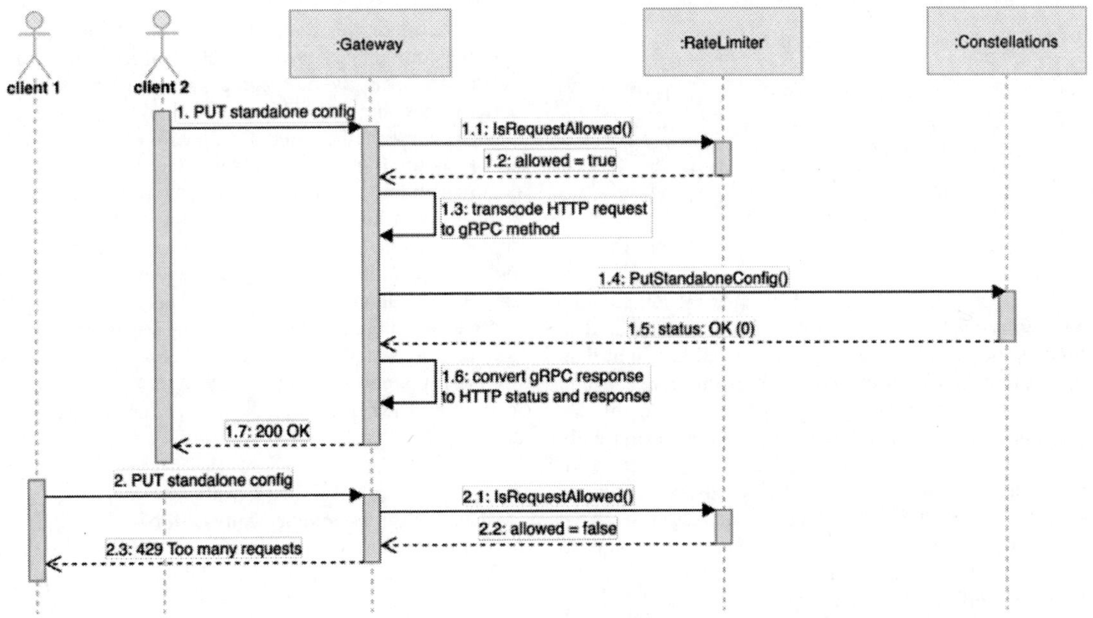

Figure 3. Sequence flow demonstrating the integration of gateway and rate-limiting services with the Constellations platform

converts the request payload to a byte stream suitable for the Protobuf format. The method name from the configuration is then used in a direct gRPC call to the rate-limiting service. The *IsRequestAllowed* method in the rate-limiting service searches for a rate limiter object based on its ID and then examines the rate limiter type to determine whether a request can be executed at the moment.

If an optional parameter is provided, the rate limiter service is also responsible for checking the user priority. Based on the examination of parameters, if the limit is reached, the method returns a false flag. Given the flag value, the gateway decides whether to invoke the actual gRPC method and transfer the request. As shown in Figure 3, for the second client, the rate limit is reached, and the request is blocked immediately. The same sequence is followed in case where a thousand users concurrently send identical requests, and the control rate is shown in Table 1, for each rate-limiting algorithm.

In Table 1, we compared the average latency introduced by different rate-limiting algorithms implemented in our service. We sent 1000 requests to the same route, configured to use the token bucket, leaky bucket, and sliding window algorithm, with the same *reqLimit* parameter set to 10. This seemed reasonable, considering the configuration is per IP address, and the average response time without a rate limit for the route was approximately 100-200ms. Both client IP address and Constellations' server were connected to the same internal network. Control rate is measured for the system rate limiter, representing the ratio between the number of successful and the number of rejected requests (those with 429 status code). Average latency represents the ratio between regular response time and response time when the rate limiter is applied.

TABLE I. A COMPARISON OF RATE-LIMITING ALGORITHMS

	Token bucket	Leaky Bucket	Sliding Window
avg. response time	0.097s	1.001s	0.095s
avg. latency	0.074s	0.043s	0.022s
control rate	0.1273	/	0.1235
total time (~1000 req)	10.502s	13.253s	10.084s

This approach enhances performance by minimizing unnecessary calls to the destination service while also providing the possibility to enforce a global rate limit that a user can achieve, regardless of the cloud service being accessed. As shown in Table 1, the control rate for the leaky bucket is not calculated, since all requests pass with a slight delay. Therefore, it is a client's responsibility to define the rate limit in advance, choosing the most appropriate algorithm depending on the use case. The transcoding process occurs at the beginning of the request call. It takes less than 5 ms, which turned out to be negligible performance-wise, especially considering that mapping is performed in the beginning, and no additional handling of routes is needed.

VI. DISCUSSION

In this research, we propose a solution to address issues in multiprotocol environments, emphasizing the need for cloud services to communicate in a predefined manner. Most cloud platforms support RPC internally and require additional time and resources to expose RPC methods as REST endpoints. Instead of the time-consuming process of refactoring existing services, we propose integration with a component that already offers protocol conversion and enables straightforward migration with API versioning. Therefore, we developed a protocol-aware gateway responsible for transcoding HTTP to RPC, following reconfigurable mapping of routes. This approach proved helpful in different settings as it supports both client reflection and the set of configuration rules described in YAML files, enabling proper connection between service methods and REST endpoints. Having this configuration separated from the internal logic of the connected services in the cloud reduces development time while making management easier. Its scheme is tested against routes with query parameters, path parameters, authorization, and custom headers, as well as with a request body, and it performs transcoding without data or header information loss. It can differentiate between unauthorized and authorized methods, preventing misuse, and could leverage access control measures if they are implemented further in the cloud environment. Moreover, the solution only requires following the schema pattern and can be easily integrated into existing cloud infrastructures, which we have demonstrated by incorporating it with the Constellations platform. However, since the proposed transcoding process heavily relies on the configuration file to extract routes, it is important to note that a strong automated YAML scheme validation is needed in order to minimize ambiguity and reduce the risk of errors.

Furthermore, this prototype relies on I/O operations to read the configuration and to track changes as new routes are added. This did not come as a bottleneck for the current setup, but it should be monitored as the number of services grows in the cloud. One possible approach would be to partition the configuration by services or their deployment location and scale horizontally. We integrated a protocol-aware gateway with the rate limiter and demonstrated its strong properties in precision rate control and manageability. With its priority queueing and system-agnostic features, it effectively enhances system safety and ensures alignment with platform requirements. Such granularity can be a trade-off between rate-limiting accuracy and performance; therefore, it is up to end users to decide whether to include fine-tuning of requests or not.

VII. CONCLUSION

The paper presents mechanisms for achieving desired performance features in a distributed cloud environment, with a focus on high availability, scalability, and robustness. To achieve these goals, we demonstrated the integration of two prototype components, namely the gateway and rate-limiting service, with an existing configuration dissemination solution. The prototype emphasizes its ease of adoption, platform-agnostic design, and the ability to enforce consistent communication patterns without sacrificing flexibility or performance. Key contributions include enabling protocol transcoding from HTTP to gRPC calls with reflection for method discovery, facilitating the transcoding of HTTP headers and body to Protobuf messages, and, in the opposite direction, packaging byte streams into readable HTTP responses in JSON format, while also ensuring proper status code mapping. This addressed the necessity for each service to expose both HTTP and gRPC endpoints. Additionally, it enhanced the availability of each service by maintaining communication within the platform on gRPC, thus boosting efficiency. Furthermore, the gateway, paired with an independent rate-limiting service, eliminates the need for each service to alter its internal logic or modify request implementation to manage and regulate network congestion. System rate limiting manages and controls overall network flow within the platform, while also allowing for the creation of specific limitations on a per-request or priority basis, which emerges as a suitable solution for subscription plans structured around request rates from cloud providers. As part of our future work, we aim to enhance rate-limiting capabilities by making them adjustable based on service telemetry and monitoring, and to extend the current solution to support distributed rate-limiting. Additionally, the goal is to further research prototype performance and general applicability by integrating it with more real-world solutions.

ACKNOWLEDGMENT

Funded by the European Union (TaRDIS, 101093006). Views and opinions expressed are however those of the author(s) only and do not necessarily reflect those of the European Union. Neither the European Union nor the granting authority can be held responsible for them.

This research has been supported by the Ministry of Science, Technological Development and Innovation (Contract No. 451-03-65/2024-03/200156) and the Faculty of Technical Sciences, University of Novi Sad through project "Scientific and Artistic Research Work of Researchers in Teaching and Associate Positions at the Faculty of Technical Sciences, University of Novi Sad" (No. 01-3394/1).

REFERENCES

[1] S. El Kafhali, I. El Mir, and M. Hanini, "Security Threats, Defense Mechanisms, Challenges, and Future Directions in Cloud Computing," *Archives of Computational Methods in Engineering*, vol. 29, no. 1, Apr. 2021, doi: https://doi.org/10.1007/s11831-021-09573-y.

[2] "constellations" *GitHub*. [Online] Available from: https://github.com/c12s [retrieved: 06, 2025]

[3] V. L. Padma Latha, N. Sudhakar Reddy, and A. Suresh Babu, "Optimizing Scalability and Availability of Cloud Based Software Services Using Modified Scale Rate Limiting Algorithm," *Theoretical Computer Science*, Jul. 2022, doi: https://doi.org/10.1016/j.tcs.2022.07.019.

[4] D. Goetz, M. Barton, and G. Lange, "Distributed rate limiting of handling requests," United States Patent 8930489, Jan. 6, 2015.

[5] L. Sarakis, N. Moshopoulos, D. Loukatos, K. Marinis, P. Stathopoulos, and N. Mitrou, "A versatile timing unit for traffic shaping, policing and charging in packet-switched networks," *Journal of Systems Architecture*, vol. 54, no. 5, pp. 491–506, Sep. 2007, doi: https://doi.org/10.1016/j.sysarc.2007.08.004.

[6] J. Rexford, F. Bonomi, A. Greenberg, and A. Wong, "Scalable architectures for integrated traffic shaping and link scheduling in high-speed ATM switches," *IEEE Journal on Selected Areas in Communications*, vol. 15, no. 5, pp. 938–950, Jun. 1997, doi: https://doi.org/10.1109/49.594854.

[7] A. W. Berger and W. Whitt, "A comparison of the sliding window and the leaky bucket," *Queueing Systems*, vol. 20, no. 1–2, pp. 117–138, Mar. 1995, doi: https://doi.org/10.1007/bf01158434.

[8] M. Niswar, R. A. Safruddin, A. Bustamin, and I. Aswad, "Performance Evaluation of Microservices Communication with REST, GraphQL, and gRPC," *International Journal of Electronics and Telecommunication*, vol. 70, no. 2, pp. 429–436, 2024, [Online] Available from: https://ijet.ise.pw.edu.pl/index.php/ijet/article/view/10.24425-ijet.2024.149562

[9] M. Śliwa and B. Pańczyk, "Performance comparison of programming interfaces on the example of REST API, GraphQL and gRPC," *Journal of Computer Sciences Institute*, vol. 21, pp. 356–361, Dec. 2021, doi: https://doi.org/10.35784/jcsi.2744.

[10] "Protocol Buffers," *protobuf.dev*. [Online] Available from: https://protobuf.dev [retrieved: 06, 2025].

[11] T. Ranković, I. Kovačević, V. Maksimović, G. Sladić, and M. Simić, "Configuration Management in the Distributed Cloud," *Lecture notes in networks and systems*, pp. 224–235, Jan. 2024, doi: https://doi.org/10.1007/978-3-031-71419-1_20.

[12] "Gateway architecture | NGINX Documentation," *Nginx.com*, 2025. [Online] Available from: https://docs.nginx.com/nginx-gateway-fabric/overview/gateway-architecture/ [retrieved: 06, 2025].

[13] "grpcurl package - Go Packages," *Go.dev*, 2025. [Online] Available from:https://pkg.go.dev/github.com/fullstorydev/grpcurl [retrieved: 06, 2025].

[14] I. Ranawaka *et al.*, "Custos: Security Middleware for Science Gateways," *Practice and Experience in Advanced Research Computing*, pp. 278–284, Jul. 2020, doi: https://doi.org/10.1145/3311790.3396635.

[15] B. Raghavan, K. Vishwanath, S. Ramabhadran, K. Yocum, and A. C. Snoeren, "Cloud control with distributed rate limiting," *ACM SIGCOMM Computer Communication Review*, vol. 37, no. 4, pp. 337–348, Oct. 2007, doi: https://doi.org/10.1145/1282427.1282419.

[16] R. Stanojevic and R. Shorten, "Load Balancing vs. Distributed Rate Limiting: An Unifying Framework for Cloud Control," *IEEE Xplore*, Jun. 01, 2009. https://ieeexplore.ieee.org/abstract/document/5199141.

Barriers and Enablers of AI Adoption in Software Testing: A Secondary Study

Katja Karhu and Jussi Kasurinen
Department of Software Engineering
LUT University
Lahti, Finland
e-mail: {katja.karhu | jussi.kasurinen}@lut.fi

***Abstract*—It seems that AI adoption in software testing is not as straightforward as promoted by the hype surrounding AI: there are a lot of expectations, but the reported practical implementations are still relatively rare. In this survey paper, we investigated the reasons behind the slow AI adoption in software testing by qualitatively analyzing recent empirical studies with industry context. In our work, we classified the barriers and enablers from the earlier studies into six categories: management, processes, human resources, technology, data and external. The main approach to AI adoption in software testing in the industry still seems to be investigation and experimentation in individual organizations without industry-wide reference implementations or standards. A major barrier for AI adoption in software testing is the lack of perceived usefulness or produced value. More research and empirical evidence of successful AI adoption in software testing is needed.**

Keywords-software testing; artificial intelligence; technology adoption; qualitative research; reflexive thematic analysis.

I. INTRODUCTION

In the industry, the interest in AI in software testing is high and growing. It is seen as a potential competitive advantage: companies that do not successfully utilize AI in software testing will lose in the competition [1]. However, the practical implementations and the AI adoption rate seem to be lagging behind [2][3].

In Perforce's [2] 2024 industry survey, 48 percent of respondents indicated they were interested in AI but have not yet started any initiatives, and only 11 percent were already implementing AI techniques in software testing. Interest in AI is still growing a year later, in Perforce's newest 2025 industry survey [3], over 75 percent of survey respondents identified AI-driven testing as a pivotal component in their strategy for 2025. But actual adoption rate is still behind, with only 16 percent of respondents reporting on having adopted AI in testing [3].

On the side of academia, the research on AI in software testing has been quite extensive [4][5]. However, Nguyen at al [6][7] found in a study conducted in 2023, that most of the existing studies on AI in software quality assurance are "experimental studies and thus do not take into consideration the industrial context". They further state that "how GenAI models deal with real-world software quality issues remains a mystery" [6][7]. King et al [8] had similar findings in 2019: "only a few of these works are backed by real-world case studies, or result in industrial tools and methods". Since some time has passed when the studies mentioned were performed, and advances in especially generative AI and large language models have been made, we wanted to explore the current state of empirical studies on AI in software testing with a strictly industry context. To our knowledge, literature surveys with this specific scope have not been conducted before.

Our first paper on AI adoption in software testing, based on the same dataset of literature, was about how AI is utilized on software testing and what are the expectations related to it [9]. There, we focused on the actual and potential use cases for AI in software testing, and their actual and expected benefits [9].

In this survey paper, we continue the reflexive thematic analysis of the literature from the point of view of barriers and enablers of AI adoption in software testing. Overall, our goal in this study is to explore, why AI adoption rate in software testing is still quite low, and what could be done about it via identifying the barriers and enablers. Our research questions are:

- RQ1: What are the issues that prevent or hinder AI adoption in software testing?
- RQ2: What are the enablers behind successful AI adoption in software testing?

The paper is structured as follows. In Section 2, we describe the data collection and research methods and process. In Section 3, we present the results of the qualitative analysis. Section 4 contains the discussion, where we further reflect on the findings. Finally, the conclusion and future work are presented in Section 5.

II. METHODS

We utilized systematic mapping study, as described by Petersen, Vakkalanka and Kuzniarz [10] to identify earlier studies on AI adoption in software testing. Then, we qualitatively analyzed the papers found via the systematic mapping study. Our primary data analysis approach in this study is reflexive thematic analysis. Braun and Clarke [11][12] define thematic analysis as a flexible qualitative analysis method, or more appropriately, a family of methods, for observing themes within data. The overall research process is documented in higher detail in the "sister paper" of this study [9].

A. Data Collection

We performed a systematic mapping study, and found 17 papers that fit our inclusion and exclusion criteria [9]. Our goal was to find recent (year 2020 or later) original empirical papers on AI in software testing where the data had been collected from testers or other QA experts. The databases we

TABLE I. NUMBER OF PAPERS PER YEAR

Year	Papers
2020	2 [13][14]
2021	0
2022	2 [1][15]
2023	4 [16]–[19]
2024	10 [20]–[28]
Total:	17

used were Scopus and Google Scholar, because they are known to include papers from a wide selection of different fields.

Over half of the papers (10) we found had been published in 2024 (see Table I). Out of the 17 papers, nine were peer-reviewed, six were theses and two were other grey literature. The reason, why we included theses and other grey literature in our study, was that they contained rich and detailed data collected from experts, making them well suited for qualitative analysis.

B. *Reflexive Thematic Analysis*

In this study, we used reflexive thematic analysis, a non-positivist approach [12], as our data analysis method. A theme is a concept that captures important patterned information and insights about the data, related to the research question [11]

We followed the phases of thematic analysis defined by Braun and Clarke [11]:

- Phase 1: familiarizing yourself with your data
- Phase 2: generating initial codes
- Phase 3: searching for themes
- Phase 4: reviewing themes
- Phase 5: defining and naming themes
- Phase 6: producing the report

In reality, the process was more iterative, where especially the phases from three to six were repeated several times. We followed an inductive approach in our analysis, and our goal was identify interesting themes in the papers. Eventually, the large number of identified themes resulted in splitting the reporting into different papers, as too many themes in one paper resulted in a very incoherent and long report. In our earlier paper, we focused on how AI is utilized in software testing, analyzing the actual and expected use cases and benefits, and the discrepancy between the expectations and reality of AI adoption in software testing [9].

In this study, we wanted to further investigate the reasons why AI adoption in software testing seems to be quite low. Therefore, we selected the barriers and enablers as our primary theme. We also tried to identify the differences between actual barriers and enablers, and expected barriers and enablers, but that proved too complicated, especially with the earlier literature, where a lot of the context was missing.

III. RESULTS

We grouped the barriers and enablers identified from the studies into six categories (see Table II): management, processes, human resources, tools, data and external. The category here describes the "source" of the barrier, or the level the barrier could be resolved. Barriers and enablers in different categories can also affect each other. For example, outsourcing can be one way of resolving the barrier of AI skill gap. It is worth noting, that the barriers of adoption are not inherently "bad" and enablers "good". For example, strict IT policies or data privacy and security issues as barriers are essential in cases where the developed software is safety-critical. Enabling the AI adoption by loosening the IT policies in this will most likely result in unwanted side-effects.

The management category describes the barriers and enablers related, for example, to the organization's finances, priorities, strategy and personnel management. The process category contains the barriers and enablers related to the daily operations within the organizations, such as policies, communication, software development processes, etc. The enablers and barriers in the human resources -category include employee-level topics, such as skills and feelings. In the tools category, we have technological barriers and enablers. The data category contains barriers and enablers related to data. And finally, in the external category, we have items that impact AI adoption in testing, but come from outside the organization, for example, societal, business ecosystem, or industry level barriers and enablers.

The obvious elephant in the room is the perceived *lack of usefulness or produced value* of AI in software testing. In Purovesi's [26] investigation of AI adoption in the test automation context, interviewees had observed that the value produced by AI is still minimal. Also, Hossain et al [27] found that in companies there was uncertainty about the usefulness of AI testing. Some felt that there was a lack of concrete estimates about the time-saving of AI assisted test automation, as the evidence was limited [26]. In the study by Amalfitano, Coppola, Distante and Ricca [20], the respondents "pointed out that while there are numerous general-purpose tools available in the domain of Large Language Models (LLM), their potential for GUI-based testing tasks remains unproven". The earlier studies reported benefits from AI adoption in software testing, but in some cases, it was difficult to quantify them [26], or respondents felt that the speed or efficiency improved only a little [24][26]. In addition, AI adoption may cause additional work that may undo the benefits: it takes more time than it saves [26]. For example, creating test cases with AI is easy, but maintenance is not: making changes to, or finetuning, AI-generated test cases takes a lot of time and effort [24].

Significant investments are required in AI adoption: especially *investments in technology and skill development* were seen as important enablers. Hossain et al [27] found that especially for software development organization that have no previous experience with AI systems, implementing AI can be both costly and time-consuming. Costs include, for example, hiring more staff or consultants, training of personnel, and infrastructure and computational resources [27]. The development of trustworthy AI systems can take a long time, months or even years, because of the experimental and iterative approach to development [27].

TABLE II. BARRIERS AND ENABLERS PER CATEGORY FROM EARLIER LITERATURE

Category	Barriers	Enablers
Management	Lack of usefulness/produced value [1][20][24][26][27] Requires significant investments [1][27] Risk aversion [1][21][27] Lack of time and resources [1][21][24][25][27]	Marketing AI benefits [1][26] Leadership support [14][16][17][25] Investments in technology [14][16][17][26] Investments in skill development [26] Outsourcing [27] Hiring new employees [27]
Processes	Incompatibility with current processes [1][13][21] Strict IT policies [25] Poor internal communication [25]	Evaluation of current processes [1][28] Change management [25] AI roadmap [27]
Human resources	AI skill gap [1][20][21][24][26][27] Lack of trust in AI [13][21][23]–[25] Resistance to change [1][25]	Personnel training [16][24]–[27] Internal communication [21][25] Collaborative experimentation and research [1] Guidelines for working with AI [20]–[22][25]
Tools	Difficulties in finding and selecting tools [20][24] Lack of transparency [13][21][28] Incompatibility with legacy systems [1][21][26] Poor usability of tools [1] Unreliability (e.g., hallucination and bias) [21][23] Tool pricing [20] Lack of domain knowledge [20]	Explainable AI (XAI) [13][21][28] Monitoring and reviewing [21] Building test automation first [1] AI tool documentation [4] Company's internal AI tools [25] Open-source AI tools [20] Formal screening process for AI tools [25]
Data	Lack of training data [1][13][20][21][23][25]–[28] Data privacy and security issues [24][27]	Purposefully collecting data for training [1][26] Creating training datasets [20][26] Tools for data cleaning and pre-processing [27] Reliable data sources [27] Proper training of AI with high quality data [20][27][28]
External	Lack of reference implementations or standards [1][21]	Education system (e.g., university level) [27] Collaboration with other organizations [27] Certifications [16][21][26]

Because of the experimental nature, someone has to make the initial commitment and investments to the development of AI-based testing solutions, but without reference implementations, it can be difficult to get organizations to commit to, or even try, AI adoption in testing [1]. Ahven [1] investigated AI adoption in testing in an IT consulting company, where their customers were not willing to commit because of the *lack of reference implementations*. And on the other hand, the consulting company was not willing to develop AI solutions internally and take the financial risk of trying something new that might result in a failure [1]. To get around this problem, the interviewee's in Ahven's [1] mentioned, that the company had started *marketing* communications (videos, webinars) to create excitement about AI-assisted testing within customers. However, on the other side of the marketing coin, aggressive marketing, unrealistic promises and a "hype peak" related AI in testing were observed [26].

Khan et al [21] found that especially small companies doing software development "may be *risk-averse* towards adopting new technologies, including AI-based software testing techniques, due to the fear of potential failures or increased costs". In addition to the financial risks, AI technologies include risks, such as risks related to security and privacy. Purovesi [26] found that, even though the interest in using AI in test automation, customers wanted to carefully consider the security and privacy before making the commitment. Uncertainty about risks was one of the reasons Hossain et al [27] also found, that reduced the willingness in organizations to commit to AI adoption in testing. In safety-critical scenarios, the uncertainty of results can be unacceptable [20]. In addition, people unaware of AI risks are a risk. Even though, in most of the studies, the interviewees were knowledgeable about the risks related to AI, a complete lack of risk awareness was also observed: some employees did not see any risks in AI utilization in software testing [25].

Time and resources are needed in many aspects of AI adoption in software testing, such as designing, building and training AI models [27], implementing AI systems for testing [1], skill development [25]. In addition, new computational resources are needed for the AI infrastructure [27]. AI adoption means time away from daily work, which may be difficult to organize and cause delays in testing work [27]. Skill development may be hindered if testers do not have working time allocated to learning about new topics that are not directly related to their current work [25].

AI adoption in software testing also requires changes in *current processes* and ways of working. Evaluating current ways of working and how things could be done differently were seen as important enablers, but it is also often blocked by lack of time [1]. Also, *resistance to change* can hinder adoption: if existing processes are working quite well already, it might be difficult to convince people to think things differently

[1]. Laine [25] suggests that *change management* efforts are therefore needed to enable successful AI adoption. Hossain et al [27] suggest creating an *AI roadmap*, and evaluating, where AI would fit in, as well as monitoring the performance indicators and milestones over time [27].

AI skill gap as a barrier was highlighted in several studies. AI as a term can contain a variety of technologies requiring specialized skills that is not usually present in a testing organization [26][27]. Verifying and validating AI model's accuracy after training requires skills, such as statistical analysis and data visualization [27]. Prompting, while seeming deceptively simple, can require significant effort and a trial-and-error approach, "which requires a fine-tuning of the prompts used and implies the possibility of wrong results of the testing activities" [20]. In order to bridge the AI skill gap, the organization must invest in skill development via, for example, personnel training, hiring new employees, developing guidelines (e.g., for prompting and creating training datasets) [20][21][27]. In one company, a study group ("future testing research unit") had been created, where testing specialists *experimented and researched* new tools and new ways of working, and presented the results to the organization [1]. Another option to resolve the AI skill gap is *hiring new personnel* [27].

The *lack of trust in AI* seems to be closely related to the *unreliability of AI tools*. In a study by Adu [23], and interviewee summarized the problem of the underlying reliability issue in LLMs: *"My main concern is that LLMs are not capable of thinking and do not really "understand" the prompts nor the content they are producing. They are rather content generators which output the statistically like response given some input. As such, the problem with using them for testing related tasks is that there is no guarantee that they are doing what you asked them to do."* [23].

Due to their inherent nature, LLMs are not therefore ideal for testing tasks that require reliability or determinism. It comes down to selecting the right AI tools for the right tasks. In addition, human supervision of AI via *monitoring and reviewing* was seen as crucial [21]. Khan et al summarized that "rule-compliant processes, monitoring systems, and external oversight contribute to reliability" [21].

Earlier it was mentioned, that marketing, and communicating the benefits of AI to customers are important. Same seems to go for the *internal communication*. Laine [25] states that "when introducing a new AI tool, the communication should emphasize the benefits, especially to the employees themselves". Poor internal communication can manifest as lack of knowledge about, e.g., the internal training materials and AI tools that are available in the company [25]. Khan et al [21] highlight also the transparent and ethical *organization culture* and communication in order to build long-term trust to AI, as well as self-regulation and self-imposed AI standards.

Clear communication is also important if, for example, utilizing public AI tools is forbidden by the IT policy due to privacy and security reasons. In addition to communication, the overall *leadership support* was seen as an important factor in engaging employees [14][16][17] and was seen as contributor to a successful adoption [25].

From the technical side, *incompatibility with legacy systems* and code was raised as a potential problem in AI adoption [21][26]. On the other hand, from the data point of view, old and complex systems were more suitable for leveraging AI, because of the large amounts of data available for AI model training [26].

The *lack of transparency* in AI models and tools can cause a lack of trust in AI, since it is difficult to understand and trust their decisions [13][20][21]. With commercial AI testing tools the black-box nature can hinder also the ability to fine-tune the tools effectively [20]. In addition, commercial tools were *difficult for testers to evaluate*, as they require subscriptions, which may lead to testers giving up on the tool evaluation completely [20].

Amalfitano, Coppola, Distante and Ricca [20] suggest *open-source AI tools* as way of increasing the transparency and explainability of AI systems. Khan et al [21] state that "*explainable AI (XAI)* is crucial for building trust, but challenges exist in achieving transparency". Solutions suggested for enabling and increasing explainability were: implementing parallel algorithms [21], knowledge distillation, saliency mapping, and symbolic reasoning [13], as well as visualization [28]

Lack of training data, and especially the *lack of high quality training* data was also a major barrier. The quality of training data directly impacts the reliability of the AI system [27]. However, potential training data was not collected systematically or it was discarded as useless [1]. Training data collection also raises *privacy and security concerns* [27]. Overall, careless handling of sensitive data in AI tools may result in compromised security [23]. Another issue was the bias in AI systems, caused by the training data. Khan et al [21] suggested using benchmark datasets in addressing the bias [21]. Overall, collecting, labeling and *cleaning* training data was seen as a challenging and high effort activity, which also requires time and investments [13][21][27].

IV. Discussion

Our research questions were: "what are the issues that prevent or hinder AI adoption in software testing" and "what are the enablers behind successful AI adoption in software testing". We went through earlier empirical studies on AI in software testing with industry context, and looked for the barriers and enablers of AI adoption. We found that AI adoption in software testing is not only a technological issue, as we classified the barriers and enablers reported in the earlier studies into six categories: management, processes, human resources, technology, data and external.

A very significant barrier for AI adoption in software testing was a lack of usefulness or produced value, combined with the lack of reference implementations. The potential reasons we identified based on the analysis of the earlier studies were:

- The early phase of adoption: the approach to AI adoption is still exploratory and investigative, as there are yet no industry-wide practices or standards

- The nature of some AI tools: for example, LLMs are not suitable for testing tasks that require reliability and determinism.

In our earlier study of the same literature dataset [9] we found that there were potential use cases for AI in software testing, such as test case generation, code analysis, and intelligent test automation, but the reported actual implementations and observed benefits were limited. Many implementations were still on the proof-of-concept level [9].

The lack of usefulness or produced value, and the lack of reference implementations, seem to be also reflected in grey literature on AI in software testing. Ricca, Marchetto and Stocco [29] have performed a multi-year analysis of grey literature in test automation, and concluded that "the nature of these sources limits to suggestions on how to use AI for TA, without presenting concrete evidence of its practical application or usage details".

For the lack of usefulness or produced value we did not identify many direct enablers. Collaborative experimentation and research, and collaboration with other organizations, could be ways for identifying useful reference AI solutions for software testing. Most of the enablers were focused on resourcing, building trust in AI/tackling resistance, skill development, and documentation.

Simmler and Frischknecht [30] have proposed a taxonomy for evaluating human-machine collaboration, that could be utilized also in software testing context to evaluate suitable AI solutions for different testing tasks, as well as the resources needed for monitoring these solutions. They define two dimensions: level of automation and level of autonomy. In short, the higher the level of automation, the less humans have control over the system, and the higher the level of autonomy is, the more the transparency decreases and it becomes more difficult to trace the machine's actions [30]. The more autonomy the AI-system has, the more important human monitoring becomes, and the higher the level of automation is, the more reliable the system needs to be [30].

It is worth noting, that the interest in AI seems to have increased significantly [2][3], even despite the lack of perceived value or usefulness. What makes companies want to invest in new technologies that do not yet have a proven track record? Gulzar and Smolander [31] provide an explanation to this: they have established that there are various motivations for new technology adoption, which can have both positive and negative effects. These motivations include [31]:

- Market dynamics - staying one step ahead, technology as a competitive edge
- Internal imperatives - goal setting by management, strategy
- Technological advancement - innovations
- Social influence - fear of missing out, hype, enthusiasm, collective feelings
- Economic considerations - reducing costs, return-of-investment (ROI)
- Operational and strategic improvements - increased efficiency, productivity, scalability

As can be seen, there are more motivations to technology adoption than just operational improvement and technological advancement. The other motivations, such as market dynamics and social influence, can weigh in more than the proven benefits of the new technology.

Monitoring is also one of the ways to tackle the barriers of lack of transparency and the lack of trust in AI. Soomro, Fan, Sohu, Soomro and Shaikh [32] have found that "negative perceptions of AI can slow down its adoption in various sectors". Open and honest internal communication on AI were highlighted by Laine [25] and Khan et at [21] as a way of addressing the lack of trust. Another issue causing lack of trust in AI are the data privacy and security issues. Kinney, Anastasiadou, Naranjo-Zolotov and Santos [33] summarized that the loss of privacy due to data needs of AI systems are a significant factor in the rejection of AI technology".

The marketing of AI benefits, whether to customers or in company's internal communication, should be based on evidence. In Purovesi's [26] study interviewees had observed aggressive marketing, unrealistic promises and a "hype peak" [26]. On the other hand, there were also reports of resistance to change [25][26]. If the lack of trust in AI and resistance is based on legitimate concerns, such as lack of produced value and usefulness, or security and data privacy problems, it should not be addressed by only trying to convince the audience of AI benefits. In summary, we need more research and empirical evidence of successful AI implementations in software testing to back up the message of AI benefits.

A. *Limitations of the study*

The studies we analyzed were from 2020-2024, so it is possible, that there have been new developments in AI adoption in software testing after their data collection phases. It can also be, that we have incomplete knowledge of AI adoption in software testing, as it may be undocumented. Companies may be unwilling to reveal their experiences of AI-assisted testing, in order to maintain business secrets or competitive edge, or even due to failed adoption attempts.

In this study we did not cover the impact of legislation and regulation to AI adoption, which could be viewed as both barriers and enablers. It was noted in the earlier studies, that for some domains, such as healthcare and banking, the laws and regulations of handling confidential data are stricter [27]. In these cases, the laws and regulations are acting as a barrier, and for a good reason. Laws and regulations were also seen as a way of increasing trust in AI, making them also an enabler. Some experts also raised the issue of problems in regulation, as it was viewed as outdated, and needed to be extended to cover AI use [27][28]. However, there were not enough details to analyze the impact of laws and legislation to AI adoption in software testing in higher detail, as this is a complex phenomenon. We also address additional limitations in our earlier study [9].

V. Conclusion and Future Work

In order to investigate the reasons behind low AI adoption rates in software testing, we performed a reflexive thematic analysis of 17 earlier empirical studies on AI adoption in software testing. We found that AI adoption is software testing is still suffering from lack of reference implementations and standards, as well as perceived usefulness and value. The limited empirical evidence on the benefits of AI in testing, combined with significant investments and resources required are one explanation for the low rates of AI adoption in software testing.

Future research is needed in evaluating the usefulness of different AI technologies (such as LLMs) in different testing tasks. We need more empirical evidence and detailed descriptions of successful AI adoptions, as well as lessons learned from unsuccessful AI adoption projects. We plan to continue our research by conducting interviews in software development organizations in order to further identify the reasons behind the slow AI adoption, as well as identifying the success factors of AI adoption in software testing.

References

[1] H. Ahven, "Utilization of artificial intelligence in software quality assurance," Finnish, M.S. thesis, University of Jyväskylä, 2022.

[2] Perforce, *The 2024 State of Continuous Testing*, 2024. [Online]. Available: https://www.perfecto.io/resources/state-of-continuous-testing, Accessed: 2025-02-14.

[3] Perforce, *The 2025 State of Continuous Testing*, Feb. 2025. [Online]. Available: https://www.blazemeter.com/resources/2025-state-of-continuous-testing-report, Accessed: 2025-02-18.

[4] D. Amalfitano, S. Faralli, J. C. R. Hauck, S. Matalonga, and D. Distante, "Artificial Intelligence Applied to Software Testing: A Tertiary Study," *ACM Computing Surveys*, vol. 56, no. 3, Oct. 2023, ISSN: 15577341. DOI: 10.1145/3616372.

[5] M. Hossain and H. Chen, "Application of machine learning on software quality assurance and testing: A chronological survey," *International Journal of Computers and their Applications*, vol. 29, no. 3, pp. 150–157, 2022.

[6] A. Nguyen-Duc *et al.*, "Generative Artificial Intelligence for Software Engineering A Research Agenda," preprint, Oct. 2023. DOI: 10.48550/arXiv.2310.18648.

[7] A. Nguyen-Duc *et al.*, "Generative Artificial Intelligence for Software Engineering A Research Agenda," *Software: Practice and Exprience*, pp. 1–38, Jun. 2025. DOI: 10.1002/spe.70005.

[8] T. M. King *et al.*, "Ai for testing today and tomorrow: Industry perspectives," in *2019 IEEE International Conference On Artificial Intelligence Testing (AITest)*, 2019, pp. 81–88. DOI: 10.1109/AITest.2019.000-3.

[9] K. Karhu, J. Kasurinen, and K. Smolander, "Expectations vs Reality – A Secondary Study on AI Adoption in Software Testing," unpublished, Apr. 2025. DOI: 10.48550/arXiv.2504.04921.

[10] K. Petersen, S. Vakkalanka, and L. Kuzniarz, "Guidelines for conducting systematic mapping studies in software engineering: An update," *Information and Software Technology*, vol. 64, pp. 1–18, Aug. 2015, ISSN: 09505849. DOI: 10.1016/j.infsof.2015.03.007.

[11] V. Braun and V. Clarke, "Using thematic analysis in psychology," *Qualitative Research in Psychology*, vol. 3, no. 2, pp. 77–101, 2006, ISSN: 14780887. DOI: 10.1191/1478088706qp063oa.

[12] V. Braun and V. Clarke, "Toward good practice in thematic analysis: Avoiding common problems and be(com)ing a knowing researcher," *International Journal of Transgender Health*, vol. 24, no. 1, pp. 1–6, 2023, ISSN: 26895277. DOI: 10.1080/26895269.2022.2129597.

[13] M. Gutiérrez, "AI-Powered Software Engineering: Integrating Advanced Techniques for Optimal Development," *International Journal of Engineering and Techniques*, vol. 2020, no. 6, pp. 1–9, 2020, ISSN: 2395-1303. DOI: 10.5281/zen.

[14] M. Barenkamp, J. Rebstadt, and O. Thomas, "Applications of AI in classical software engineering," *AI Perspectives*, vol. 2, no. 1, pp. 1–15, Dec. 2020. DOI: 10.1186/s42467-020-00005-4.

[15] S. Ramchand, S. Shaikh, and I. Alam, "Role of Artificial Intelligence in Software Quality Assurance," in *Intelligent Systems and Applications*, K. Arai, Ed., Cham: Springer International Publishing, 2022, pp. 125–136, ISBN: 978-3-030-82196-8.

[16] J. Bhuvana, V. Ranjan, and N. Bhaduariya, "Integration of AI in the Realm of Software Development," in *2023 International Conference on Advances in Computation, Communication and Information Technology, ICAICCIT 2023*, Institute of Electrical and Electronics Engineers Inc., 2023, pp. 974–978, ISBN: 9798350344387. DOI: 10.1109/ICAICCIT60255.2023.10465893.

[17] R. Kumar, V. Naveen, P. Kumar Illa, S. Pachar, and P. Patil, "The Current State of Software Engineering Employing Methods Derived from Artificial Intelligence and Outstanding Challenges," in *1st IEEE International Conference on Innovations in High Speed Communication and Signal Processing, IHCSP 2023*, Institute of Electrical and Electronics Engineers Inc., 2023, pp. 105–108, ISBN: 9798350345957. DOI: 10.1109/IHCSP56702.2023.10127112.

[18] S. Qazi, I. Memon, B. Q. Hashmi, M. S. Memon, and E. A. Qazi, "Software Quality Assurance Using Artificial Intelligence Techniques: A Survey of the Software Industry of Pakistan," *Journal of Hunan University Natural Sciences*, vol. 50, no. 12, pp. 1–9, 2023. DOI: 10.55463/issn.1674-2974.50.12.1.

[19] A. I. Amarasekara, "Challenges of outdated software test automation tools in the sri lankan it industry and the proposal of suitable ml strategies for a sustainable quality assurance process," M.S. thesis, Uppsala University, 2023.

[20] D. Amalfitano, R. Coppola, D. Distante, and F. Ricca, "AI in GUI-Based Software Testing: Insights from a Survey with Industrial Practitioners," in *Quality of Information and Communications Technology*, A. Bertolino, J. Pascoal Faria, P. Lago, and L. Semini, Eds., Cham: Springer Nature Switzerland, 2024, pp. 328–343, ISBN: 978-3-031-70245-7.

[21] S. A. Khan *et al.*, "AI-Based Software Testing," in *Proceedings of World Conference on Information Systems for Business Management*, A. Iglesias, J. Shin, B. Patel, and A. Joshi, Eds., Singapore: Springer Nature Singapore, 2024, pp. 323–334, ISBN: 978-981-99-8346-9.

[22] R. Santos, I. Santos, C. Magalhaes, and R. De Souza Santos, "Are We Testing or Being Tested? Exploring the Practical Applications of Large Language Models in Software Testing," in *Proceedings - 2024 IEEE Conference on Software Testing, Verification and Validation, ICST 2024*, Institute of Electrical and Electronics Engineers Inc., 2024, pp. 353–360, ISBN: 9798350308181. DOI: 10.1109/ICST60714.2024.00039.

[23] G. K. Adu, "Artificial Intelligence in Software Testing: Test scenario and case generation with an AI model (gpt-3.5-turbo) using Prompt engineering, Fine-tuning and Retrieval

augmented generation techniques," M.S. thesis, University of Eastern Finland, 2024.

[24] H. Jauhiainen, *Artificial Intelligence In Software Testing*, 2024, Bachelor's thesis. HAMK.

[25] A. Laine, "A Change Management Approach to Incorporating AI into Software Testing," M.S. thesis, LUT University, 2024.

[26] R. Purovesi, "Test Automation and AI," M.S. thesis, LUT University, 2024.

[27] T. Hossain *et al.*, "AI based solutions for Software Testing in Bangladeshi software companies," unpublished, Jan. 2024. DOI: 10.13140/RG.2.2.17371.95526.

[28] L. Layman and R. Vetter, "Generative Artificial Intelligence and the Future of Software Testing," *Computer*, vol. 57, no. 1, pp. 27–32, Jan. 2024, ISSN: 15580814. DOI: 10.1109/MC.2023.3306998.

[29] F. Ricca, A. Marchetto, and A. Stocco, "A multi-year grey literature review on ai-assisted test automation," *Information and Software Technology*, vol. 186, p. 107 799, 2025, ISSN: 0950-5849. DOI: https://doi.org/10.1016/j.infsof.2025.107799.

[30] M. Simmler and R. Frischknecht, "A taxonomy of humanmachine collaboration: capturing automation and technical autonomy," *AI and Society*, vol. 36, no. 1, pp. 239–250, Mar. 2021, ISSN: 14355655. DOI: 10.1007/S00146-020-01004-Z/FIGURES/1.

[31] M. Gulzar and K. Smolander, "Explaining the motivational drivers in technology adoption: Triggers & Consequences," in *Proceedings of the 58th Hawaii International Conference on System Sciences*, 2025, ISBN: 9780998133188.

[32] S. Soomro, M. Fan, J. M. Sohu, S. Soomro, and S. N. Shaikh, "AI adoption: a bridge or a barrier? The moderating role of organizational support in the path toward employee well-being," *Kybernetes*, vol. ahead-of-print, no. ahead-of-print, 2024, ISSN: 0368492X. DOI: 10.1108/K-07-2024-1889/FULL/XML.

[33] M. Kinney, M. Anastasiadou, M. Naranjo-Zolotov, and V. Santos, "Expectation management in AI: A framework for understanding stakeholder trust and acceptance of artificial intelligence systems," *Heliyon*, vol. 10, no. 7, e28562, Apr. 2024, ISSN: 24058440. DOI: 10.1016/J.HELIYON.2024.E28562/ASSET/4DE3D17E-E79C-41C4-9450-0E69B166AC58/MAIN.ASSETS/GR1.JPG.

Ethical Considerations of Using Generative AI in Software Development

Tiina Tuomisto
Lasse Harjumaa
Kokkola University Consortium Chydenius
University of Jyväskylä
Kokkola, Finland
e-mail: tii2tuo@gmail.com | lasse.m.harjumaa@jyu.fi

***Abstract*—Generative Artificial Intelligence (GenAI) is gaining more and more popularity among different professions, and it is also transforming software development by enabling automated text, code, and image generation, enhancing productivity across various tasks. This study examines the most common use cases of GenAI tools in software development, alongside software professionals' experiences, ethical concerns, and awareness of ethical guidelines related to GenAI. Through qualitative semi-structured interviews with IT professionals in Finland, the research identifies that GenAI tools are primarily used for programming, software testing, and general problem-solving. While these tools accelerate workflows, challenges such as unreliable outputs, outdated training data, and ethical concerns - particularly regarding transparency, bias, and data security - remain significant. The findings align with previous research, highlighting both the benefits and risks of GenAI adoption. Ethical considerations, though acknowledged, are rarely integrated into daily practices, emphasizing the need for clearer guidelines and education. This study contributes to the discourse on the evolving role of AI in software engineering, underscoring the importance of ethical awareness and responsible AI utilization.**

***Keywords*-Generative artificial intelligence; ethics; software development; GenAI; GenAI tools.**

I. INTRODUCTION

GenAI is one of the most influential technological innovations of recent years. While traditional systems utilizing artificial intelligence follow predetermined patterns and rules, GenAI systems can create more imaginative items, such as text, images, sounds and videos. This ability makes it an attractive tool for various purposes, including tasks related to software development. Instead of having to search through repositories of previously written questions and answers by other developers, such as searching through StackOverflow, GenAI tools will create an answer based on huge amounts of data, which has been used to train them. To improve the answers over time, they are further trained based on the feedback given on the generated responses.

Generative AI can improve productivity in various software development tasks, including coding, testing, debugging, documentation, reviewing and brainstorming. At best, the quality of the product and productivity of the developers can improve significantly [1].

It has been predicted that generative AI will have a significant impact on software practitioners' work, permanently changing the roles of software engineers. Developers will need to have new kinds of competencies to master and fully utilize the potential of GenAI systems [2]. Since generative AI does not have a comprehensive knowledge of the context in which it generates a solution, or human language, the engineers' who is authoring the prompt has the responsibility to verify the conformity of the generated outcome.

GenAI tools also pose numerous issues, many of which are related to ethics. For example, Weidinger et al. [3] identify six ethical and social risk areas related to language models: 1. Discrimination, Exclusion and Toxicity, 2. Information Hazards, 3. Misinformation Harms, 4. Malicious Uses, 5. Human-Computer Interaction Harms, 6. Automation, Access and Environmental Harms. Tanaka et al. [4] further decompose these risk classes into more detailed subcategories to help mitigate risks by either removing the risk sources, avoiding the hazard, or managing the impact.

Due to the potential ethical problems associated with GenAI tools, several entities have developed ethical guidelines for the developers and users of AI systems. An example of this is the High-Level Expert Group on Artificial Intelligence (AI HLEG) established by the European Commission [5], which has created ethical guidelines for developing trustworthy AI systems. However, adhering to various ethical guidelines and principles is not easy. As Ryan and Stahl [6] point out, they do not provide sufficient advice for implementing the principles in practice. Consequently, software practitioners encounter various ethical issues when using GenAI tools.

This study brings forward the experiences and opinions of software practitioners regarding the benefits and drawbacks of utilizing GenAI tools, as well as the awareness of AI ethical guidelines and the prevalence of ethical issues. Our study extends prior research by offering insights into how practitioners engage with ethical issues specifically in the context of generating software engineering artifacts and by examining the extent to which they follow relevant guidelines, if any. We also integrate perspectives on software quality, the ethics of software development more broadly, and existing ethical guidelines for AI to outline the foundations of guidelines specifically intended for the use of GenAI in software development tasks.

The rest of the paper is arranged as follows. Section 2 describes the basic concepts of generative artificial intelligence and its utilization in the various phases of software development, as well as the ethical issues related to AI within the domain. Section 3 describes the research approach and the main findings of the study, and the contributions and limitations of the study are discussed in Section 4. Finally,

Section 5 concludes the paper.

II. Generative AI in Software Development

This section provides a brief overview of the tasks that typically comprise the software development process and examines how GenAI has been applied to these tasks, as reported in academic research. It then discusses how ethical issues related to GenAI have been addressed in guidelines issued by major organizations.

A. Software Development Tasks

Software development process models - such as the waterfall model, agile, spiral, and DevOps - provide structured guidance to build high-quality software efficiently. These models help developers, project managers, and stakeholders manage resources, improve predictability, and standardize outcomes. Regardless of the model, key development tasks remain consistent.

Development usually begins with planning and a feasibility study, where project goals, risks, and viability are assessed. Requirements engineering follows, focusing on gathering and documenting user needs, either through formal specifications in traditional models or iterative collaboration in agile methods. System design defines architecture, components, and interfaces. In the implementation phase, developers choose suitable tools and follow best practices to ensure maintainable, high-quality code. Testing and reviews are critical for quality assurance: testing includes unit, integration, and acceptance levels, often automated to enhance efficiency. Reviews help detect defects early. In agile development, testing is continuous and central to rapid feedback. Deployment moves the finished product to production, ensuring it is accessible and operational. Finally, maintenance and support address issues post-launch, keep the software secure, and adapt it to evolving needs. Together with project management tasks, these stages form a cycle that ensures user-focused, robust, and maintainable software delivery.

B. Applications of GenAI

GenAI tools have been widely studied for their ability to support software development tasks. These tools can generate code [7], fix coding errors, translate between programming languages [8], and assist with writing comments [9] or answering programming queries [10]. The effectiveness of GenAI varies by user experience. While Copilot-generated code provides a good starting point [11], it does not always speed up development. Moradi Dakhel et al. [12] noted that experienced developers gain the most, as they can spot and correct errors. Inexperienced users benefit from guidance and learning opportunities, provided they evaluate the output critically. Across skill levels, GenAI reduces time spent consulting documentation and offers real-time advice - though its suggestions should be validated, as it lacks full context awareness.

GenAI also supports software testing. Studies have explored its use in generating unit tests [13], for example. Although generated test data may contain errors, it forms a useful foundation when properly reviewed. In maintenance, GenAI enables anomaly detection and automatic code fixes, as shown in a study by Khlaisamniang et al. [14]. In design, GenAI aids in producing diagrams [1], UI development, and prototyping [15]. Project planning is another emerging area, where GenAI helps with scheduling, cost estimation, and risk analysis [16]. GenAI also assists in requirements engineering: language models help gather, summarize, and complete requirements [17], including user story generation. Despite occasional inaccuracies, GenAI tools offer significant value across the software development life cycle by providing inspiration, automating routine tasks, and enhancing productivity.

C. Generative AI Tools

Studies evaluating the code quality of GenAI tools show mixed results. GitHub Copilot and Microsoft Copilot have been rated highest in code generation [18][19]. ChatGPT has also demonstrated strong performance, though it is considered less effective in implementation and testing [1]. Google Gemini and Claude received lower evaluations in multiple studies, while Amazon Q Developer was also criticized [19]. GenAI tool performance varies by programming language, making it essential to align tool selection with project-specific needs.

Error correction capabilities have been studied primarily in ChatGPT and GitHub Copilot, showing moderate success but with limitations in complex problem-solving [8]. Effective prompting is crucial to improving output quality. Other tools, such as Claude and Gemini, lack extensive evaluation in this area. GenAI tools like ChatGPT and GitHub Copilot also assist with information retrieval and development guidance, though their utility beyond programming is limited. ChatGPT remains the most researched tool across software development tasks, including documentation and design, while others have been studied mainly for coding purposes.

The reliability of GenAI tools depends heavily on the comprehensiveness of their training data. When the data is insufficient or misaligned with the problem, tools may produce vague or incorrect responses, requiring users to spend time validating and refining the output [8]. Developers must also provide clear prompts, as vague inputs can degrade response quality. Although tools like Copilot can reduce vulnerabilities [7], other studies show they may introduce more errors than inexperienced developers [12] and obscure error sources [20]. Programming language and problem familiarity affect response accuracy, with GenAI tools performing better on common tasks with ample training data [19]. While GenAI supports learning and boosts productivity for novices, overreliance may hinder skill development. Understanding a tool's inner workings is also vital, as misconceptions about how suggestions are generated can mislead users [20].

D. Ethics in Software Development And Issues Related to Generative AI

The IEEE-CS/ACM Joint Task Force (2021) outlines eight ethical principles for software developers, covering responsibilities to the public, clients, employers, products, professional judgment, management, the profession, colleagues, and self. These guidelines, which are also adopted nationally (e.g., in Finland by TIVIA), emphasize that developers must ensure their work is safe, lawful, and ethical.

Software must not harm people, nature, or society, and any risks must be reported. Developers must communicate honestly about project feasibility, costs, and risks, and should not misuse confidential information or overstate their skills. They must deliver products that meet quality standards and are properly documented, tested, and maintained. Developers are expected to act impartially, avoid conflicts of interest, and reject unethical practices like bribery. Managers must ensure team members understand ethical practices, treat staff fairly, and handle project resources responsibly.

Professionalism involves educating others, complying with laws, and taking accountability for software quality and errors. Developers should also support and evaluate colleagues fairly, protect confidentiality, and continually improve their skills in areas like design, maintenance, and testing. Ultimately, ethical software development requires responsibility, transparency, fairness, and ongoing self-improvement.

Various organizations, including AI HLEG [5], IEEE [23][24][26][27], Adobe [25], Google [21], and IBM [22], have developed ethical guidelines for AI to address risks throughout its lifecycle. Despite this, no specific, comprehensive ethical standards exist solely for generative AI, highlighting a gap amid its rapid development and increasing use. These ethical guidelines and principles for AI are not legally binding. They therefore act as incentives for ethical behavior. Table I represents the summary of the ethical principles of these major organizations.

III. Research Setting and Key Findings

This section describes the research approach adopted in the study and summarizes the main findings that emerged from the interviews.

A. Research Approach

This study examines whether IT companies utilize any ethical guidelines when using GenAI tools and how familiar the guidelines for artificial intelligence are to IT-professionals. The research questions are as follows:

RQ1. What software development tasks are Generative AI tools used for in practice?

RQ2. What are the benefits and drawbacks of Generative AI tools as perceived by software developers?

TABLE I. Summary of the Ethical Principles.

Ethical Principle	Description	Organizations
Privacy	Users must be able to control their own data and be informed about why the data is collected and how it is used. User data must be kept intact and must not be misused.	[5], [21], [22], [23]
Security and resistance to threats	AI must withstand exceptional situations, such as attacks, without causing harm. It must perform as intended in varying conditions and its results must be repeatable. The results of AI must be accurate, and the probability of incorrect predictions must be disclosed openly. AI should also have security measures.	[5], [21], [22], [24]
Explainability	Explainability refers to the comprehensibility of information provided about artificial intelligence. In this case, the explanation provided should be formulated according to the level of expertise of the recipients of the information so that the explanation is understandable. This guideline is closely related to transparency.	[5], [22], [23]
Transparency	The user must gain an understanding of how artificial intelligence works, how data is used and stored. This helps to understand how and why the system reaches a certain result. Traceability must be ensured so that if an error occurs, the cause of the error can be determined and prevented in the future. The user must be informed whether they are working with another person or artificial intelligence. This guideline is closely related to explainability.	[25], [5], [21], [23]
Justice and equity	The aim is to treat different groups and individuals equally. It prevents bias, which refers to bias towards a position, object or person, which can lead to unfair results. Data sets, such as training data, can contain unintentional biases that exacerbate discrimination and prejudice against individuals and groups.	[25], [5], [21], [24]
Sustainability and well-being	Artificial intelligence should operate in an environmentally friendly manner and support the well-being of people and society. The aim is to ensure that the artificial intelligence being developed brings clearly more benefits to society than disadvantages and challenges.	[5], [21], [26]
Accountability	Assessing artificial intelligence and identifying and reporting its negative impacts. Impact assessments can be used to prevent negative impacts. Users have the right to appeal if a decision made by an artificial intelligence negatively affects them. The guideline also includes the principle of fairness.	[25], [5], [21]
Self-determination	This guideline aims to protect human rights. Artificial intelligence must not endanger people's right to self-determination and artificial intelligence can be monitored by a human to overturn decisions made by the artificial intelligence, if necessary. Also includes features of explainability, transparency and accountability.	[5], [21]
Avoiding damage	Artificial intelligence should not cause harm to people or nature and should not be able to be misused. This principle consists of several other principles, such as fairness and sustainable development and well-being.	[5], [21], [22], [23], [24], [26], [27]

RQ3. Have developers encountered ethical issues when using Generative AI tools?

RQ4. How are ethical guidelines related to AI taken into consideration in software development when using Generative AI tools?

The research methodology employed was a qualitative semi-structured interview, incorporating elements of thematic interviewing as introduced by Hirsjarvi and Hurme [28]. Invitations for interviews were sent to randomly chosen IT companies with offices in the middle part of Finland, in a region known for active software industry. A total of nine individuals with long experience in software engineering participated in the interviews, which were conducted remotely. The gathered research data were transcribed, coded and analyzed. The full interview template including all questions is available at [29].

Interview requests were sent to 74 different sized companies, of which seven companies participated in this study. From these seven companies, a total of nine IT professionals agreed to be interviewed. Seven of the interviewees have worked in IT for at least 15 years, which allows them to analyze the changes that the GenAI tools have brought to the field. Eight of the interviewees have experience as software developers, while one interviewee's responsibility seems to be the quality control of software products.

The data analysis begins with open coding in which Urquhart [30] suggests analyzing the data systematically by reading paragraphs one by one to create codes. Once the text has been coded, they can then be categorized in a phase called axial coding. According to Williams and Moser [31] in this phase, relations between the codes found in open coding are examined and then they can be categorized into groups. Williams and Moser [31] also showcase that these categories can then be combined into themes in the selective phase. To create the final themes, the relations between codes are actively compared as were the relations between categories. The research questions were then answered based on the found themes. An example of formulating codes, categories and themes is represented in Table 2. The table shows issues that were mentioned concerning the code that GenAI tools produce. Both issues pertain to the trustworthiness and quality of the generated responses and are therefore categorized under the same theme.

TABLE II. AN EXAMPLE OF CODING

Comment	**Open code**	**Axial coding: Categories**	**Selective phase: Themes**
"...if I just copy paste the generated response and use it as it is in my code it never works. They rarely work." (I)	Errors in code	Faulty responses	GenAI tools generate low quality and untrustworthy responses
"... they [GenAI tools] generate repetitive amateur level code..." (E)	Amateurish code	Low quality responses	

B. Findings

1) Tasks for Which GenAI Tools Are Utilized: The most popular tools used among the interviewees are GitHub Copilot and different versions of ChatGPT. Based on the interviews, the tools are used for different tasks according to their strengths and weaknesses.

While ChatGPT is used for various tasks, GitHub Copilot is a popular choice for programming and testing. Eight out of nine interviewees mention that they have used GenAI tools for programming tasks while two interviewees have also used them for testing. Three of the interviewees also compliment the quality of GitHub Copilot's autocompletion ability. GitHub Copilot's autocompletions and integration to an IDE helps to streamline different coding tasks. ChatGPT is also considered a user-friendly tool because it allows the users to have conversational interactions with the tool.

Six interviewees mention that GenAI tools can also be useful for different word processing tasks. Especially ChatGPT is used for many tasks that require word processing. The interviewees have used it for content creation for websites and documentation. One interviewee also mentions that Microsoft Copilot has potential in making presentations. Creative work. Three of the interviewees have used GenAI tools in visual and creative tasks. They have been used to generate process images, promotional videos and ideas. The tools lack understanding of causality, which is the reason they are not suitable for creating pictures that showcase logic. One of the interviewees mentions that GenAI tools seem promising in generation of game graphics, but they seem to be lacking in animation tasks.

Among the interviewees, GenAI tools were most frequently used for tasks that are already well-documented, such as programming, testing, and word processing. Despite this, the tools appear to hold considerable potential, even though significant development is still required. The participants appeared interested in experimenting with the tools to reduce the amount of repetitive or monotonous tasks, for example.

2) Benefits and Drawbacks: The interviewees identify several pros and cons of using GenAI tools. They streamline a variety of tasks and are easy to use but can generate incorrect or untrustworthy answers. Users must assess and fix low-quality outputs and know enough about the subject to create effective prompts. If problems are frequent, the tools may be seen as unnecessary.

Interviewees agree that GenAI tools can speed up tasks, though their usefulness depends on the quality of training data. They support testing, coding, and writing by generating templates and offering simple integration. GitHub Copilot, for instance, integrates into programming environments and provides automatic suggestions, which three interviewees rated as high-quality. These tools help with repetitive tasks, allowing users to focus on more interesting work, increasing job satisfaction.

ChatGPT can substitute for Stack Overflow by helping users solve programming problems efficiently. Information retrieval is quicker, and tools provide concise answers without web browser distractions. ChatGPT is especially effective in word processing, and interviewees generally viewed it more favorably for this than for coding. Two interviewees noted that GenAI tools can outperform people in some tasks. They possess broader domain knowledge and are unaffected by fatigue, potentially reducing users' mental burden.

Despite the benefits, two interviewees do not use GenAI tools due to poor output quality. All interviewees noted the risk of incorrect answers, which require user verification and correction. Prompt quality impacts output, and ineffective prompts may force users to restart conversations. Thus, users need enough expertise to evaluate answers and formulate prompts.

Even with good prompts, hallucinations—confident but incorrect outputs—are common. If answers are unreliable, as one interviewee experienced, users may abandon the tools. Quality also varies across programming languages, with some tools struggling with niche tasks or using outdated libraries. Poor training data may lead to overly generic or unusable outputs. Three participants raised concerns about censorship and moderation, limiting use in ethically sensitive projects. One interviewee mentioned accessibility issues and memory limitations. Two interviewees noted the tools can't generate diagrams showing causality and context. Since many limitations are outside user control, it's important not to over-rely on GenAI tools and to retain traditional methods when needed.

3) Ethical Issues: Lack of knowledge on ethical issues related to GenAI and how they emerge during software development may shape interviewees' experiences. Developers often focus on their own ethical conduct and may overlook ethical problems caused by GenAI tools. Although some interviewees encountered issues while using GenAI, they might not recognize them as ethical in nature. Even without identifying specific ethical concerns, users may still avoid these tools, as in the case of one interviewee who stopped using them due to potential ethical risks. Only two interviewees explicitly mentioned ethical concerns. However, when considering inequality, such as GenAI's varying performance across programming languages, the number rises to six. Four of these six did not identify this inequality as an ethical issue, highlighting a lack of awareness.

Six interviewees bring up that GenAI tools lack transparency and three of these interviewees also mention that AI models can be black boxes. The generated answers may also be derived from copyright-protected and licensed material. The interviewees are aware of this risk, even though they have not faced it themselves while using GenAI tools. The interviewees agree that the GenAI tools can produce untrustworthy answers. GenAI tools need to be more explainable and transparent so that they can be trusted. Because the tools can generate inaccurate and incorrect information users should develop their critical thinking abilities.

Two interviewees noticed that the tools may repeat the same answers while solving programming tasks. They reported that the tools tend to replicate the same programming mistakes and problem-solving methods, which may indicate a bias.

Six of the nine interviewees also recognize that GenAI tools may cause information security risks. The tools may gather information from customers and companies to be used for its training. Users must also consider carefully what information can be given to the tool via prompts. Two interviewees also mention the communication platform, Slack, having a potential ethical issue where they use the user data to train their AI models.

AI development can also impact societal well-being and the environment. Two of the nine interviewees expressed concern about the impact that AI can have on the environment because their development and usage require a lot of resources. Three interviewees also believe that the tools may cause inequality between societies, companies and people. Four interviewees noticed that the code produced by GenAI tools varies in its quality according to the used programming language. This may also cause inequality among software developers because the training data does not represent all programming languages extensively.

In general, the interviewees are not worried about AI replacing them. This might partly be because of their long work experience in the IT field. Though, they do agree that AI can replace people to some extent in software development, especially in software testing and possibly in coding. Three interviewees are also worried about the impact that the tools might have on the professional skills of the software developers. These worries are especially related to programming when the tools can generate code quickly and effortlessly. As a result, users may be less likely to think about the problem independently but instead strives to solve the problem as fast as possible.

4) Ethical Guidelines: Five of the nine interviewees had little to no awareness of the existing ethical guidelines for AI. Though, even if the guidelines were unknown for these interviewees, the ethical terms and subjects related to ethics of AI were familiar to them. The interviewees have gotten information about the ethics of AI through the internet, colleagues and training but only two interviewees have gotten information from official sources, for example, the ethical guidelines made by AI HLEG. Four of the interviewees mention that they get most of their information about the ethics of AI from the internet by reading and listening to discussions. The responsibility of understanding and learning about the ethics of AI seem to fall on the employees.

Seven of the companies do not comply with any ethical guidelines meant for AI. Because of this the ethical discussions and decisions are left to the users of GenAI tools. This means that the users are most likely guided by their own morals and other guidelines and requirements in software development.

Two interviewees mention that their companies have methods to avoid possible ethical issues. One of the companies has appointed a group that handles ethics and informs and guides the employees on these matters. The other company is aware of different ethical guidelines provided by the Digital and Population Data Services Agency of Finland, for example. Two interviewees also mention that it's possible to forbid the use of GenAI tools in a project to avoid ethical issues. Though, it's possible that the clients are not aware or informed about the use of these tools in their projects.

Three interviewees mention that their companies are currently updating their ethical guidelines to include AI. Companies seem to develop their processes according to the changes brought by AI but updating the guidelines and understanding the different ethical aspects takes time. One interviewee also brings up that the use of ethical guidelines of AI not only help with understanding how to use these tools ethically, but they also help the user to decide whether these tools should be used at all when making a product.

IV. Discussion

This section summarizes the main contributions of the study and discusses its limitations and threats to validity.

A. Main Contributions

The study reveals that GenAI tools are primarily used for programming, testing, and problem-solving, with occasional use in text processing. Although earlier research suggests broader applicability, real-world use remains limited, especially in visual tasks due to poor output quality. GitHub Copilot is preferred for coding, while ChatGPT is assigned more varied tasks. GenAI tools help accelerate work, but users must critically evaluate outputs due to frequent hallucinations, errors, and outdated code - especially with newer libraries. Effective use requires strong prompt design skills, as tools struggle with context, particularly in visual logic tasks.

Ethical considerations are largely overlooked in practice. Most professionals are unfamiliar with formal AI ethics guidelines, though they recognize concepts like transparency and explainability. Ethical concerns raised include data security, response repetition, and inequality due to uneven support for different languages and frameworks. While many companies lack formal ethical policies, internal discussions are increasing. Additionally, broader concerns such as unauthorized data use, data leaks, and bias are acknowledged. The findings align with earlier studies and highlight the growing need for ethical awareness as adoption increases across development workflows.

The results show that ethical guidelines related to artificial intelligence are poorly known. Based on this, it could be useful to know how companies that develop or specialize in developing artificial intelligence systems follow ethical guidelines. These companies could also provide practical advice on preventing ethical problems. The concern is that ethical guidelines related to artificial intelligence may also be ignored in companies that develop artificial intelligence systems. An interesting topic for further research would therefore be to examine the knowledge of ethics and related practices of companies that provide artificial intelligence systems.

B. Limitations and Threats to Validity

Because the sample is small, the results cannot provide a comprehensive picture of the entire software development field. The results of the study can provide an indication of typical problems, benefits and uses, as well as compliance with ethical guidelines, but they lack more specific perspectives on, for example, the use of tools in game development.

Some interviewees reported having only limited experience with GenAI tools, which may have constrained the depth of their engagement. Nonetheless, even these participants were able to articulate a range of challenges they had encountered, with many indicating that such difficulties constituted the primary reason for their discontinuation of tool use. Furthermore, the specific purposes for which study participants used GenAI tools do not necessarily reflect typical usage patterns, but rather serve as illustrative examples of the tools' potential applications.

V. Conclusion and Future Work

Addressing ethical issues related to AI and large language models is vital for achieving trustworthiness of the tools and requires a multidisciplinary approach involving professionals from the fields of technology, ethics, law and policy. However, it seems that even though the software professionals are familiar with the concepts of ethical principles related to AI, they do not know the ethical guidelines provided by several organizations, and the employer companies do not utilize the guidelines.

The issues related to transparency and explainability of the generated answers were particularly familiar to the interviewees. In addition, it seems that recurring responses generated by the tools seem to be an issue. Concerns were also raised about the security of the tools. Furthermore, many felt that the quality of the responses provided by the tools was insufficient.

This study illustrates and raises discussion on ethical issues that may arise in software development, as well as examines the awareness of AI ethics among software professionals. Currently, GenAI tools support various work tasks, but they have several weaknesses that require users to actively evaluate the quality and reliability of responses. Additionally, not all users benefit equally from these tools. While guidelines published by different organizations aim to prevent potential ethical issues and enable the development of reliable AI systems, it appears that GenAI tools still have significant room for improvement.

Since it is expected that awareness of ethical problems caused by AI systems will increase among users, companies will likely create their own guidelines to avoid them. In the future, it may be useful to find out how considering the ethical perspective is developing in companies that utilize AI tools, or whether the developers of the tools have created their own guidelines.

References

[1] Z. Özpolat, Ö. Yildirim, and M. Karabatak, "Artificial intelligence-based tools in software development processes: Application of chatgpt," *Eur. J. Technic*, vol. 13, no. 2, pp. 229–240, 2023.

[2] C. Ebert and U. Hemel, "Technology trends 2023: The competence challenge," *IEEE Softw.*, vol. 40, no. 3, pp. 20–28, 2023.
[3] L. Weidinger *et al.*, *Ethical and social risks of harm from language models*, https://arxiv.org/abs/2112.04359, retrieved: August, 2025, 2021.
[4] H. Tanaka *et al.*, "Taxonomy of generative ai applications for risk assessment," in *Proc. IEEE/ACM 3rd Int. Conf. AI Eng.-Softw. Eng. AI*, 2024, pp. 288–289.
[5] AI HLEG, *Ethics guidelines for trustworthy ai*, https://www.europarl.europa.eu/meetdocs/2014_2019/plmrep/COMMITTEES/JURI/DV/2019/11-06/Ethics-guidelines-AI_FI.pdf, retrieved: June, 2025, Apr. 2019.
[6] M. Ryan and B. C. Stahl, "Artificial intelligence ethics guidelines for developers and users: Clarifying their content and normative implications," *J. Inf. Commun. Ethics Soc.*, vol. 19, no. 1, pp. 61–86, 2021.
[7] O. Asare, M. Nagappan, and N. Asokan, "Is github's copilot as bad as humans at introducing vulnerabilities in code?" *Empirical Software Engineering*, vol. 28, no. 129, 2023.
[8] M. A. Haque and S. Li, "The potential use of ChatGPT for debugging and bug fixing," *EAI Endorsed Trans. AI Robot.*, vol. 2, 2023.
[9] T. Kumari and A. Das, "Towards development of an effective ai-based system for relevant comment generation," in *Proc. 15th Annu. Meet. Forum Inf. Retrieval Eval.*, 2023, pp. 118–120.
[10] G. Giunti and C. P. Doherty, "Cocreating an automated mhealth apps systematic review process with generative ai: Design science research approach," *JMIR Med. Educ.*, vol. 10, e48949, 2024.
[11] P. Vaithilingam, T. Zhang, and E. L. Glassman, "Expectation vs. experience: Evaluating the usability of code generation tools powered by large language models," in *CHI Conf. Hum. Factors Comput. Syst. Ext. Abstr.*, 2022, pp. 1–7.
[12] A. M. Dakhel *et al.*, "Github copilot ai pair programmer: Asset or liability?" *J. Syst. Softw.*, vol. 203, p. 111 734, 2023.
[13] M. Schäfer, S. Nadi, A. Eghbali, and F. Tip, "An empirical evaluation of using large language models for automated unit test generation," *IEEE Trans. Softw. Eng.*, vol. 50, no. 1, pp. 85–105, 2024.
[14] P. Khlaisamniang, P. Khomduean, K. Saetan, and S. Wonglapsuwan, "Generative ai for self-healing systems," in *Proc. 18th Int. Joint Symp. Artif. Intell. Nat. Lang. Process. (iSAI-NLP)*, 2023.
[15] V. Bilgram and F. Laarmann, "Accelerating innovation with generative ai: Ai-augmented digital prototyping and innovation methods," *IEEE Eng. Manag. Rev.*, vol. 51, no. 2, pp. 18–25, 2023.
[16] A. Barcaui and A. Monat, "Who is better in project planning? generative artificial intelligence or project managers?" *Project Leadership and Society*, vol. 4, p. 100 101, 2023.
[17] D. Luitel, S. Hassani, and M. Sabetzadeh, "Improving requirements completeness: Automated assistance through large language models," *Requirements Eng.*, vol. 29, pp. 73–95, 2024.
[18] H. Hochmair, L. Juhász, and T. Kemp, "Correctness comparison of chatgpt-4, gemini, claude-3, and copilot for spatial tasks," *Trans. GIS*, vol. 28, no. 7, pp. 2219–2231, 2024.
[19] B. Idrisov and T. Schlippe, "Program code generation with generative ais," *Algorithms*, vol. 17, no. 2, p. 62, 2024.
[20] S. Barke, M. B. James, and N. Polikarpova, "Grounded copilot: How programmers interact with code-generating models," *Proc. ACM Program. Lang.*, vol. 7, pp. 85–111, 2023.
[21] Google, *Our principles*, https://ai.google/responsibility/principles/, retrieved: August, 2025, Oct. 2023.
[22] IBM, *IBM artificial intelligence pillars*, https://www.ibm.com/policy/ibm-artificial-intelligence-pillars/, retrieved: August, 2025, Aug. 2023.
[23] IEEE Standard 7001, *IEEE standard for transparency of autonomous systems*, IEEE, 2022.
[24] IEEE Standard 7002, *IEEE standard for data privacy process*, IEEE, 2022.
[25] Adobe, *Adobe's Commitment to AI Ethics*, https://www.adobe.com/content/dam/cc/en/ai-ethics/pdfs/Adobe-AI-Ethics-Principles.pdf, retrieved: June, 2025, Oct. 2023.
[26] IEEE Standard 7009, *P7009 standard for fail-safe design of autonomous and semi-autonomous systems*, IEEE, 2024.
[27] IEEE Standard 7010, *IEEE recommended practice for assessing the impact of autonomous and intelligent systems on human well-being*, IEEE, 2020.
[28] S. Hirsjärvi and H. Hurme, *Tutkimushaastattelu : teemahaastattelun teoria ja käytäntö*, H. Hurme, Ed. Helsinki: Yliopistopaino, 2000, retrieved: February, 2025. [Online]. Available: https://jyu.finna.fi/Record/jykdok.829757.
[29] T. Tuomisto, "Generatiivisen tekoälyn käyttö ja etiikka ohjelmistokehityksessä," retrieved: August, 2025, M.S. thesis, University of Jyväskylä, 2024. [Online]. Available: https://urn.fi/URN:NBN:fi:jyu-202411287512.
[30] C. Urquhart, *Grounded Theory for Qualitative Research: A Practical Guide*. 55 City Road: SAGE Publications, Ltd, 2013.
[31] M. Williams and T. Moser, "The art of coding and thematic exploration in qualitative research," *Int. Manag. Rev.*, vol. 15, no. 1, pp. 45–55, 2019.

Software Engineering for Educational AI Applications: Insights from Student Requirements for a VR Coaching System

Yvonne Sedelmaier
Department Education
SRH University of Applied Sciences Heidelberg
Fuerth, Germany
Yvonne.sedelmaier@srh.de

Jens Grubert, Dieter Landes
Center for Responsible Artificial Intelligence
University of Applied Sciences Coburg
Coburg, Germany
{ jens.grubert, dieter.landes }@hs-coburg.de

***Abstract*—This paper presents findings of a study which explored students' perspectives on a virtual reality (VR)-based AI coach designed to support preparation for oral examinations. It highlights the complex interplay between user experience, acceptance, and software development priorities. The qualitative data collected from informatics students provides important insights into their learning goals, expectations, and specific requirements for such a tool and reveals significant implications for the design and development process.**

The study shows that students are generally open to the use of AI-based VR applications in exam preparation. They express strong interest in virtual coaching — particularly to build confidence and reduce exam-related anxiety in oral settings. Students value the opportunity to engage in realistic simulations, receive authentic and useful feedback, and benefit from a personalized learning environment that adapts to their individual needs.

The students articulated high expectations regarding the realism of the virtual coaching scenarios, the accuracy and completeness of the content, and the degree of individualization provided by the system.

In summary, the student feedback underscores the critical role of user experience and perceived value in the development of educational technologies. When prospective developers are also the users, their standards become even more stringent. To succeed, a VR-based coaching system must not only be technically functional but also pedagogically credible and emotionally acceptable from its very first use. These insights challenge typical development rhythms and require a raised awareness of the experiential dimension of educational software.

Keywords-AI-based learning; virtual reality; VR; educational software engineering; oral examination; requirements.

I. Introduction

Digital transformation has become a key driver in reshaping educational practices in higher education. In recent years, the rapid advancement of Artificial Intelligence (AI) and immersive technologies such as Virtual Reality (VR) has opened new possibilities for designing personalized and interactive learning environments. Particularly large language models (LLMs) like ChatGPT have catalyzed discussions about the potential of AI to enhance teaching and learning experiences.

Despite these technological innovations, the formats of academic assessments have remained largely unchanged. Written examinations still dominate the assessment landscape, followed by oral examinations. While students are generally accustomed to preparing for written assessments, oral examinations are often associated with discomfort, anxiety, and uncertainty. Many students report feelings of nervousness or even fear when faced with the challenge of articulating knowledge in a face-to-face examination setting.

These emotional barriers can significantly affect performance and learning outcomes. To address this, AI-based learning companions – specifically, virtual coaches using VR and conversational AI – may offer a promising approach. By simulating realistic examination situations, providing feedback, and offering adaptive support, such tools could help students prepare more effectively and confidently for oral assessments.

This paper presents an exploratory study investigating students' goals, preferences, and requirements for an AI-based VR coach designed to support oral examination preparation. Through qualitative content analysis of open-ended questionnaire data, we aim to understand better how such a tool should be designed to meet learners' needs. It derives some implications for software engineering for educational AI applications.

II. Related Work

The development of virtual and AI-based coaching systems for educational purposes is interlinked with numerous research approaches, including virtual reality in higher education, user-centered design in educational software engineering, and adaptive feedback mechanisms for oral communication training.

A. Virtual Reality in Higher Education

The use of VR technologies in education has gained momentum over the past decade, especially in domains that benefit from immersive, scenario-based learning environments. VR has been applied in healthcare (e.g., surgery) [1], [2], engineering (e.g., simulation of hazardous environments) [3], and language learning (e.g., simulated dialogues) [4], [5] to enhance experiential learning and motivation [6], [7]. Recent studies highlight that VR can support cognitive, affective, and behavioral learning when used in well-structured instructional designs [8], [9].

In the context of assessment preparation, however, research is still emerging. Some initial works have investigated VR as a means to reduce anxiety [10], [11] and increase speaking fluency [12], [13], [14]. Others have explored virtual exam situations [15] but often in context of healthcare [16], [17]. The integration of adaptive, AI-based elements, especially for open-ended oral interactions, is still relatively novel.

B. Coaching Systems and AI in Educational Feedback

AI-based coaching systems are increasingly used to provide personalized feedback and scaffolded learning environments. Intelligent tutoring systems have been shown to improve learning outcomes by offering adaptive support based on user input, performance history, or predefined instructional rules [18], [19]. Recent approaches leverage natural language processing and machine learning to model open-ended communication, such as in empathic pedagogical conversational agents [20].

In oral exam preparation, however, such systems are rarely used. While virtual agents have been developed for interview training or job application scenarios [21], [22], the level of pedagogical alignment and realism required in academic oral examinations presents unique challenges. The present study addresses this gap by investigating learner expectations for a VR-based AI coach in this high-stakes educational context.

III. Research Question and Research Design

A. Research Questions

This study primarily aims at better understanding students' needs and expectations regarding the use of a virtual coach to prepare for oral examinations in higher education. Specifically, the research explores if students are generally open to learning with a virtual coach, and if so, what their intended learning outcomes are. Furthermore, the study aims to identify students' requirements and preferences for a virtual coach that supports the preparation for oral examinations.

The following questions guided the study:

- Would students be willing to use a virtual coach for exam preparation? (RQ1)
- What are their learning goals when using such a tool? Which purposes do students associate with using a virtual coach? (RQ2)
- Which requirements and expectations do they have with respect to the functionality and behavior of a virtual coach? (RQ3)
- Which features or behaviors would lead students to reject or avoid using such a coach? (RQ4)

B. Research Design

The study employed a qualitative design based on a paper-and-pencil questionnaire containing open-ended questions. These questions invited students to complete sentence prompts related to their expectations, goals, and concerns regarding a virtual coach for oral examination preparation. We asked the following questions:

"Imagine you had the ability to prepare for oral exams with the support of virtual reality. What should such a VR-based training system look like, what should it be able to do? Please complete the following sentences:

- The most stressful thing for me before or during an oral exam is ...

- From a VR-coach I expect ...

- I would like to train with a VR coach...

- I'd love to...

- It's not possible that ..."

Participants included a total of 44 participants from informatics (bachelor) and data science (master). The survey was conducted in the middle of the term.

Qualitative content analysis (QCA) following Mayring [23] was applied to analyze the data. This approach allows a structured, category-based, and research question–oriented evaluation of the open responses [24]. QCA was chosen because it is systematic and transparent, ensuring that results are understandable and intersubjectively verifiable.

The analysis followed the eight standard steps of QCA:

1) Definition and Selection of Material

The first step determines the type and scope of the material to be analyzed. A representative subset of the complete data corpus should be selected, ensuring relevance and alignment with the research questions. The selection criteria are informed by the aim to capture the diversity and key dimensions of the material in a manageable, yet meaningful way. In our case, no selection was necessary because we can include all 44 questionnaires received.

2) Analysis of the Context of Material Production

To understand the material in its original context, the circumstances of its creation should be examined. This includes identifying the individuals or institutions responsible for compiling the material, their motivations, and the intended purposes. Particular attention should be paid to the broader socio-institutional and thematic context in which the material was produced, which is essential for interpreting its content appropriately. This step was not relevant for us as we conducted the survey ourselves.

3) Formal Characterization of the Material

The selected material should be formally described with respect to its type and structure. This includes documentation of the transcription conventions and other formatting rules applied, ensuring transparency and reproducibility of the analytical process. The questionnaire was answered by our students in a paper-and-pencil survey.

4) Determination of the Analytical Perspective

The focus of the analysis should be defined by specifying which aspects of the material would be explored. This study primarily concentrated on students' requirements and preferences for an AI-based VR coach, in accordance with the overarching research interest.

5) Theory-Guided Differentiation of the Research Question

The main research question should be refined into several sub-questions, based on relevant theoretical considerations. This step allows for a more nuanced investigation and facilitates the development of a structured analytical framework. In our case, section III.A. describes the detailed research questions.

6) Selection of Analytical Techniques

Based on the nature of the material and the research aims, appropriate analytical techniques should be selected. These include elements of summarizing, explicating, and structuring content. In our study, we focus on summarizing the content [25, p. 64ff] and analyzing frequencies.

7) Definition of Units of Analysis

According to Mayring, "the focus [of CQA] is always on the development of a category system. These categories are developed in a relationship between the theory (question) and the concrete material, defined by construction and assignment rules and revised during the analysis." [25]

In principle, both an inductive and a deductive approach to category formation is possible. In deductive category formation, a coding guideline clearly defines the category system. These category definitions are formulated in advance from the theoretical background. Only then the material processing starts and searches for relevant sections of text. This approach is often used for explicating and structuring content analysis.

In contrast, we chose summarizing content analysis as analyzing technique. The summary content analysis tries to take all material into account and systematically reduce it to the essentials. If only certain components (to be determined according to a definition criterion) are taken into account in such reductive text analysis processes, this is a kind of inductive category formation [25]. Therefore, inductive category development was used in our study, allowing categories to emerge from the data in close relation to the research questions. Inductive category definition derives categories directly from the material in a generalization process, without referring to previously formulated theoretical concepts [25, p. 84].

8) Conducting the Material Analysis

The material was analyzed according to the established procedure. The category system was applied iteratively, allowing for dynamic interplay of the coding process and the refinement of categories. When the category system was adjusted substantially, previously coded material was re-examined to ensure consistency and validity.

IV. Results

Participants included bachelor students in their second or third year (Informatics) and master students in Data Science. The survey was conducted in the middle of the semester, and 22 students from each course (a total of 44 participants) completed the questionnaire.

Bachelor students attach much more importance to the goal of "gaining certainty, reducing excitement" (21), while this is only a marginal phenomenon for master students (6). The latter put more emphasis on closing knowledge gaps and achieving understanding of the content (18), while bachelor students prefer to learn answers to all possible questions (7) and thus build knowledge (2). There is a striking shift during the course of studies from the "soft" focus on gaining security and reducing examination anxiety to content-related and knowledge-related aspects.

Interaction and feedback are also becoming increasingly important for training with a VR coach during the course of studies, even though bachelor students already have high demands here. 12 bachelor students want real feedback rather than an imposed, standardized interaction. This aspect becomes even more important for the master students (17).

It is also striking that bachelor students prefer to be motivated by a VR coach (2, in the master's program only one person), while master students want the VR coach to develop an individual schedule for further learning together with them.

Overall, individualization and personalization gain relevance along with the study progress: while only one bachelor student expects personalized feedback from the VR coach, there are already 7 master students who wish to do so.

The main requirement for a VR coach is particularly striking: about 70 percent of students (15 bachelor and 16 master students) expect realistic scenes and as real situations as possible from a VR coach. 5 bachelor and 5 master students wish to have images of the real examiners and sometimes even a picture of the real examination room. In terms of proximity to reality, both groups are very similar in their statements and see this as an essential requirement and also a prerequisite for using the VR coach.

The statements of the students can be summarized into two super-categories with sub-categories:

1. One category puts a focus on learning goal-related aspects (RQ2), which in turn can be subdivided into personal and content-related learning outcomes.
2. The second category relates to aspects of the learning process (RQ3 and RQ4), including realistic scenarios and the simulation of real instructors and assessors as well as the examination room. Another sub-category is real interaction and individualized feedback. A third aspect is personalized and individualized support of the learning process including the motivation and development of learning paths.

V. Discussion of Results

The results of the QCA provide valuable insights into students' learning goals and expectations regarding the use of a virtual coach to prepare for oral examinations. Regarding RQ1, all but two students have no fundamental reservations against using a virtual coach.

Regarding learning goals (RQ2), students expressed both personal and cognitive motivations for using a virtual coach. On a personal level, many bachelor students emphasized a desire to gain confidence in their performance, reduce examination anxiety, and manage nervousness prior to the exam. This shows a strong emotional component in preparing for oral assessments, which a virtual coach might address through repeated exposure to realistic exam-like settings.

On the cognitive level, students wish to identify and close knowledge gaps and assess their own level of understanding. This indicates that learners are not only looking for emotional support but also expect the virtual coach to contribute to their academic progress by offering feedback that enhances metacognitive awareness and supports self-regulated learning.

Regarding the requirements for the VR-coach (RQ3), students highlighted several key expectations. First and foremost, authenticity and realism are essential. Students expect the simulation to closely mirror real-life examination scenarios, including realistic examiners, spaces, and question types. Furthermore, the coach must enable real interaction and provide meaningful, situation-specific feedback. Simple or generic responses were considered insufficient.

A second major requirement is personalization. Students want the virtual coach to support their individual learning processes by offering customized feedback, motivation, and structured guidance, such as helping to create a personalized preparation schedule.

Notably, although most participants were in favor of using a virtual coach, two students preferred not to engage with such a tool. One key reason cited was physical discomfort or motion sickness when using VR/AR devices, illustrating that technical accessibility and user comfort must be considered in system design.

Students were also clear on what would be unacceptable in a virtual coach (RQ4). These "no-go" criteria include predefined or incorrect answers, impolite or insensitive behavior, and above all a lack of personalization or the use of unrealistic or artificial scenarios. Such deficiencies would undermine the coach's credibility and usefulness and might even exacerbate exam-related stress rather than reduce it.

Taken together, these findings suggest that a virtual coach can be a valuable tool for preparing oral examinations – but only under certain conditions. Technically limited or overly generic solutions are unlikely to be accepted by students. From a development perspective, this implies that the virtual coach must be technically mature, pedagogically sound, and tailored to the needs of individual learners. While iterative development methods such as agile approaches offer flexibility, they can only be applied within narrow limits if the product is to meet user expectations from the outset. In particular, iterative and agile approaches often develop solutions in short iterations that result in increments which can be rolled out to users even way before the system is complete. This does not seem to be a viable option here since a large share of students declines to learn with an incomplete or partly faulty VR tutor. Consequently, incremental development may kill user acceptance due to bad user experience.

In conclusion, the data point toward a clear user demand for realistic, interactive, and personalized virtual learning environments. If these criteria are met, a virtual coach may not only support cognitive preparation but also help students overcome emotional barriers, ultimately contributing to more confident and competent oral performance.

VI. CONCLUSIONS FROM THE USER SURVEY

This study investigated students' perspectives on a VR-based AI coach developed to support preparation for oral examinations. Overall, the findings point to clear priorities for educational software engineering and challenge assumptions about early-stage development and user tolerance.

A. High Expectations rather than Skepticism

Students exhibit general openness and interest in the concept of a VR-based coach, especially regarding managing exam-related anxiety, building oral communication confidence, and enabling repeated, self-directed practice. They want to use the VR coach also for preparing content. The survey also revealed that students see the VR-based coach primarily as a means to an end, i.e. a tool to improve their exam performance. Yet, this openness is paired with very high expectations. From the outset, the system is expected to deliver accurate content, reflect realistic exam scenarios, and provide individualized responses. Core requirements include realism, individualization, and content accuracy. Rather than accepting early-stage imperfections, students only consider the VR coach useful if it works meaningfully from the very first interaction. This leaves little room for gradual quality improvements or tolerance of rough, minimally functional prototypes. A "wobbly" first impression, as several students implied, would result in the tool's immediate rejection.

B. Tension between Virtual and Real Examiners

The potential trade-off between realism and emotional safety emerged as an implicit theme. While real examiners might represent the gold standard for authenticity, the idea of a virtual coach offers psychological advantages—especially the ability to practice without judgment, make mistakes safely, and repeat scenarios as needed. This tension between learning in a realistic environment and practicing in a protected space suggests a need for further exploration into the pedagogical positioning of virtual coaches. Students' responses indicate that the VR coach is not expected to replace real examiners but rather to supplement preparation in a way that increases emotional readiness and perceived control.

C. Shifting Perspectives: From Developer to User

Nearly all surveyed students had a technical background, often engaging in software development themselves. In particular, the bachelor students were enrolled in a course that deals with requirements elicitation and analysis. Interestingly, their expectations changed when viewing the VR system not as developers, but as users. When eliciting requirements in the course, they often complained that customers did not care about a system's technical issues but were only interested in getting a solution for their problem. Now, they were not interested in specific VR features of the tutor system but showed a marked shift toward usability and outcome orientation. Likewise, while they typically accept early-stage, technically incomplete prototypes in development contexts, they became far less tolerant when taking a user role themselves. In that mindset, the technical implementation became secondary to the learning outcome. When imagining themselves as users of the VR-based coach, students showed less concern about the underlying technology and focused instead on whether the system would provide real value in preparing them for exams.

This shift illustrates a known but often underestimated cognitive bias in software development: when students are in the user role, their tolerance for imperfection and experimentation decreases dramatically. Their focus shifted from "how the system works" to "what the system enables". This highlights a critical insight: when students are the end users, their standards for usability, reliability, and educational effectiveness rise sharply—regardless of their technical empathy for the development process. This also underlines the importance of integrating user-centered perspectives early and consistently in the software engineering process.

D. *Implications for Development: Beyond Classical Agile Approaches*

The findings raise questions about the applicability of conventional agile development practices in this context. While agile methodologies promote early user feedback and continuous improvement, the survey responses suggest that in this particular use case, this can backfire if early iterations do not meet the expected level of realism and content quality. In the case of educational technologies used in emotionally charged situations—such as oral exam preparation—careless early releases may compromise user acceptance.

This is not an argument against agile principles as such but calls for cautious and strategically staged implementation of increments. Each release must meet high quality standards in terms of usability, realism, and content correctness, even in early stages. Thus, an adapted or hybrid approach is required: agile principles may be maintained but with greater emphasis on upfront planning, anticipatory design, and thorough quality assurance in each increment to ensure that early impressions do not jeopardize the tool's acceptance.

VII. Summary and Outlook

This study presented a qualitative analysis of students' expectations for a VR-based AI coach to support oral exam preparation. The qualitative data collected from undergraduate and graduate informatics students provides important insights into students' learning goals, expectations, and specific requirements for such a tool.

The results clearly show that students appreciate the idea of a virtual coach and express a strong interest in using it, especially to manage examination anxiety and improve their confidence in oral settings.

The results underline that while students are highly receptive to the concept, they also hold clear and demanding expectations: Students are critical of systems that feel inauthentic, lack individualization, or provide overly generic responses. They value realism, personalized feedback, and content accuracy, and they require these features to be present from the very first use.

The pedagogical potential of such systems is evident. Students appreciate the chance to train in a psychologically safer space and repeat challenging scenarios without social consequences. Yet, the virtual coach's success hinges on more than functionality: it must offer a credible learning experience and be perceived as professionally valuable.

Crucially, informatics students—mostly with development experience—demonstrated a significant shift in mindset when viewing the system as users rather than as developers. While technically-minded in many academic contexts, they deprioritized implementation details in favor of usability, effectiveness, and emotional relevance. This highlights the importance of continuous, user-centered validation throughout the development process.

A further question that emerges from the data concerns the relationship between virtual and real-life exam preparation: Is a real examiner ultimately the better coach, or can a realistic virtual alternative offer distinct advantages? On the one hand, the authenticity of real-life interaction may provide the highest degree of realism and thus better prepare students for actual exams. On the other hand, a well-designed virtual coach could offer a psychologically safer and more flexible environment for iterative practice—free from fear of judgment—allowing students to practice more calmly, make mistakes without embarrassment, and build confidence over time. The real examiner may be most authentic, but a virtual system could lower emotional barriers, enabling deeper, repeated engagement with the exam format.

This tension between realism and psychological safety presents a promising area for future comparative studies. Such studies should empirically examine the relative benefits of human versus virtual coaching scenarios, particularly in terms of learner outcomes, confidence development, and long-term skill retention.

These insights have important implications for educational software engineering. First, they underline a strong pedagogical demand for immersive, user-adaptive technologies that support oral communication skills in realistic settings. Second, they point to a need for development strategies that prioritize the user experience—not only in terms of interface design, but also regarding the system's pedagogical effectiveness and credibility; otherwise, the technology may neither be accepted, nor used effectively. The findings further suggest that a purely technical focus or minimal-viable approach may fall short if it does not align with learners' expectations for realism and relevance. A VR coach that fails to simulate realistic examiner behavior or classroom dynamics may even increase insecurity rather than alleviate it.

In terms of outlook, further research and iterative development with student involvement are necessary. Future work should investigate how adaptive AI systems can dynamically tailor content and feedback to individual learners and how the realism of examiner behavior can be technically modeled in VR. Moreover, long-term studies may also provide valuable insights into the actual learning impact of such systems on learning outcomes, examination performance, and user acceptance over time.

The next step for our project is a prototype development phase, in which a minimal viable product will be co-created and evaluated with student feedback loops. Special attention will be paid to usability, immersion, content reliability, and pedagogical effectiveness from the start. By addressing users' expectations proactively, we aim to ensure that the VR-based coach is not only technically sound, but also pedagogically credible and emotionally supportive. The challenge will be to strike the right balance between technical feasibility, psychological comfort, and educational impact—ensuring that the VR-based coach becomes a credible, accepted, and effective tool in students' academic journeys.

REFERENCES

[1] R. Q. Mao *et al.*, 'Immersive Virtual Reality for Surgical Training: A Systematic Review', *J. Surg. Res.*, vol. 268, pp. 40–58, Dec. 2021, doi: 10.1016/j.jss.2021.06.045.

[2] A. Luca *et al.*, 'Innovative Educational Pathways in Spine Surgery: Advanced Virtual Reality–Based Training', *World Neurosurg.*, vol. 140, pp. 674–680, Aug. 2020, doi: 10.1016/j.wneu.2020.04.102.

[3] R. Toyoda, F. Russo-Abegão, and J. Glassey, 'VR-based health and safety training in various high-risk engineering industries: a literature review', *Int. J. Educ. Technol. High. Educ.*, vol. 19, no. 1, p. 42, Aug. 2022, doi: 10.1186/s41239-022-00349-3.

[4] L. Hsu, 'Exploring EFL learners' acceptance and cognitive absorption at VR-Based language learning: A survey and experimental study', *Heliyon*, vol. 10, no. 3, p. e24863, Feb. 2024, doi: 10.1016/j.heliyon.2024.e24863.

[5] I. W. E. D. Rahmanu and G. Molnár, 'Multimodal immersion in English language learning in higher education: A systematic review', *Heliyon*, vol. 10, no. 19, p. e38357, Oct. 2024, doi: 10.1016/j.heliyon.2024.e38357.

[6] G. Makransky, T. S. Terkildsen, and R. E. Mayer, 'Adding immersive virtual reality to a science lab simulation causes more presence but less learning', *Learn. Instr.*, vol. 60, pp. 225–236, Apr. 2019, doi: 10.1016/j.learninstruc.2017.12.007.

[7] J. Radianti, T. A. Majchrzak, J. Fromm, and I. Wohlgenannt, 'A systematic review of immersive virtual reality applications for higher education: Design elements, lessons learned, and research agenda', *Comput. Educ.*, vol. 147, p. 103778, Apr. 2020, doi: 10.1016/j.compedu.2019.103778.

[8] M. Conrad, D. Kablitz, and S. Schumann, 'Learning effectiveness of immersive virtual reality in education and training: A systematic review of findings', *Comput. Educ. X Real.*, vol. 4, p. 100053, 2024, doi: 10.1016/j.cexr.2024.100053.

[9] M. Poupard, F. Larrue, H. Sauzéon, and A. Tricot, 'A systematic review of immersive technologies for education: Learning performance, cognitive load and intrinsic motivation', *Br. J. Educ. Technol.*, vol. 56, no. 1, pp. 5–41, Jan. 2025, doi: 10.1111/bjet.13503.

[10] Y. Wang, M. Hu, and Q. Wan, 'The application and prospects of artificial intelligence in the treatment of anxiety disorders', in *Proceedings of the 2023 4th International Symposium on Artificial Intelligence for Medicine Science*, Chengdu China: ACM, Oct. 2023, pp. 923–926. doi: 10.1145/3644116.3644274.

[11] J. Grubert, Y. Sedelmaier, and D. Landes, 'Towards Embodied Conversational Agents for Reducing Oral Exam Anxiety in Extended Reality', in *IEEE International Symposium in Mixed and Augmented Reality (ISMAR-Adjunct)*, IEEE, 2025.

[12] S. A. SalsabilaHadi, M. S. Putri, F. Ismiarti, A. A. Santoso Gunawan, and F. S. Pramudya, 'A Systematic Literature Review:Virtual Reality's in Decreasing Public Speaking Anxiety (PSA)', in *2023 International Conference on Information Technology and Computing (ICITCOM)*, Yogyakarta, Indonesia: IEEE, Dec. 2023, pp. 1–5. doi: 10.1109/ICITCOM60176.2023.10442335.

[13] S. Saufnay, E. Etienne, and M. Schyns, 'Improvement of Public Speaking Skills Using Virtual Reality: Development of a Training System', in *2024 12th International Conference on Affective Computing and Intelligent Interaction Workshops and Demos (ACIIW)*, Glasgow, United Kingdom: IEEE, Sept. 2024, pp. 122–124. doi: 10.1109/ACIIW63320.2024.00025.

[14] J. Schneider, G. Romano, and H. Drachsler, 'Beyond Reality—Extending a Presentation Trainer with an Immersive VR Module', *Sensors*, vol. 19, no. 16, p. 3457, Aug. 2019, doi: 10.3390/s19163457.

[15] N. Badve *et al.*, 'Development of Online Exam System for the Institution', *Int. J. Res. Appl. Sci. Eng. Technol.*, vol. 11, no. 4, pp. 4303–4311, Apr. 2023, doi: 10.22214/ijraset.2023.50576.

[16] A. Shomorony, R. Weitzman, H. Chen, and A. P. Sclafani, 'Augmented otorhinologic evaluation in telemedical visits', *Am. J. Otolaryngol.*, vol. 45, no. 1, p. 104088, Jan. 2024, doi: 10.1016/j.amjoto.2023.104088.

[17] S. Moroz, R. Andrade, L. Walsh, and C. L. Richard, 'Student Performance on an Objective Structured Clinical Exam Delivered Both Virtually and In-Person', *Am. J. Pharm. Educ.*, vol. 87, no. 7, p. 100088, July 2023, doi: 10.1016/j.ajpe.2023.100088.

[18] D. Landes, Y. Sedelmaier, F. Böck, A. Lehmann, M. Fraas, and S. Janusch, 'Combining Data- and Knowledge-Driven AI with Didactics for Individualized Learning Recommendations', in *2024 IEEE Global Engineering Education Conference (EDUCON)*, Kos Island, Greece: IEEE, May 2024, pp. 01–08. doi: 10.1109/EDUCON60312.2024.10578640.

[19] R. Britto, W. G. De Oliveira Filho, C. G. Barros, and E. C. Lopes, 'Intelligent tutor system model applied to basic electronics', in *2017 12th Iberian Conference on Information Systems and Technologies (CISTI)*, Lisbon, Portugal: IEEE, June 2017, pp. 1–5. doi: 10.23919/CISTI.2017.7975832.

[20] E. Ortega-Ochoa, M. Arguedas, and T. Daradoumis, 'Empathic pedagogical conversational agents: A systematic literature review', *Br. J. Educ. Technol.*, vol. 55, no. 3, pp. 886–909, May 2024, doi: 10.1111/bjet.13413.

[21] M. J. Smith *et al.*, 'Mechanism of Action for Obtaining Job Offers With Virtual Reality Job Interview Training', *Psychiatr. Serv.*, vol. 68, no. 7, pp. 747–750, July 2017, doi: 10.1176/appi.ps.201600217.

[22] M. D. Bell and A. Weinstein, 'Simulated Job Interview Skill Training for People with Psychiatric Disability: Feasibility and Tolerability of Virtual Reality Training', *Schizophr. Bull.*, vol. 37, no. suppl 2, pp. S91–S97, Sept. 2011, doi: 10.1093/schbul/sbr061.

[23] P. Mayring, *Qualitative Content Analysis*. London: SAGE Publications Ltd, 2021. Accessed: Feb. 06, 2023. [Online]. Available: https://uk.sagepub.com/en-gb/eur/qualitative-content-analysis/book269922

[24] P. Mayring, 'Qualitative Content Analysis: Demarcation, Varieties, Developments'.

[25] P. Mayring, *Qualitative Inhaltsanalyse: Grundlagen und Techniken*, 13th edn. Weinheim Basel: Beltz, 2022.

On the Keeping Models in the System Design and Implementation

Radek Kočí

Brno University of Technology, Faculty of Information Technology,
IT4Innovations Centre of Excellence
Bozetechova 2, 612 66 Brno, Czech Republic
email: koci@fit.vut.cz

***Abstract*—An essential criterion for software design and implementation is the effectiveness of requirements specification, development, and verification. One possibility is the use of high-level models and languages. A particular disadvantage is the need to transform models into a production environment, either manually or automated. In both cases, the link to the original models is often lost, degrading their usability in the future. In this paper, using a demonstration example, we will look at the possibility of modeling requirements using Object-Oriented Petri Nets (OOPN) and then transforming them into Java to maintain the model's and implementation's correlation. We will discuss the automation of this process and possible ways to increase efficiency.**

Keywords*—*Object Oriented Petri Nets; model transformation; Java.

I. INTRODUCTION

Model and Simulation-Based System Design (MSBD) refers to a set of techniques and tools for developing software systems that are based on formal models and simulation techniques throughout the development process. The fundamental problem with model transformations is often the impossibility of a fully automated process and, therefore, the mismatch between models and their implementation. In this paper, using a demonstration example, we will look at the possibility of modeling requirements using Object-Oriented Petri Nets (OOPN) and then transforming them into Java to maintain the model's and implementation's correlation. We will discuss the automation of this process and possible ways to increase efficiency.

There are many approaches to code generation. First, the generation of models in the chosen language from UML models [1]–[3], the transformation of different levels of diagrams [4], or the transformation of conceptual models described, e.g., in SysML into simulation models [5]. Second, more accurate code generation from simplified variants of UML models (xUML or fUML) [6][7]. The biggest pitfall of these approaches at the moment is tool support. Freely available tools often fail to exploit the full potential of the underlying principles. Our closest approaches are probably the Network-within-a-Network (NwN) formalism and the associated tool Renew [8]. Like us, NwN combines Petri nets and the Java language, and the models are directly translated into Java. Nevertheless, our approach works not only with one language, but we can combine Smalltalk, Java, or C++, including directly writing the code within models. We aim to create a system and tool for more efficient modeling and model deployment, including code generation on languages like Java and C++.

The paper is structured as follows. In Section II, we introduce the basics of the OOPN formalism. Section III introduces the demonstration example and describes the basic principles of modeling components and layers based on the Discrete Event System Specification (DEVS) formalism. Section IV describes the way we can move from DEVS like components to objects. Section V discusses possibilities of code generation in two ways – unsupervised and sipervised.

II. OBJECT ORIENTED PETRI NETS FORMALISM

An OOPN is a set of classes specified by high-level Petri nets [9]. Formally, an OOPN is a triple (Σ, c_0, oid_0) where Σ is the class set, c_0 is the initial class, and oid_0 is the name of the initial object of c_0. A *class* is determined primarily by the object net and the set of method nets. Object nets describe the possible autonomous actions of objects, while method nets describe the reactions of objects to messages sent to them from outside.

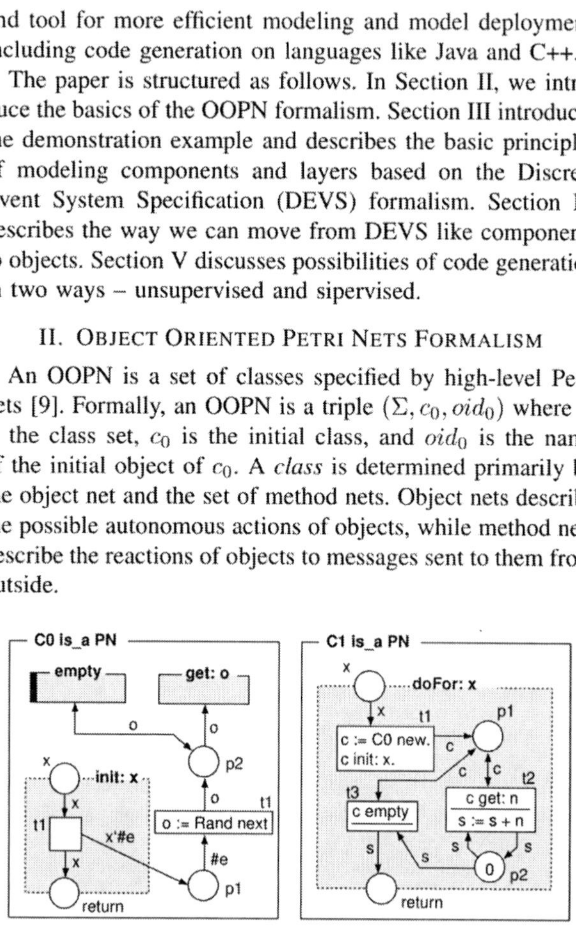

Figure 1. Example of the OOPN model.

An example illustrating the essential elements of the OOPN formalism is shown in Figure 1. Two classes are depicted, *C0* and *C1*. The object net of the class *C0* consists of places *p1* and *p2* and one transition *t1*. The object net of the class *C1* is empty. The class *C0* has a method *init:*, a synchronous port *get:*, and a negative predicate *empty*. The class *C1* has the method *doFor:*. An invocation of the method *doFor:* leads to the random generation of *x* numbers and a return of their sum.

Object nets consist of places and transitions. Each place has an initial marking. Each transition has conditions (i.e., inscribed test arcs), preconditions (i.e., inscribed input arcs), guard, action, and postconditions (i.e., inscribed output arcs).

Method nets are similar to object nets, but each net has a multiplicity of parameter places and the return place. Method nets can access the places of the corresponding object nets to allow running methods to change object states.

III. Requirements Modeling

This section presents a demonstration example and the essence of requirements modeling using the OOPN and DEVS formalisms.

A. Demonstration Example

Let us start with the following example, which is inspired by the simple game LightBulb. First, let's give the basic text description. The game board consists of fields that are either empty, contain connections (only the edges of a square can be connected), an energy power, or a light (bulb). Connectors can connect two, three, or four edges. There is just one source and at least one bulb in the game. The player can rotate each field 90 degrees to the right. At the beginning, the fields are rotated so there is no connection between the power and the bulbs. The game's goal is to rotate the boxes so that the source connects with all the bulbs and thus lights them up. If a field is energized (connected to the power), indicate this by changing color. We will focus here on defining the behavior of each field.

B. Components and Layers in the Model

In the specification and design, we will assume that a field is a component that operates on specific input values and passes information about changes through outputs. It will settle the initial design and reasoning over the requirements and their modeling. We can combine the OOPN (behavioural model) and DEVS (structure and component model) formalisms for these purposes. We start specifying a field as a DEVS component with four input and four output ports. Each input and output pair represents the information transfer between fields adjacent to the corresponding edge, as shown in Figure 2.

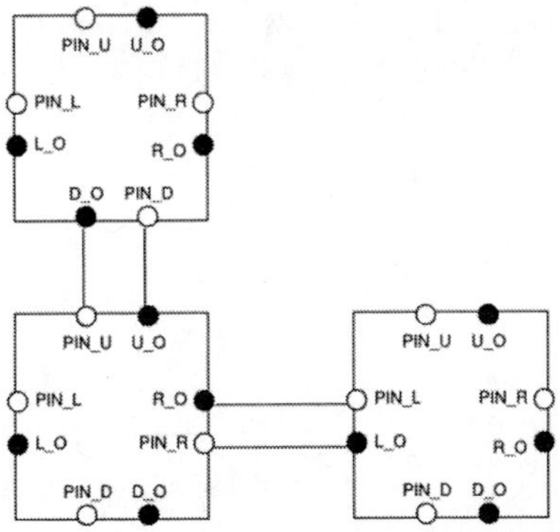

Figure 2. Component model using DEVS formalism.

The behaviour will be defined using the OOPN formalism, where we will create so-called layers. Each layer represents a separate functionality, which can then be modeled as part an object net or a method net. Working with layers allows us to structure behavior better and manipulate the distribution of responsibilities.

C. Initial Requirements Model and Layers

In specifying the requirements, we will start from the elements that follow from the specification, model them using the OOPN formalism, and gradually reveal other essential components.

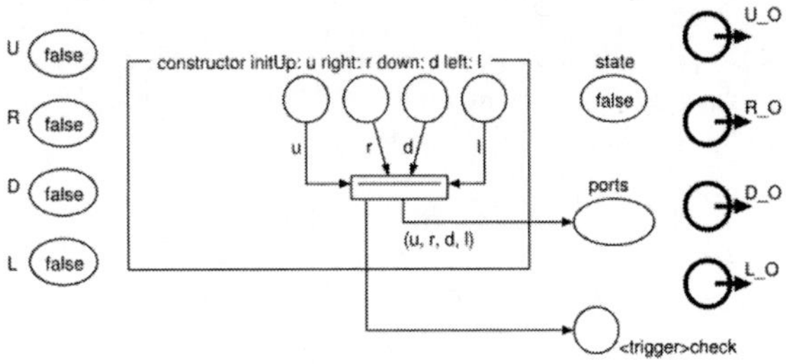

Figure 3. Initial model of the Field component.

The basic definition assumes that each field knows whether an edge is part of a connection. The information is stored in the place ports and can be modeled by a sequence of true/false values indicating whether the edge is connected. The sequence always starts with the top edge and proceeds clockwise. For example, the sequence (true, true, false, false) corresponds to the left bottom field shown in Figure 2. The field stores information about the surrounding fields (modeled as U, R, D, and L places) and informs the surrounding fields of the change (modeled as U_O, R_O, D_O, and L_O output ports). The information indicates whether the field is connected to power. Finally, the place state indicates whether this field is under the power (values true or false). Figure 3 shows the basic model of the Field component. The model is initialized by the constructor initUp:right:down:left:.

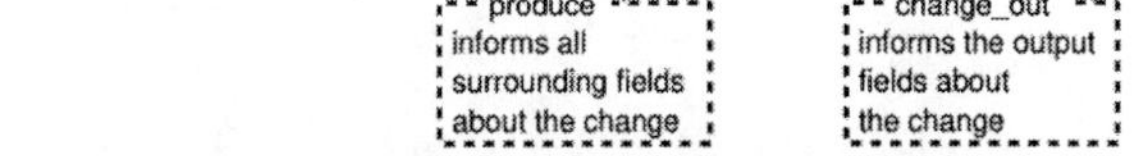

Figure 4. The model flow including layers.

Depending on the task, we can distinguish three basic actions – initialization, rotation, and reaction to a change coming from the surroundings. Figure 4 depicts the basic flows. When the corresponding event is triggered (i.e., the trigger place receives a token), the field is always checked to see whether the field is connected to the energy source, i.e., whether the triggered action caused the change. However, the subsequent actions differ according to the originator, so that we can find two basic flows. In the case of initialization and rotation, we have to inform all the surrounding fields, since a link between fields may have been created or broken. In the case of a change coming from the surroundings, we only inform the fields connected through existing links of the change, if any.

D. Basic Layers

Now, we will look at the model's layers. First, the check layer, which is shown in Figure 5. The model clearly shows how the new state is evaluated.

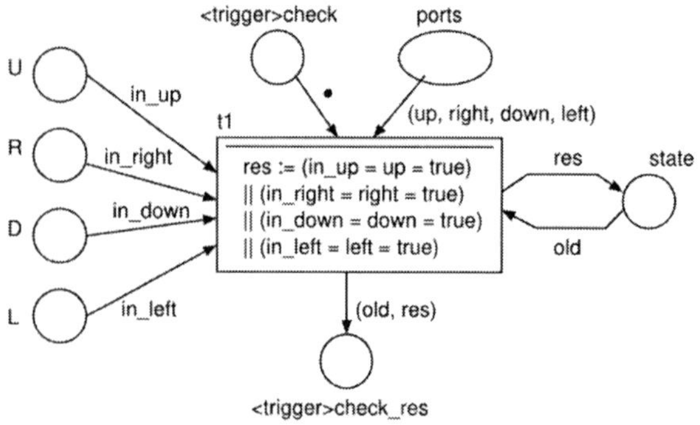

Figure 5. The check layer.

The evaluation is based on the knowledge of the state of the surrounding fields (places U, R, D, and L) and whether the corresponding edge contains a connection to the corresponding fields (see the place ports). If at least one edge containing a connection is true, this field is connected to the energy power. The new value has been rewritten in the state place. The execution of the layer is conditioned by the token in the place *check*, and termination is indicated by inserting the previous and new state pairs in the place check_res.

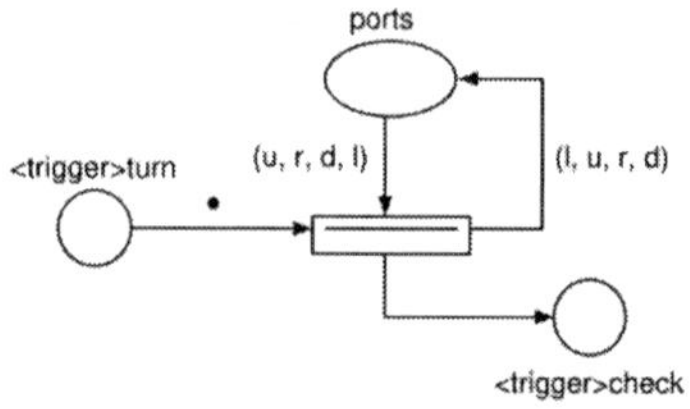

Figure 6. The turn layer.

The next layer is turn, which is captured in Figure 6. The principle of modeling this functionality is evident from the model – the original sequence is removed from the place ports and new sequence, which rotates one position to the right, is inserted back. The execution of the layer is conditioned by the token in the trigger place turn. The termination can be indicated by the addition of an exit place, similar to the check layer. The necessity of such an addition will become apparent during model creation.

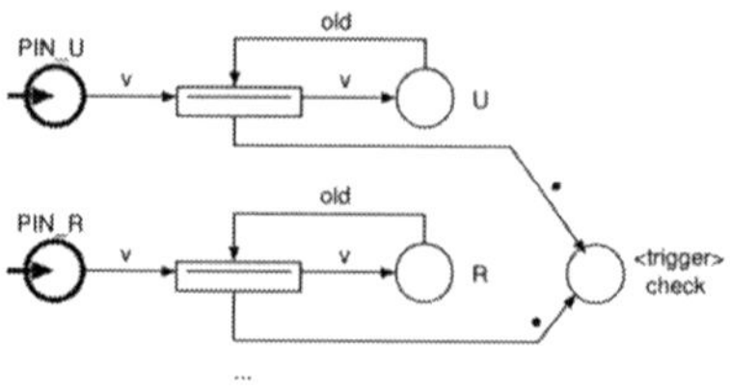

Figure 7. The change_in layer.

The next layer is change_in, which is captured in Figure 7. This layer responds to a change in an input port value and ensures that the contents of the corresponding places are changed. Ports are modeled by special places; see, e.g., PIN_U in Figure 7. If the new value is accepted from the surrounding, it is placed to the input port. The layer updates field's information about the surrounding and activates the check layer by inserting a token in the place check. The model assumes that the change occurs at exactly one input port at a time.

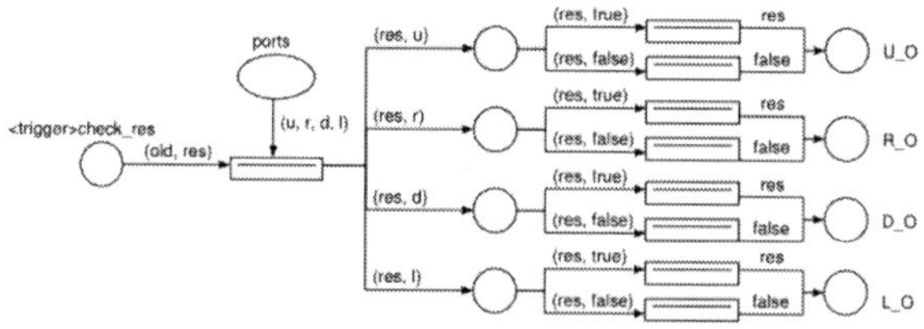

Figure 8. The produce layer.

The next layer is produce, which is captured in Figure 8. This layer is activated by inserting a pair of values of the original and new value of the field state. The layer ensures that the new value is distributed to the surrounding patches through the output ports. However, the insertion of the new value is conditional on a connection on the corresponding edge. If there is no connection, it informs the connected patch of the false state (if there was a connection in the previous state, the connected patch must process this change).

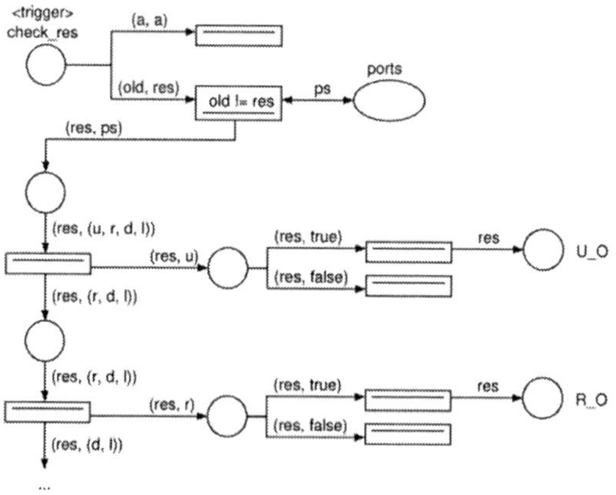

Figure 9. The change_out layer.

The next layer is change_out, which is captured in Figure 9. This layer is fundamentally similar to the layer produce, it captures an alternative modeling option. First, it checks whether the state has changed. If so, all surrounding fields are informed, i.e., the new value is inserted into the appropriate output port if it exists on that link edge. If there is no connection on the edge, no value is inserted (the field is not informed).

IV. Transformation of DEVS Components to Objects

So far, we have considered the model of the field as a DEVS component that communicates with its surroundings through ports. However, we need a conventional approach for use in classical programming languages and environments, i.e., communication via messaging. At the same time, in the modeling, we worked with a sequence of logical values at the port location, which determined which edges contained the connector. It carries specific modeling implications, e.g., repetitive capture of the same functionality over different edges, since the result must always be placed in a different component output port. This section illustrates two steps. First, the edges are named for more flexible handling, and then the DEVS component is transformed into an object component.

A. Ports identification

For our simple example, we choose naming using symbols that bind to the pair (name, exist) in the place ports.

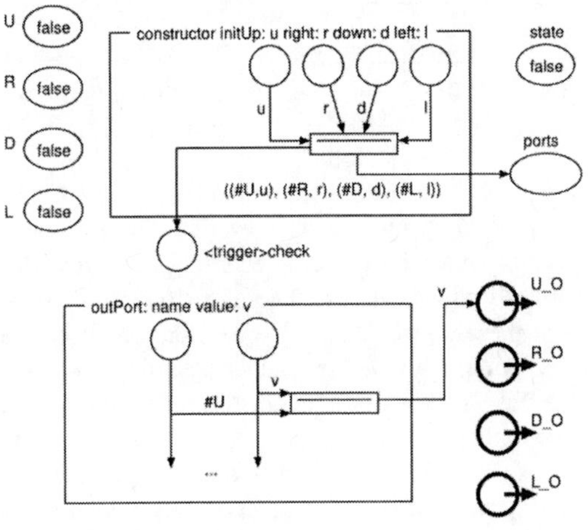

Figure 10. Modification of the init layer.

Figure 10 shows a preview of the change at the init layer. At the same time, we introduced the outPort:value: method, which inserts the specified value into the output port identified by name. We make similar modifications for the check and turn layers (see Figures 11 and 12).

B. Replacement of Ports

We will show more substantial modifications to the produce layer. Since we have the output ports named, we can use the concept of foreach as shown in Figure 13. The basic idea

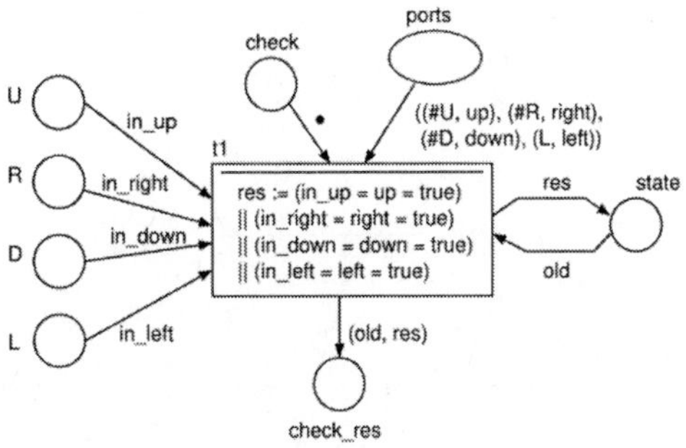

Figure 11. Modification of the check layer.

of the foreach loop is based on list processing in the Prolog language.

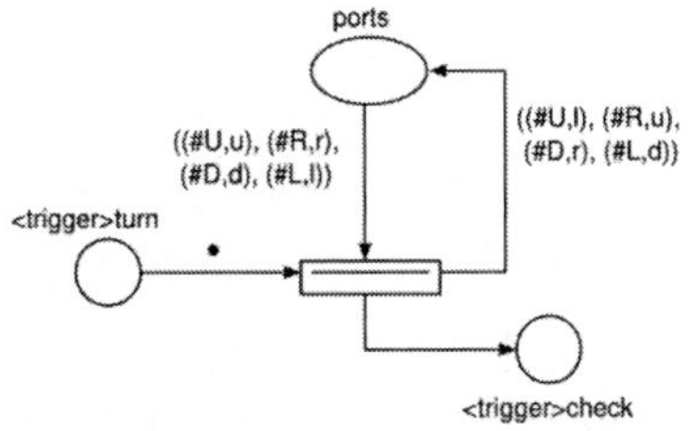

Figure 12. Modification of the turn layer.

Let us return to the produce layer (Figure 13). We build on the original solution, but instead of inserting a value into a specific output port, we call the outPort:value: method. This evaluation is done only once for all edges stored in the place ports. A similar modification could be made for the check_out layer.

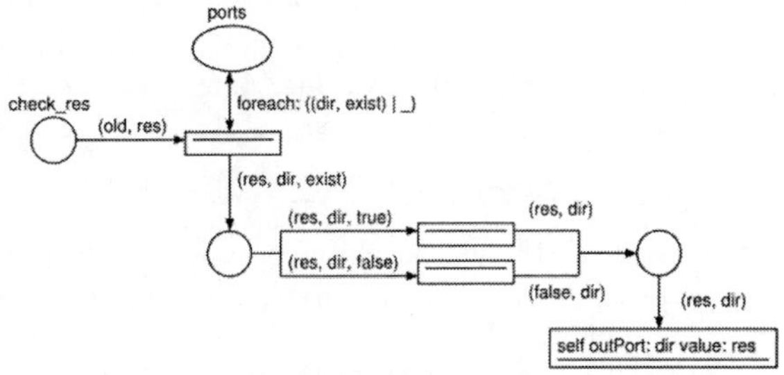

Figure 13. Modification of the produce layer.

Finally, we replace ports with methods or method calls. We generate a corresponding method for each input port with the same name and one argument. Instead of passing data through DEVS components, objects will send messages to each other. An example of changing the PIN_U input port to a method is shown in Figure 14.

Output ports are replaced by calling the corresponding method. For instance, for the output port U_O, it is necessary to call the method PIN_D:, because the output of the up field corresponds to the down input of the connected field (see the

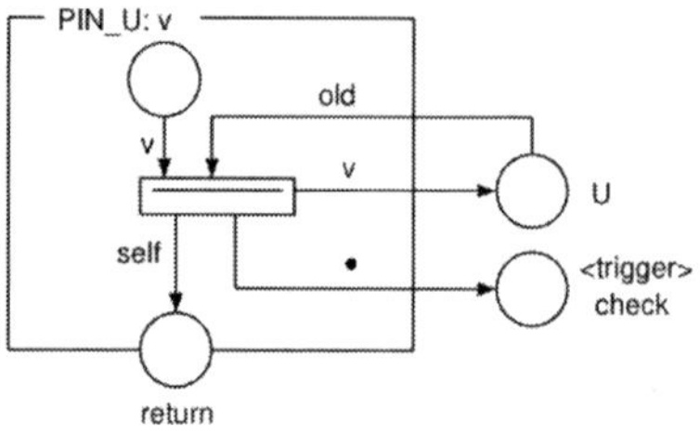

Figure 14. Replacing the input port with the method.

DEVS component model in Figure 2). An example is shown in Figure 15.

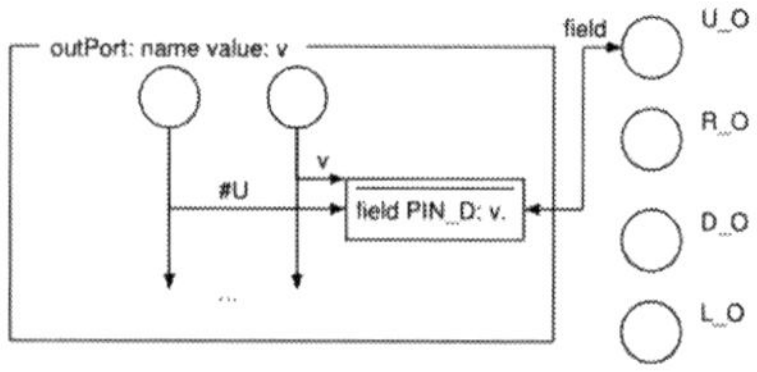

Figure 15. Replacing the output port with the method call.

Figure 16 schematically depicts the resulting OOPN model – places, methods, and basic layers initiated by trigger places.

V. Code Generation

This section presents the possible outputs of the model transformation into Java. We build on the work of [10]. Due to the generality of the OOPN formalism, the fundamental transformation mechanism is cumbersome (*unsupervised generation*), but introducing some additional information can make code generation more efficient (*supervised generation*). This information can be supplied manually, or it can be derived by automated analysis of the model. We will present examples of generated code for only one part of the model. In both cases, we obtain executable code that differs in complexity and efficiency.

A. Basic Framework Classes

The created OOPN models, which correspond to the principles mentioned so far, can be automatically translated into Java. The resulting class system needs a basic framework prepared for these purposes [10]. Figure 17 shows the basic structure of classes and interfaces required to transform OOPN models into Java.

The class Place represents the collection corresponding to a place. The OOPN class is always derived from the PN class, which provides the primary means for object handling and communication. The object net is represented by the constructor. The object net's places can be considered attributes (object variables) of the object, and their declarations are, therefore, placed in the member fields space. Because the OOPN language is typeless, the common type of all variables is the PNObject class, and communication, i.e., sending messages, must be done specially.

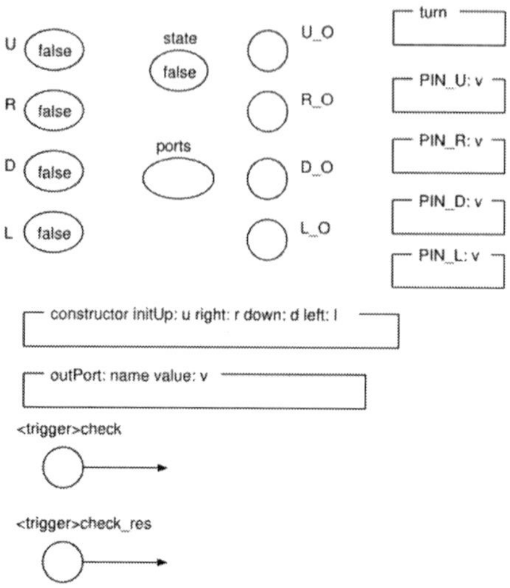

Figure 16. Model of the class Field overview.

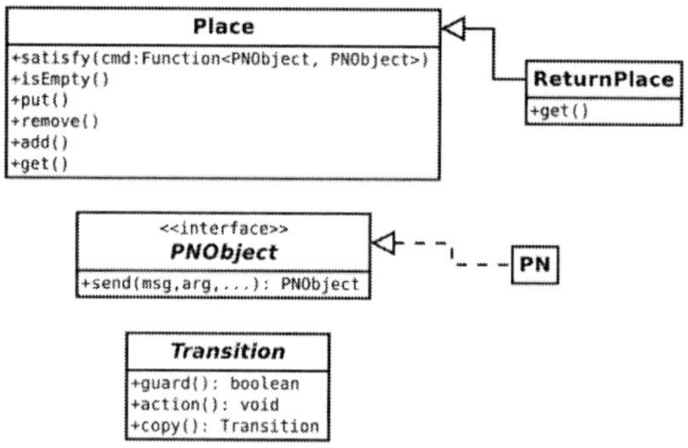

Figure 17. Basic Java classes for OOPN transformation.

PNObject is the interface implemented by the PN class and, thus, by all OOPN classes. However, we must consider that models also work with other objects (e.g., primitive Java data types and other Java classes). Therefore, we need wrappers for objects of these classes that implement the PNObject interface to ensure compatibility. For each transition, a class derived from the Transition class is generated, containing methods to verify the input conditions (guard) and a method containing the actual actions of the transition (action). A place corresponds to an unordered collection of objects from which objects can be read and removed, and new objects can be added.

B. Unsupervised Generation

As mentioned, we will demonstrate the transformation (code generation) capabilities only on selected parts of the model. The model consists of a single class *Field*. Figure 18 shows the generated code for the model layer captured in Figure 16 in the basic (unsupervised) version.

All variables and values are typed as class *PNObject*. A special class *PNList* is used to implement the list of values. This figure does not capture the whole listing; it is only an outline of the generated code.

```
public class Field extends PN {
   protected boolean state;
   protected List<List<Dir, Boolean>> ports;
   protected boolean U, R, D, L;
   protected boolean U_O, R_O, D_O, L_O;
   public enum Dir {U, R, D, L};
   public Cl(boolean u, boolean r, boolean d,
             boolean l) {
      state = false;
      ports = new ArrayList<>();
      ports.put(new ArrayList<>(Dir.U, u));
      ports.put(new ArrayList<>(Dir.R, r));
      ports.put(new ArrayList<>(Dir.D, d));
      ports.put(new ArrayList<>(Dir.L, l));
      ...
   }
}
```

Figure 19. Supervised translation of the class Field into Java.

C. Supervised Generation

For supervised generation, we use the constraints introduced in [9], which allow us to define different constraints on models. The constraints can be defined manually or derived by analyzing the model or its simulated run [11]. This analysis finds the following constraints on the model under consideration.

```
public class Field extends PN {
   protected Place state;
   protected Place ports;
   protected Place U, R, D, L;
   protected Place U_O, R_O, D_O, L_O;
   public Cl(PNObject u, PNObject r, PNObject d,
             PNObject l) {
      state = new Place(this);
      ports = new Place(this);
      fields = new Place(this);
      inputs = new Place(this);

      state.add(false);
      PNlist lst = new PNList();
      lst.add(new PNList("#U", u));
      lst.add(new PNList("#R", r));
      lst.add(new PNList("#D", d));
      lst.add(new PNList("#L", l));
      ports.add(lst);
      ...
   }
}
```

Figure 18. Unsupervised translation of the class Field into Java.

context Field::state: Boolean
context Field::ports: OrderedList
context Field::ports element: OrderedList (Dir, Boolean)
context Dir: enum(U, R, D, L)
...

The generated code can be simplified and streamlined based on the defined constraints, as shown in Figure 19.

VI. Conclusion

This paper presented the possibilities of modeling requirements using OOPN formalisms (for behavior definition) and DEVS-like components (for structure description). The model can then be gradually transformed into a more efficient form and a programming language (currently Java). The essential feature we want to achieve is that the resulting code does not need to be further modified, because the original model allows the use of code and objects from the target environment. Thus, all changes and modifications occur at the model level.

In the future, we want to focus on fully automated constraint derivation over the model (while retaining the possibility of manual intervention) and automated support for model modifications. For these purposes, we plan to explore the possibilities of involving artificial intelligence, particularly large language models (LLMs). It also assumes tool support, which we will continue to work on.

Acknowledgment

This work has been supported by the internal BUT project FIT-S-23-8151.

References

[1] T. Hussain and G. Frey, "UML-based Development Process for IEC 61499 with Automatic Test-case Generation," in *2006 IEEE Conference on Emerging Technologies and Factory Automation*. IEEE, 2006, pp. 1277–1284.

[2] C. A. Garcia, E. X. Castellanos, C. Rosero, and Carlos, "Designing Automation Distributed Systems Based on IEC-61499 and UML," in *5th International Conference in Software Engineering Research and Innovation (CONISOFT)*, 2017, pp. 61–68.

[3] I. A. Batchkova, Y. A. Belev, and D. L. Tzakova, "IEC 61499 Based Control of Cyber-Physical Systems," *Industry 4.0*, vol. 5, no. 1, pp. 10–13, November 2020.

[4] S. Panjaitan and G. Frey, "Functional Design for IEC 61499 Distributed Control Systems using UML Activity Diagrams," in *Proceedings of the 2005 International Conference on Instrumentation, Communications and Information Technology ICICI 2005*, 2005, pp. 64–70.

[5] G. D. Kapos, V. Dalakas, A. Tsadimas, M. Nikolaidou, and D. Anagnostopoulos, "Model-based system engineering using SysML: Deriving executable simulation models with QVT," in *IEEE International Systems Conference Proceedings*, 2014, pp. 531–538.

[6] F. Ciccozzi, "On the automated translational execution of the action language for foundational uml," *Software and Systems Modeling*, vol. 17, no. 4, p. 1311–1337, 2018, doi: 10.1007/s10270-016-0556-7.

[7] E. Seidewitz and J. Tatibouet, "Tool paper: Combining alf and uml in modeling tools: An example with papyrus," in *15th Internation Workshop on OCL and Textual Modeling, MODELS 2015*, pp. 105–119, [retrieved: June, 2025]. [Online]. Available: http://ceur-ws.org/Vol-1512/paper09.pdf

[8] L. Cabac, M. Haustermann, and D. Mosteller, "Renew 2.5 - towards a comprehensive integrated development environment for petri net-based applications," in *Application and Theory of Petri Nets and Concurrency - 37th International Conference, PETRI NETS 2016, Toruń, Poland, June 19-24, 2016. Proceedings*, 2016, pp. 101–112. [Online]. Available: http://dx.doi.org/10.1007/978-3-319-39086-4_7

[9] R. Kočí and V. Janoušek, "The Object Oriented Petri Net Component Model," in *The Tenth International Conference on Software Engineering Advances*. Xpert Publishing Services, 2015, pp. 309–315.

[10] R. Kočí, "On the object oriented petri nets model transformation into java programming language," in *The Nineteenth International Conference on Software Engineering Advances, ICSEA 2024*. Xpert Publishing Services, 2024, pp. 38–42.

[11] R. Kočí and V. Janoušek, "Tracing and Reversing the Run of Software Systems Implemented by Petri Nets," in *ThinkMind ICSEA 2018, The Thirteenth International Conference on Software Engineering Advances*. Xpert Publishing Services, 2018, pp. 122–127.

VR-DeltaDebugging: Visualization Support for Delta Debugging in Virtual Reality

Roy Oberhauser[0000-0002-7606-8226]
Computer Science Dept.
Aalen University
Aalen, Germany
e-mail: roy.oberhauser@hs-aalen.de

Abstract – **Debugging is a challenging activity involved in software development and maintenance processes. Delta Debugging (DD) is an automatic debugging algorithm and methodology that applies a scientific recurrent hypothesis, trial, and result loop to systematically reduce failure-inducing inputs to a minimal set. Yet, especially for larger (structured) input sets, how DD arrived at its results and its intermediate inputs and test results may not be intuitively evident to practitioners. This paper contributes our solution concept VR-DeltaDebugging for an immersive visualization in Virtual Reality to support comprehension, analysis, and collaboration. A prototype demonstrates its feasibility, and a cased-based evaluation on execution, comprehension and analysis, and scalability provides insights into its capabilities and potential.**

Keywords – delta debugging; visualization; virtual reality; debugging; software engineering.

I. INTRODUCTION

Debugging is a costly and time-consuming activity incurred during software development and maintenance processes. A 2021 study [1] found debugging sessions (even during programming) occurred on average every eight minutes, with sessions lasting from less than a few minutes to over 100 minutes. A 2020 survey [2] of 73 developers reported that roughly a quarter of their time (26%) was spent reproducing and fixing failing tests, averaging 13 hours to fix a single bug. A study on debugging [3] found that almost half of the 303 developers (47%) spend 20-40% of their time debugging, with 26% spending even 40–60%. Over half had no formal debugging knowledge or training, and over 70% were unaware of more advanced debugging tools or approaches, which only very few applied.

Among automated software fault localization techniques and tools, Delta Debugging (DD) [4] is a method and algorithm that *simplifies and isolates failure-inducing input automatically and systematically* by testing subsets and complements of the input. This can reduce debugging effort by narrowing the relevant inputs that cause a test to fail. Debugging and testing are often performed contemporaneously, and one application area that exemplifies DD's applicability and benefit is fuzzing. Fuzzing (or fuzz testing) is an automated dynamic test technique that injects random, invalid, or unexpected inputs and observes a software's behavior (crash, memory leak, vulnerabilities, etc.). Yet fuzzing can result in a large (random) input set for a test failure. DD has been shown to be effective and efficient at isolating some input to the minimum set that still reproduces the failure [5]. DD is also applied in compiler development when dealing with program code as structure text inputs, as exemplified in [6]. As to DD's benefits, the empirical study on DD by Yu et al. [7] found that two thirds of isolated changes in the studied programs were helpful in terms of accuracy and efficiency, providing (in)direct clues in locating regression bugs; yet a third were superfluous changes or incorrect isolations. Thus, DD practitioners should have better analysis and process support tooling for insights into determining the validity of a DD result. This is a problem and underlying motivation for this paper's contribution. We seek a solution that can support DD practitioners in comprehending and analyzing the DD reduction input sets and results, and thus more readily determine valid results (or input or test case issues) and the intermediate steps that led to it. Visualization could support DD and make advanced debugging approaches more accessible to practioners. While 2D debugging tools (textual, visual, or Integrated Development Environment (IDEs)) are prevalent, there has been relatively little investigation into the potential of Virtual Reality (VR) for debugging support, in particular for DD and structured inputs.

In this paper, we propose and investigate applying immersive VR to support the DD method. In prior work, we investigated the application of VR to various other areas. A selection of our prior VR-related contributions in the Software Engineering (SE) space: VR-SDLC [8] models development lifecycles, VR-Git [9] models Git repositories, VR-DevOps [10] models Continuous Development pipelines, VR-SBOM [11] models Software Bill of Materials (SBOM) and software supply chains. HyDE [12] showed a VR-based multi-display IDE that could also be used for debugging support. This paper contributes our VR-DeltaDebugging solution concept towards immersive visualization support for Delta Debugging in VR. A prototype demonstrates its feasibility, while a case-based evaluation provides insights into its capabilities and potential for supporting comprehension, analysis, and collaboration.

This paper is structured as follows: the next section discusses related work. Section 3 describes our solution. In Section 4, our realization is presented, which is followed by our evaluation in Section 5. Finally, a conclusion is provided.

II. RELATED WORK

Regarding DD, the survey by Wong et al. on software fault localization [13] analyzed 587 papers and 68 theses, with the discussion also encompassing DD - yet there is no mention of visualization or VR. Further, all searches found no work directly involving DD visualization. Any work, tools, or libraries are text-based or involve a Command Line Interface (CLI). As to IDE integration, DDinput [14] was an Eclipse plugin (appears to no longer appears be supported [15]). Work regarding DD tools or libraries includes Picire [16] as described in [17], and that cited in Wong et al. above [13].

As to debugging in general, VR-based work includes Mauer et al. [18] with a VR-based 3D-debugging prototype, demonstrating how VR can be used for programming comprehension and debugging. Our own prior work HyDE [12] demonstrated a VR-based multi-display IDE (Integrated Development Environment), which could also be used for direct programming and debugging support. 3D visualization work includes Code Park [19], which provides a code-centric environment for code comprehension, yet offers no debugging or editing support. Examples of 2D visualization tools supporting fault localization include Tarantula [20] and GZoltar [21], which showed that visualizations can drastically reduce debugging time.

In contrast, VR-DeltaDebugging is a VR solution directly addressing DD visualization support for (un)structured inputs.

III. Solution Concept

Our solution concept is grounded on prior VR research in areas related to modeling, analysis, and collaboration, some of which is highlighted here. Akpan & Shanker's systematic meta-analysis [22] in discrete event modeling found VR/3D to be advantageous for model development, analysis, and Verification and Validation (V&V). 95% of 23 papers concluded 3D was more potent and provided better analysis than 2D (e.g., evaluating model behavior or what-if analysis). Another finding was a consensus that 3D/VR can present results convincingly and understandably for decision-makers. In 74% of 19 papers, model development tasks improved significantly in 3D/VR (team support, precision, clarity).

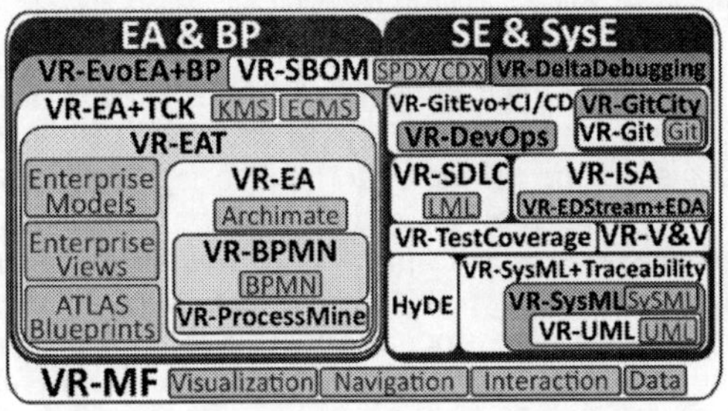

Figure 1. Conceptual map of our published VR solution concepts highlighting their differentiation (VR-DeltaDebugging highlighted in blue).

Our conceptual map of Figure 1 shows our VR-DeltaDebugging solution concept (blue) within the SE and SysE (Systems Engineering) area and in relation to our other prior VR solutions. VR-MF, our generalized VR Modeling Framework (detailed in [23]), provides the basis, providing a domain-independent hypermodeling framework addressing the VR aspects of visualization, navigation, interaction, and data integration. We have published VR-based solutions specific to the Enterprise Architecture (EA) and Business Process (BP) space (EA & BP): VR-EA [23] for mapping EA models to VR, VR-BPMN for BPMN models, VR-EAT for enterprise repository integration, VR-EA+TCK [24] for knowledge and content integration, and VR-EvoEA+BP [25] for EA evolution and business process animation, and VR-SBOM [11]. Solutions in the SE and SysE areas include: VR-Git [9], VR-GitCity, and VR-GitEvo+CI/CD for git-related solutions, VR-DevOps [10], VR-V&V (Verification and Validation), VR-TestCoverage, VR-SDLC [8], VR-ISA for Informed Software Architectures, and VR-UML and VR-SysML for software and systems modeling. HyDE [12] is our VR-based multi-display IDE, and while it can be used for debugging, hitherto none of our work focused directly on supporting debugging in VR.

With regard to structured inputs, Hierarchical Delta Debugging (HDD) [26] has been proposed as a variant to improve DD's effectiveness. However, the study by Yu et al. [27] found that HDD suprisingly did not improve accuracy nor efficiency. Thus, while our solution concept is compatible with HDD, our prototype initially focuses on DD support, incorporating HDD in future work. Since HDD is an AST-oriented reducer, our AST-based nexus can be seen as a precursor to eventual AST-based input support for HDD.

A. Visualization in VR

For text visualization (both input and test code), an interactive scrollable billboard analogy is used for the main screen, similar to terminal screens but enhanced for DD support. It offers a large interaction and viewing space for text-centric analysis. A menu is provided on the side to readily offer interaction without interfering in the analysis. The nexus view is kept synchronized and to the side of the billboard.

For structured DD text inputs, a common alternative graphical visualization form is an Abstract Syntax Tree (AST) (e.g., source code input to debug a compiler/interpreter, or any JSON/XML/HTML/YAML inputs). In VR, we visualize this AST as a *nexus* graph of nodes and edges on the surface of an invisible sphere. 3D nodes depict syntactical elements (classes, functions), while the edges (directed lines) are used to indicate semantic relationships, such as calls or class affiliations. A sphere was chosen to reduce dependency collisions while holding the entire graph spatially compact for immersive flythrough navigation. A Boundary Box (BB) is used to delimit the context of the visual model in case multiple models or model versions are loaded.

B. Navigation in VR

Dual navigation modes are supported in our solution: default gliding controls for fly-through VR, and teleporting to instantly place the camera at a selected position in space. Although teleporting can be potentially disconcerting, it may reduce the likelihood of VR sickness.

C. Interaction in VR

User-element interaction is supported through the VR controllers. A *DD Replay* capability is provided via a slider above the main screen. It is labeled with the total number of DD steps invoked. By adjusting the slider, the DD step and its result are correspondingly displayed on the main screen. Green line numbers indicate the input that passed, and red denotes inputs that failed. Since during main screen interaction no movement is involved, DD interaction controls are offered either directly on the main screen, or via a side screen with a menu to change the context of the main screen. The VR-Tablet travels with the VR camera to support nexus interaction, in particular AST filtering by node type, and can provide detailed context-specific information for a selected element (e.g., node or relations) from the AST data.

IV. REALIZATION

The logical architecture of our prototype realization is shown in Figure 2. The VR visualization aspects of our prototype (referred to as our frontend) were realized in C# using Unity 2022.3.5f1 (LTS) with the XR Interaction Toolkit 2.3. Our backend consists of our Data Hub that contains a data repository and adapters for invocation and data transformation using Python 3.10. While the Data Hub is conceptually separated via a communication channel, in our prototype this would have created unnecessary overhead. The necessary JSON data could be readily transferred via a socket or Web API. Thus, invocation from C# of the Python adapters utilized subprocesses instead.

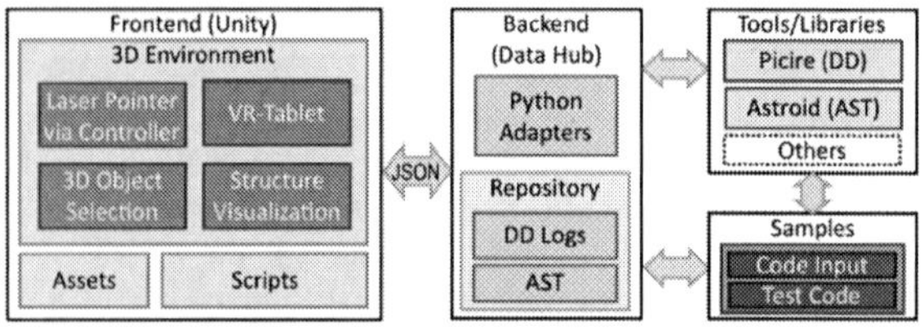

Figure 2. Logical architecture.

```
1  {
2    "steps": [
3      {
4        "step": 1,
5        "result": "FAIL",
6        "lines": [
7          "'N&+slk%hyp5'\n",
8          "\"'@[3(rW*M5W]tMFPU4\\\P@tz%[X?uo\\\17b4T;1bDeYtHx #UJ5\"\n",
9          "'w}pMmPodJM,_%%BC~dYN6*g|Y*Ou9I<P94}7,99ivb(9`=%jJj*Y*d~OLXk!;J'\n",
10         "'V\"/+!aF~{V4EOz**s/Q,7}2@0_'\n",
11         "\"!iOU8]hqg00?u(c);>:\\\\=V<ZV1=*g#UJA'No5QZ}~~{})Sdv#m*L\"\n",
12         "'0iHh[-MzS.U.X}fG7aA:G<bEI\\'0fn[\",Mx{@jfto}i3D?7%V7XdtO6BjYEa#I1}~]'\n",
13         "\"E`h7h)ChX0G*m,|sosJ.mu/\\\c'EpaPi0(n{\""
14       ],
15       "line_numbers": [
16         1,
17         2,
18         3,
19         4,
20         5,
21         6,
22         7
23       ]
24     },
25     ...
26     {
27       "step": 9,
28       "result": "FAIL",
29       "lines": [
30         "'V\"/+!aF~{V4EOz**s/Q,7}2@0_'\n"
31       ],
32       "line_numbers": [
33         4
34       ]
35     }
36   ],
37   "meta": {
38     "message": "Reduction complete"
39   }
40 }
```

Figure 3. Extract snippets of DD execution step log output in JSON (intermediate results removed at line 25 for brevity), showing step number, input and corresponding line numbers, and test result for that subset.

A. Backend

We utilized the Picire [16] Python DD implementation. It splits input (by characters or lines) into n chunks (we used n=2), testing these to see if any remain interesting. We created a generic DD logging proxy for testcases, which tracks separate testcase invocation sequences, storing corresponding step, input, line numbers, and result, shown in our JSON-based log output snippet in Figure 3. This retains DD execution state for subsequent playback and analysis.

Visual analysis for structured DD inputs (like source code for compilers/interpreters, JSON, markup) is supported via an AST. We exemplify feasibility by initially supporting Python. The Python Astroid module (extends the Python ast module) provides an enhanced AST with additional semantic information. We then generate a JSON-based AST data model with the following features:

- Nodes for syntactic units: classes, functions, variable assignments, imports.
- Edges between semantically-linked nodes, such as method calls or class affiliations.
- Additional data such as line numbers, code snippet, node type, and parent nodes.

B. Frontend

The nexus assists with structured inputs, exemplified with Python source code. The nexus layout is based on the Fibonacci sphere algorithm for spatial separation together with a force-directed graph algorithm, which adjusts node placement proximity based on relations, the results of which is illustrated in Figure 4. To depict directed relations between elements, rather than adding arrow heads, direction is indicated by coloring from the source (black) to the destination (white) as a gradient, as seen in Figure 5.

To support immersive interaction in the nexus sphere, a VR-Tablet offers a Nexus Stepper check box: when unchecked, the entire AST is depicted; if checked, only the corresponding portion of the input for that step is shown. It also offers a filtering capability (to ghost or make opaque in the nexus) of the visible node types using checkboxes, as shown in Figure 5. To simplify tablet interaction while keeping its size small, pagination was used instead of scrolling. The node type options depend on the loaded AST, and can include, e.g.: Module, Import, classdef, functionsdef, arguments, assign, assignname, assignattr, etc. The BB around the nexus offers a legend of the node type color assignment, and well as metrics such as the total number of nodes visible. To retain and utilize a user's spatial memory, rather than optimize spatial distance, the nexus is not relocated or its layout changed once instantiated, even if steps or filtering cause far fewer nodes to be visible.

Support for selecting a DD Replay step was implemented as a slider on top of the main screen, ranging from initial input on the left to the final result on the right. During Replay interaction in VR, the corresponding input is shown, and the line numbers are colored according to the step and test result (green for pass, red for fail). A menu screen to the right of the main screen provides the ability to load and execute a different DD context.

Figure 4. Input nexus of AST code graph.

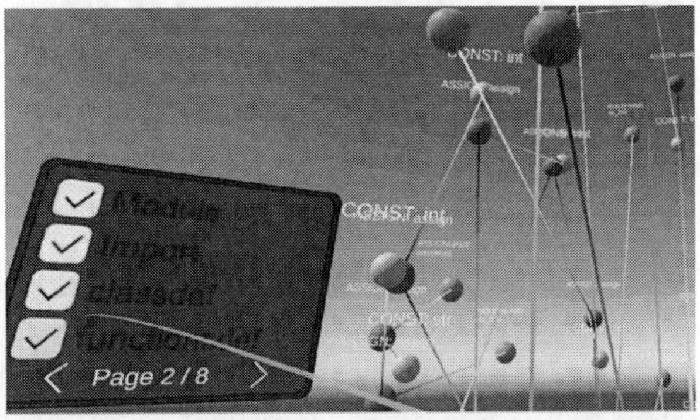

Figure 5. Nexus closeup showing directional dependencies via gradients and the node type filtering ability in the VR-Tablet.

As our evaluation did not necessitate text entry, a virtual keyboard was not included. The implementation could readily be enhanced with a virtual keyboard using laser pointer key selection, as demonstrated in our other VR solutions.

V. EVALUATION

The evaluation of our VR solution concept is based on the design science method and principles [28], in particular a viable artifact, problem relevance, and design evaluation (utility, quality, efficacy). A case study is used based on the following scenarios: DD execution support, DD comprehension and analysis support, and nexus scalability.

A. DD Execution Support in VR

To evaluate DD execution capability in VR, various tests with structured and unstructured inputs were run. The nexus only applies to structured input. To illustrate unstructured input support, input and a Python test from a DD reference site [29] were slightly adapted for our implementation, shown in Figure 6 and Figure 7 respectively.

```
'N&+slk%hyp5'
"'@[3(rW*M5W]tMFPU4\\P@tz%[X?uo\\1?b4T;1bDeYtHx #UJ5"
'w}pMmPodJM,_%%BC~dYN6*g|Y*0u9I<P94}7,99ivb(9`=%jJj*Y*d~0LXk!;J'
'V"/+!aF-(V4EOz*+s/Q,7)2@0_'
"!iOU8]hqg00?u(c);>:\\=V<ZV1=*g#UJA'No5QZ)~--[})Sdv#m*L"
'0iHh[-MzS.U.X}fG7aA:G<bEI\'Ofn[",Mx{@jfto}i3D?7%V7XdtO6BjYEa#Il)~]'
"E`h7h)ChX0G*m,|sosJ.mu/\\c'EpaPi0(n{"
```

Figure 6. Example unstructured text input. Adapted from [29].

```
from picire.outcome import Outcome


def run_test(code_str):
    try:
        mystery(code_str)
        outcome = Outcome.PASS
    except Exception:
        outcome = Outcome.FAIL
    return outcome


def mystery(inp: str) -> None:
    x = inp.find(chr(0o17 + 0o31))
    y = inp.find(chr(0o27 + 0o22))
    if x >= 0 and y >= 0 and x < y:
        raise ValueError("Invalid input")
```

Figure 7. Example provided Python DD testcase. Adapted from [29].

After execution, the initial result (Step 1/9) is as shown in Figure 8, and moving the stepper to the end (Step 9/9) shows the final result of the line found that causes the test to fail, shown in Figure 9.

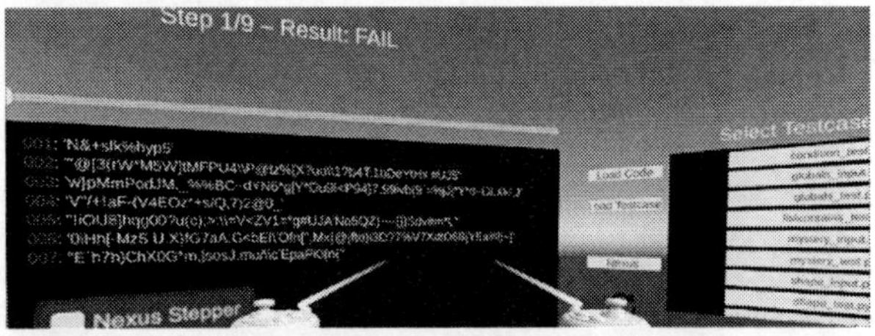

Figure 8. Unstructured input (left) and step and result status (top). Unclear as yet if the input can be further reduced to a single line (or set of characters).

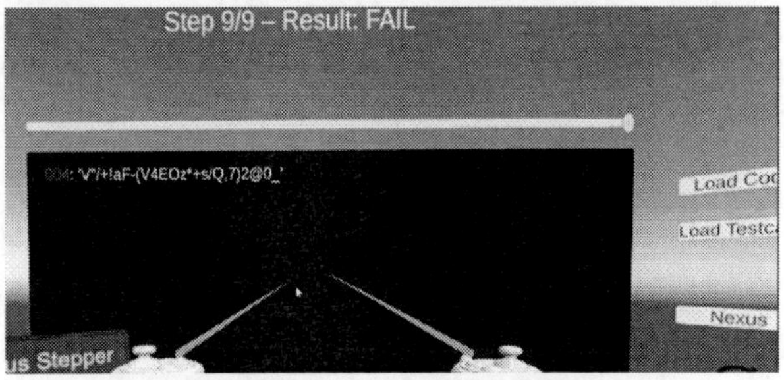

Figure 9. A single input line found to cause the DD test to fail.

B. DD Comprehension and Analysis Support in VR

DD comprehension and analysis are supported in two ways: DD Replay (via the stepper slider) and the graphical DD nexus, which provides a synchronized graphical view for structured DD input, which text-based tools do not offer.

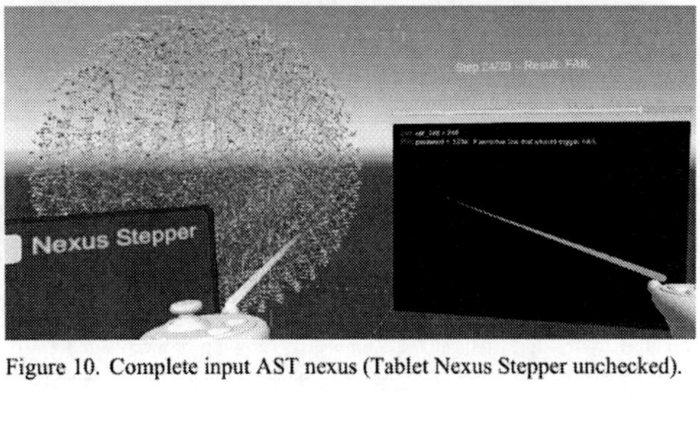

Figure 10. Complete input AST nexus (Tablet Nexus Stepper unchecked).

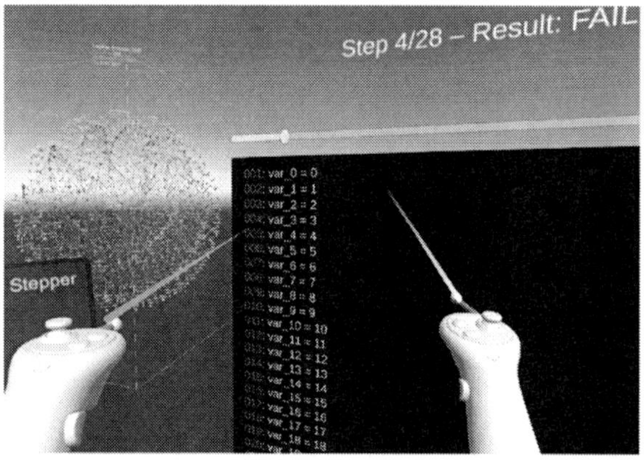

Figure 11. Replay synchronized AST nexus (left) shows reduced input set for Step 4 of 28 on screen (red line numbers indicate set in testcase failure).

To illustrate the comprehension capability, a full AST nexus (since the Nexus Stepper is unchecked on VR-Tablet) of 1500 elements, based on the complete structured text input of 500 lines of assignments in Python code, is shown in Figure 10. A faulty line was intentionally placed on line 250. The nexus view supports DD comprehension by also depicting any known structural relations of the input in a graphical and immersive form, allowing the user to better understand large structured input sets as they may relate to the DD (intermediate) results. A Python AST was used to illustrate this capability, but any structures that can be transformed to a graph-based form could use this capability.

To support analysis of DD results, with the Nexus Stepper checked, moving the slider to Step 4 shows a reduced nexus as well as a reduced textual input set on the main console, as shown in Figure 11. At Step 8, the nexus is further reduced, and the main console shows the passing input (via green line numbers), as seen in Figure 12. The Replay final result shows the failing line found, with a reduced nexus visible on the left that contains only 3 elements, shown in Figure 13.

Immersion in the nexus allows the user to perceive the relations between element types in structured input. The filtering capability by node type is illustrated in Figure 14. Here, the assign nodes were deselected in the VR-Tablet and thus ghosted, enabling the user to focus on (a) specific AST node type(s) of interest.

Figure 12. Replay synchronized AST nexus showing reduced input set on Step 8 (main screen green line numbers indicate input passing testcase).

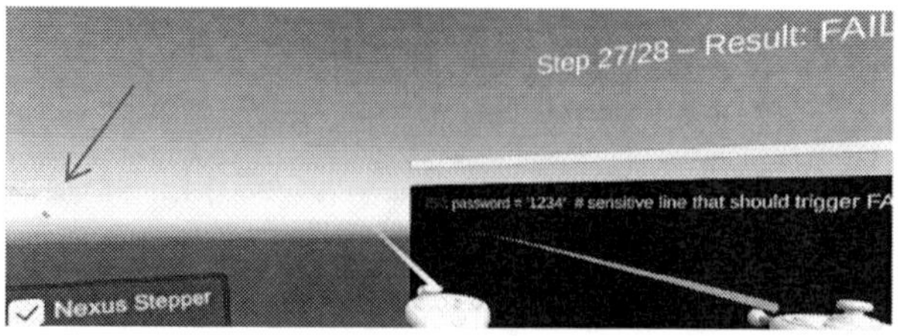

Figure 13. Replay final result showing failing line (reduced nexus on left contains only 3 elements, pointed to by red arrow annotation).

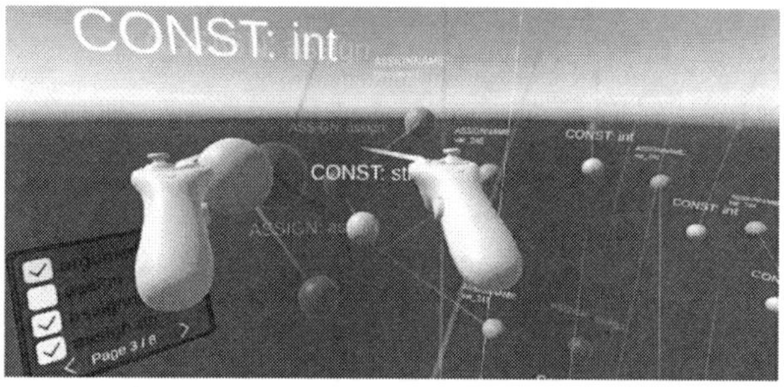

Figure 14. AST nexus filtering (assign nodes are ghosted since deselected).

Figure 15. DD test execution input and result status.

C. Nexus Scalability in VR

VR has no theoretical spatial limitations. However, the number of visible elements depicted affects the frame rates, which are dependent on software and hardware capabilities. For our scalability scenario, the setup was a desktop Win 11 PC AMD Ryzen 9 7900X with 32GB RAM and NVIDIA RTX 4070 using Unity 2022.3.5f1 (LTS). A large structured input (500 lines of Python code) was depicted as an AST as shown in Figure 4. It consists of 1500 visible elements of three different types (ASSIGN, ASSIGNNAME, CONST) of 500 each and their associated dependencies, as shown on the BB in No negative usability issues were encountered, and it demonstrates the feasibility and scalability of the nexus visualization concept for structured inputs such as ASTs. Future work will evaluate larger code repositories.

VI. CONCLUSION AND FUTURE WORK

Debugging has received relatively little visualization support, especially investigating 3D and VR enhancements opportunities and integration with automated debugging tools. This paper described our VR-DeltaDebugging solution concept that offers immersive visualization support for Delta Debugging in VR. Instead of relying on purely text-based DD invocation, comprehension, and analysis, it offers an interactive cockpit with visual support offering intermediate DD result replay the DD steps that led to the DD result. Structured DD inputs are enhanced with an optional graphical nexus visualization that depicts elements and relations within the input, which might affect the failure, and it's depiction is synchronized with the DD Replay results.

The prototype demonstrates its feasibility. The case-based evaluation provided insights into its capabilities and potential for supporting comprehension, analysis, and scalability. VR could also offer a collaboration space regarding DD issues.

Future work includes support for Hierarchical Delta Debugging (HDD), git-bisect integration, and a comprehensive empirical study that also includes usability.

ACKNOWLEDGMENT

The author would like to thank Umut Dönmez and Jonas Kling for their assistance with the implementation, screenshots, and data preparation.

REFERENCES

[1] A. Alaboudi and T. D. LaToza, "An exploratory study of debugging episodes," arXiv preprint arXiv:2105.02162, 2021.

[2] Cambridge University Judge Business School: The business value of optimizing CI pipelines (2020). [Online]. Available from: https://info.undo.io/ci-research-report 2025.08.19

[3] M. Perscheid, B. Siegmund, M. Taeumel, and R. Hirschfeld, "Studying the advancement in debugging practice of professional software developers," Software Quality Journal, 25(1), 2017, pp.83-110.

[4] A. Zeller, "Yesterday, My Program Worked. Today, It Does Not. Why? " in Proc. Seventh European Software Eng. Conf., Seventh ACM SIGSOFT Symp. Foundations of Software Eng., (ESEC/FSE '99), vol. 1687, 1999, pp. 253–267.

[5] A. Zeller and R. Hildebrandt, "Simplifying and isolating failure-inducing input," in IEEE Transactions on Software Engineering, vol. 28, no. 2, 2002, pp. 183-200.

[6] D. Stepanov, M. Akhin, and M. Belyaev, "ReduKtor: How We Stopped Worrying About Bugs in Kotlin Compiler," In: 34th IEEE/ACM International Conference on Automated Software Engineering (ASE 2019), IEEE, 2019, pp. 317-326.

[7] K. Yu, M. Lin, J. Chen, and X. Zhang, „Towards automated debugging in software evolution: Evaluating delta debugging on real regression bugs from the developers' perspectives," Journal of Systems and Software, 85(10), 2012, pp.2305-2317.

[8] R. Oberhauser, "VR-SDLC: A Context-Enhanced Life Cycle Visualization of Software-or-Systems Development in Virtual Reality," In: Business Modeling and Software Design (BMSD 2024), LNBIP, vol 523, Springer, Cham, 2024, pp. 112-129.

[9] R. Oberhauser, "VR-Git: Git Repository Visualization and Immersion in Virtual Reality," 17th Int'l Conf. on Software Engineering Advances (ICSEA 2022), IARIA, 2022, pp. 9-14.

[10] R. Oberhauser, "VR-DevOps: Visualizing and Interacting with DevOps Pipelines in Virtual Reality," Nineteenth International Conference on Software Engineering Advances (ICSEA 2024), IARIA, 2024, pp. 43-48.

[11] R. Oberhauser, "VR-SBOM: Visualization of Software Bill of Materials and Software Supply Chains in Virtual Reality," In: Business Modeling and Software Design (BMSD 2025), LNBIP, vol 559, Springer, Cham, 2025, pp. 52-70.

[12] R. Oberhauser, A. Matic, and C. Pogolski, "HyDE: A Hyper-Display Environment in Mixed and Virtual Reality and its Application in a Software Development Case Study," International Journal on Advances in Software, 11(1 & 2), 2018, pp.195-204.

[13] W. E. Wong, R. Gao, Y. Li, R. Abreu, and F. Wotawa, "A survey on software fault localization," IEEE Transactions on Software Engineering, 42(8), 2016, pp.707-740.

[14] P. Bouillon, M. Burger, and A. Zeller, "Automated debugging in Eclipse: (at the touch of not even a button)," In: Proceedings of the 2003 OOPSLA workshop on eclipse technology eXchange, 2003, pp. 1-5.

[15] DDinput. [Online]. Available from: https://www.st.cs.uni-saarland.de/eclipse/ 2025.08.19

[16] Picire. [Online]. Available from: https://github.com/renatahodovan/picire/ 2025.08.19

[17] R. Hodován and Á. Kiss, "Practical improvements to the minimizing delta debugging algorithm," In: International Conference on Software Engineering and Applications, Vol. 2, SciTePress, 2016, pp. 241-248.

[18] S. T. Mauer et al., „A Novel Approach for Software 3D-Debugging in Virtual Reality," In: International Conference on Human-Computer Interaction (HCII 2024), LNCS, vol 14708. Springer, Cham, 2024, pp. 235-251.

[19] P. Khaloo, M. Maghoumi, E. Taranta, D. Bettner and J. Laviola, "Code Park: A New 3D Code Visualization Tool," 2017 IEEE Working Conference on Software Visualization (VISSOFT), 2017, pp. 43-53, doi: 10.1109/VISSOFT.2017.10.

[20] J. A. Jones, M. J. Harrold, and J. T. Stasko, "Visualization for fault localization," In: Proceedings of ICSE 2001 Workshop on Software Visualization, 2001, pp. 71-75

[21] C. Gouveia, J. Campos, and R. Abreu, "Using HTML5 visualizations in software fault localization," In: Proceedings of the First IEEE Working Conference on Software Visualization, IEEE, 2013, pp. 1–10.

[22] I. J. Akpan and M. Shanker, "The confirmed realities and myths about the benefits and costs of 3D visualization and virtual reality in discrete event modeling and simulation: A descriptive meta-analysis of evidence from research and practice," Computers & Industrial Engineering, 112, 2017, pp. 197-211

[23] R. Oberhauser and C. Pogolski, "VR-EA: Virtual Reality Visualization of Enterprise Architecture Models with ArchiMate and BPMN," In: Business Modeling and Software Design (BMSD 2019), LNBIP, vol. 356, Springer, Cham, 2019, pp. 170-187.

[24] R. Oberhauser, M. Baehre, and P. Sousa, "VR-EA+TCK: Visualizing Enterprise Architecture, Content, and Knowledge in Virtual Reality," In: Business Modeling and Software Design (BMSD 2022), LNBIP, vol 453, Springer, 2022, pp. 122-140. https://doi.org/10.1007/978-3-031-11510-3_8.

[25] R. Oberhauser, M. Baehre, and P. Sousa, "VR-EvoEA+BP: Using Virtual Reality to Visualize Enterprise Context Dynamics Related to Enterprise Evolution and Business Processes," In: Business Modeling and Software Design (BMSD 2023), LNBIP, vol 483, Springer, 2023, pp. 110-128, https://doi.org/10.1007/978-3-031-36757-1_7.

[26] G. Misherghi and Z. Su, "HDD: Hierarchical delta debugging," In: International Conference on Software Engineering (ICSE 2006), ACM, 2006, pp. 142–151.

[27] K. Yu, M. Lin, J. Chen, and X. Zhang, „Towards automated debugging in software evolution: Evaluating delta debugging on real regression bugs from the developers' perspectives," Journal of Systems and Software, 85(10), 2012, pp. 2305-2317.

[28] A.R. Hevner, S.T. March, J. Park, and S. Ram, "Design science in information systems research," MIS Quarterly, 28(1), 2004, pp. 75-105.

[29] A. Zeller, "Reducing Failure-Inducing Inputs." [Online]. Available from: https://www.debuggingbook.org/html/DeltaDebugger.html 2025.08.19